"The ongoing Mormon-evangelical dialogue has been a model of charitable listening and mutual education, but also of challenging confrontations expressed in just the right way. This book features high-level exchanges growing out of that dialogue, with an unusually compelling mix of exposition, apologetics and evangelism (from both sides to both sides). It is an important landmark on an important journey."

Mark Noll, Francis McAnaney Professor of History, University of Notre Dame, author of *Protestantism: A Very Short Introduction*

"Some people wonder why they should engage in conversation with persons of other faiths. Short of conversion, what is to be gained? Here is the answer from Mormons and evangelicals who have been talking to one another for many years. They tell you what they learned and how these conversations changed their lives. One cannot help but wonder if this is not the kind of talk the world needs more of."

Richard Bushman, Gouverneur Morris Professor Emeritus of History, Columbia University, author of *Joseph Smith: Rough Stone Rolling*

"Fifteen years ago, the prospect of evangelicals and Mormons engaged in theological conversation struck some as preposterous and others as hopeful. *Talking Doctrine* demonstrates that the balance tilts decisively toward the latter rather than the former."

Randall Balmer, Dartmouth Professor in the Arts & Sciences, chair of the department of religion, Dartmouth College, author of *The Making of Evangelicalism*

"Richard Mouw and Robert Millet have compiled an outstanding collection of essays that place Jesus' core message at the center of interfaith dialogue: true disciples interact in love and mutual respect. These pioneers of the evangelical-Mormon conversation have much to teach us all by their words and examples alike."

Terryl Givens, Bostwick Professor of English, University of Richmond, author of *Wrestling the Angel: The Foundations of Mormon Thought*

"Times are changing. For nearly two centuries, wariness—if not hostility—has marked the relationship between Mormons and evangelicals. But in the past fifteen years a small but courageous band of academics on both sides has met to see what could be done. These thoughtful essays by dialogue participants mark a major contribution to that effort. They describe the history of the project, designate places where bridges might be built and call for honest respect where they cannot. Simply put, the book offers a valuable moment of repose for measuring the past, taking stock of the present and offering hope for the future."

Grant Wacker, Gilbert T. Rowe Distinguished Professor of Christian History, Duke University, author of *Heaven Below: Early Pentecostals and American Culture*

TALKING DOCTRINE

MORMONS & EVANGELICALS IN CONVERSATION

EDITED BY

RICHARD J. MOUW
& ROBERT L. MILLET

IVP Academic

An imprint of InterVarsity Press
Downers Grove, Illinois

InterVarsity Press
P.O. Box 1400, Downers Grove, IL 60515-1426
ivpress.com
email@ivpress.com

InterVarsity Press® is the book-publishing division of InterVarsity Christian Fellowship/USA®, a movement of students and faculty active on campus at hundreds of universities, colleges and schools of nursing in the United States of America, and a member movement of the International Fellowship of Evangelical Students. For information about local and regional activities, visit intervarsity.org.

While any stories in this book are true, some names and identifying information may have been changed to protect the privacy of individuals.

Cover design: Cindy Kiple
Interior design: Beth McGill
Images: cross and steeple: © Strathdee Holdi Ltd./iStockphoto
  golden angel and steeple: © meshaphoto/iStockphoto

ISBN 978-0-8308-4080-9 (print)
ISBN 978-0-8308-9882-4 (digital)

Printed in the United States of America ∞

Library of Congress Cataloging-in-Publication Data

Talking doctrine : Mormons and Evangelicals in conversation / edited by Richard J. Mouw and Robert L. Millet.
   pages cm
  Includes bibliographical references.
  ISBN 978-0-8308-4080-9 (pbk. : alk. paper)
  1. Evangelicalism—Relations—Church of Jesus Christ of Latter-day Saints. 2. Evangelicalism—Relations—Mormon Church. 3. Church of Jesus Christ of Latter-day Saints—Relations—Evangelicalism. 4. Mormon Church--Relations—Evangelicalism. 5. Evangelicalism. 6 Church of Jesus Christ of Latter-day Saints—Doctrines. I. Mouw, Richard J., editor. II. Millet, Robert L., editor.
  BR1641.M67T35 2015
  289.3'32--dc23

                                                                                          2015014884.

| **P** | 23 | 22 | 21 | 20 | 19 | 18 | 17 | 16 | 15 | 14 | 13 | 12 | 11 | 10 | 9 | 8 | 7 | 6 | 5 | 4 | 3 | 2 | 1 |
| **Y** | 35 | 34 | 33 | 32 | 31 | 30 | 29 | 28 | 27 | 26 | 25 | 24 | 23 | 22 | 21 | 20 | 19 | 18 | 17 | 16 | 15 |

Contents

Prefaces by the Editors

Richard J. Mouw

Since I am one of the essay-writers in this book it is probably quite immodest to say so, but I will say it anyway: this is an amazing collection of essays. Even if the essays were poorly done—which is certainly not the case!—this would be an amazing book. Who would have thought, fifteen years ago, that the group of Mormons and evangelicals who gathered for the first time on the Provo campus of Brigham Young University would eventually produce the kinds of essays gathered in this volume? The past encounters between our two faith communities had been, from the beginnings of Mormonism in the early decades of the nineteenth century, typified by angry accusations and denunciatory rhetoric. And now, in the following pages we find thoughtful, respectful and nuanced engagements with each other's perspectives on some of the most controversial topics that have inflamed our passions in the past.

As Robert Millet reports in chapter two, at that first Provo meeting we all felt awkward and anxious, sensing that we were stepping out on a path that was pretty much uncharted. To be sure, we had a strong hint that something good might come of our efforts. Our joint decision to form the dialogue group had been influenced in good part by the appearance of a wonderful volume, *How Wide the Divide: A Mormon and an Evangelical in Conversation*, published by InterVarsity Press in 1997. Indeed, the coauthors of that volume, Stephen Robinson and Craig Blomberg, were both present at our first session on the Brigham Young campus. We saw the two of them as courageous pioneers who had been willing to take the risk of initiating a new kind of conversation, and then of agreeing to go public with their provisional assessments of the nature of the "divide." And it also took some courage for an evangelical press to publish what they were reporting! But

Stephen and Craig knew that they had only begun to scratch the surface, and that their explorations had to probe more deeply.

For those of us who have contributed to this volume, it is clear that we can look back to that first meeting in 2000 and say—to paraphrase 1 John 3:2, a text that loomed large in our later discussions of what it means for humans to be "divinized"—that it did not yet appear what we could be in our commitment to becoming dialogue partners. The essays here show the great sensitivity and clarity we developed in our efforts to build bridges across what in the past had looked like an unbridgeable divide.

While the essays in this book nicely document our efforts, they also point beyond themselves to more profound personal engagements that cannot be captured in the written record. For several of us representing evangelicalism, we will never forget our depth of feeling when we were gathered on the eastern bank of the Mississippi River, listening to a moving account by a Latter-day Saints historian and colleague of what it was like for the Nauvoo Mormons to flee from that very spot westward after the murder of Joseph Smith in the nearby Carthage jail. Or what is was like to grieve together over the death from cancer of one of our much-loved friends, Brigham Young University's Paul Peterson, whose life we celebrated by singing together "How Great Thou Art," the one hymn that he had insisted be featured at his funeral. Or what it meant to request each other's prayers in times of illness or family crisis.

While those experiences have for many of us a significance for matters of the heart, this book of essays, is an important—yes, an amazing—written record of an intellectual journey taken together thus far. We publish these essays at a time when we have paused to think about ways we might explore new initiatives on several different fronts. Where those initiatives might take us in another fifteen years "doth not yet appear." But this volume serves as an encouraging signpost on a path that we are firmly convinced is leading us to more amazing engagements along the way.

ROBERT L. MILLET

For a very long time—longer than should be the case—evangelical Christians and Latter-day Saints (Mormons) have "enjoyed" a relationship that could at best be described as guarded and suspicious and at worst as antagonistic and hostile. Evangelicals have seen their Mormon counterparts as sheep stealers, competitors for the souls of men and women, enemies of the Christian faith. Mormons have frequently characterized evangelicals as overly exclusionary, arrogant and filled with rancor. Consequently, harsh rhetoric and angry discourse have been the order of the day. No matter what "side" one may be on, when observed from a loftier perch, such wranglings surely must come across as anything but Christian, an affront to the Savior's plea in his great intercessory prayer that his followers, those who profess faith in his name, all may be one.

In recent years, however, evangelicals and Mormons have frequently found themselves laboring as cobelligerents against influences in our world that threaten to tear at the very fabric of our society—militant atheism, growing secularism, ethical relativism and frontal attacks on marriage, the family and religious liberty. No doubt some measure of nervousness has existed on the part of participants in these battles, but at least many socially active men and women on both fronts have had to acknowledge that members of evangelical Christian churches and members of the Church of Jesus Christ of Latter-day Saints share a common moral code, and both yearn for a better world for their children and grandchildren than now exists.

In addition, on a small scale to be sure, there has been an effort underway since 2000, at least among a handful belonging to both faith traditions, to better understand and appreciate one another, an effort to speak cordially, to listen attentively and to discuss, of all things, theological matters, even theological differences. Neither group came to the enterprise with an ecclesiastical imprimatur in hand, and neither group ever purported to represent anything other than their own private views of what they believed. In the spring of 2000 at the top of the N. Eldon Tanner Building at Brigham Young University in Provo, Utah, a gathering of very anxious and uncertain religious scholars took place, an endeavor that would affect the participants in ways they never would have supposed. It would result in friendships that would prove to be long-lasting, travel to various sites of "sacred space" for each group, and for some a new way of viewing one's fellow men and women and the overall plans and purposes of Almighty God. This book is the story of that singular endeavor. It is a report of the Mormon-evangelical dialogue from 2000–2014, a careful consideration of what took place at several of the doctrinal discussions and what was decided—definite and seemingly irreconcilable differences, matters deserving of continued exploration and areas of surprising similarity.

In speaking of the formative days of Mormonism, one Latter-day Saint leader, Oliver Cowdery, commented that "these were days never to be forgotten." And so it was with us. The Mormon-evangelical dialogue was a distinctive and memorable experience, one that has changed us, for the better. Our sincere hope is that the reader will find the report of these "vexations of the soul" to be not only intellectually stimulating, and even entertaining reading, but also motivational, in the sense of prompting readers to reach out to those who are different, to strike up a conversation, to listen with empathy and to be willing to learn and to be affected. Richard Mouw suggested in his important work *Uncommon Decency* that interfaith dialogue is always helped along by a healthy dose of curiosity, and so we extend the challenge to those who may read this book, even if only in the name of sheer curiosity, to "go, and do thou likewise." The results just might surprise you.

PART ONE

The Nature
of the Dialogue

1

The Dialogue

Backgrounds and Context

Derek J. Bowen

EVANGELICALS AND MORMONS are relative newcomers to the practice of interfaith dialogue. The genesis of modern interfaith dialogue is generally traced back to the 1893 World's Parliament of Religions held in conjunction with the Chicago World's Fair.[1] Although Christianity largely dominated the conference, nine other religions were represented. Mormons and many evangelicals were among those groups missing, and it wasn't by accident. For Mormons, their "representation was not wanted nor solicited by the organizers of the 1893 Parliament."[2] Even after inclusion was reluctantly granted, further discrimination caused the Mormon delegation to walk out in protest. As for evangelicals, the identification of interfaith dialogue with liberal Protestantism was enough to keep conservatives like Dwight L. Moody and the archbishop of Canterbury away from the event, believing the parliament symbolized the compromise of Christianity.[3] Consequently Mormons and evangelicals did not participate in the beginnings and early practice of interfaith dialogue—due to the discriminatory exclusion of Mormons, as opposed to the deliberate avoidance of evangelicals. Despite their differing reasons for absence, both groups have generally continued to remain aloof from this movement for most of its existence. Yet ironically, two of the groups most averse to interfaith dialogue decades ago now have among their ranks some of the greatest beneficiaries and practitioners of the enterprise in the present-day Mormon-evangelical scholarly dialogue. It is equally surprising that the dialogue is specifically occurring between Mormons and evangelicals, two groups who take the Lord's Great Commission very seriously, but who also share a long history of antagonism toward one another.

Several factors coalesced to cause the Mormon-evangelical scholarly dialogue to occur by the late twentieth century. One significant factor was the loss of what many historians have referred to as the American evangelical Protestant empire of the nineteenth century.[4] Between the years 1860 and 1926, the population of the United States grew from 31.5 million to over 117 million.[5] Although evangelicalism also grew during this time, it could not keep pace with the massive number of immigrants entering the country. By 1890, Roman Catholicism surpassed Methodism as the single largest Christian denomination in America, and has remained so ever since.[6] In addition to immigration, Protestantism's division into liberal and fundamentalist camps over issues like evolution and higher criticism of the Bible, further weakened evangelical influence. These and other developments caused evangelicals to lose their majority status—from approximately half of the American population to 26 percent of Americans currently.[7] Although their fundamentalist forebears first reacted with a separatist approach, neo-evangelicals, with their commitment to cultural engagement, began to see dialogue as a new method of evangelism. For some evangelicals, dialogue became a means by which to negotiate the new reality of religious pluralism as a smaller group within the American mosaic of religion.[8]

Meanwhile, a series of changes occurred within Mormonism that in many ways brought it closer to evangelicalism, in both doctrine and practice. Although early nineteenth-century Mormonism resembled evangelicalism in many particulars, the followers of Joseph Smith gradually followed a path of radical differentiation from the dominant Protestant culture of nineteenth-century America. As Richard Mouw will discuss later in this volume, Latter-day Saints did not simply step forward and offer to the world new books of Scripture; they announced that God had chosen to restore the prophetic office. Mormonism introduced a worldview that combined the temporal and the spiritual, uniting religion with economics and politics (see Doctrine and Covenants 29:34). Mormonism introduced a priesthood hierarchy and let it be known that the divine apostolic power to perform salvific ordinances (sacraments), the power once held by the early Christian church

(Matthew 16:19; 18:18), had been restored as well. In other words, in spite of the fact that Mormonism arose in a Protestant world, its ecclesiastical structure resembled Roman Catholicism. And with the claim of modern prophets and continuing revelation came the renewal and spread of spiritual gifts, including the gift of tongues, and the reports of miracles and signs and angelic visitations. By the end of Joseph Smith's life, in 1844, he had introduced the practice of polygamy, or plural marriage, as well as the startling and for some repulsive belief that men and women could become like God.

The Mormon movement into the twentieth century and into the traditional American society began quite dramatically in 1890, when Latter-day Saints (LDS) Church president Wilford Woodruff declared an end to polygamy. From 1890 on, Mormonism followed a new path of assimilation into American and evangelical cultural norms, which to a great extent continues today. Besides forsaking polygamy in favor of monogamy, Mormonism also forsook communal economics for capitalism and theocratic politics for democracy.[9] Later social assimilation included joining the evangelical cause of Prohibition, a move that reflected the LDS adherence to what the Saints called the "Word of Wisdom"—a health law first introduced in 1833—a ban on alcohol, tobacco, tea and coffee. By the early decades of the twentieth century, the complete observance of the Word of Wisdom became a requirement for members in good standing to enter their temples.[10] Mormonism also adopted to some extent the anti-intellectual heritage of fundamentalism, dismissing both evolution and scientism and looking askance at what religionists came to know as the "higher criticism" of the Bible.[11] With the later emergence of neo-evangelicalism, Mormonism soon found a moral and political ally within the Republican Party who supported causes like antiabortion legislation and traditional marriage amendments. But none of these changes would have been enough to foster the Mormon-evangelical dialogue without accompanying shifts in Mormon theological emphases.

Two related intellectual movements within Mormonism during the twentieth century brought Mormon theology closer to evangelical doctrine than ever before. Beginning around the mid-century point, there was a greater emphasis placed on the belief in an infinite God, the plight of fallen humanity and salvation by the mercy and grace of God. Sociologist Kendall White has called this movement "Mormon neo-orthodoxy."[12] White argues that Mormon neo-orthodoxy, like Protestant neo-orthodoxy, was a "crisis theology," in that both movements developed out of a response to the crisis of modernity. In the case of Mormonism, White suggests that "Mormons have traditionally believed in a finite God, an optimistic assessment of human nature, and a doctrine of salvation by merit. In contrast, most Mormon neo-orthodox theologians have tended to embrace the concept of an absolute God, a pessimistic assessment of human nature, and a doctrine of salvation by grace."[13] White proposes that a traditional Mormonism somewhat compatible with modernism gave way to a Mormon neo-orthodoxy compatible with evangelicalism and to some extent fundamentalism. Observing such change, Richard Mouw wondered in a 1991 *Christianity Today* article whether an "Evangelical Mormonism" was developing.[14] Building on the foundation of Mormon neo-orthodoxy, John-Charles Duffy has suggested that another intellectual movement developed, one he coins "Mormon Progressive Orthodoxy."[15] Duffy defines Mormon Progressive Orthodoxy as "the effort to mitigate Mormon sectarianism, the rejection of Mormon liberalism, and the desire to make Mormon supernaturalism more intellectually credible."[16] Some observers of the Mormon-evangelical dialogue would classify a majority of the LDS participants in the dialogue as adherents of Mormon Progressive Orthodoxy, although none have specifically identified themselves as such. The recognition of such developments has brought some evangelicals to the dialogue table in order to encourage what they perceive as spiritually healthy developments within the LDS faith. (Most of the LDS dialogists would, however, claim that they have no such inclinations or ambitions, only a desire to assist their evangelical brothers and sisters to come to appreciate the "Christian" foundations of Mormonism.)

Into these prime conditions walked Pastor Gregory C. V. Johnson of "Standing Together," a parachurch evangelical ministry in Utah.[17] As a young child Johnson had joined the Church of Jesus Christ of Latter-day Saints with his family, but later as a teenager converted to evangelicalism following what he describes as a born-again experience. This joint experience with and exposure to both Mormonism and evangelicalism created a natural interfaith dialogue within Johnson himself, a passion to help bridge what had for decades been an unbridgeable gulf. Over time, this inner dialogue organically evolved into an outer dialogue between groups of Mormons and evangelicals organized by Johnson. As student body president of Denver Seminary, Johnson introduced one of his professors, Craig Blomberg, to religion professor Stephen Robinson of Brigham Young University (BYU). Through their interaction, and with the encouragement of Johnson, in 1997 Blomberg and Robinson wrote *How Wide the Divide? A Mormon and an Evangelical in Conversation* (InterVarsity Press). As the first public step toward a more formal Mormon-evangelical scholarly dialogue, the book received a mixed review of praise and disdain. Most of the Mormon appraisal was positive, whereas the evangelical assessment was generally split between encouraging remarks from scholars and bitter criticism from professional counter-cultists.[18] In April of 1997 Johnson became acquainted with BYU religion professor Robert L. Millet, and their monthly lunch conversations gradually evolved into a public forum titled "A Mormon and an Evangelical in Conversation," a two-hour program that discussed the value of religious exchange and also addressed doctrinal similarities and differences between the two faith traditions. To date, Millet and Johnson have been invited to hold their public dialogues some seventy times to churches (both LDS and evangelical), universities, civic organizations and law schools, throughout the United States, Canada and even in Great Britain. Besides their own presentations, Millet and Johnson helped organize an interfaith gathering, "An Evening of Friendship," in the Salt Lake Mormon Tabernacle with Christian apologist Ravi Zacharias in 2004, the first time an evangelical had spoken in that venue since Dwight L. Moody in 1899. Zacharias returned to the Tabernacle a decade later, to a packed house.

After three years of meeting together, Johnson suggested to Millet the possibility of expanding their conversation to include scholars from both faiths. This resulted in a semiannual dialogue that has continued since 2000. The first meeting occurred at Brigham Young University in Provo, Utah. Among the first evangelical participants were Greg Johnson, Richard Mouw (Fuller Theological Seminary), Craig Blomberg (Denver Seminary), Craig Hazen (Biola University), David Neff (editor of *Christianity Today*) and Carl Moser, at the time a doctoral student in Scotland and later a professor of religion at Eastern University in Philadelphia. On the LDS side, participants included Robert Millet, Stephen Robinson, Roger Keller, David Paulsen,

Daniel Judd and Andrew Skinner, all from BYU.[19] Additions and subtractions in participants have taken place over the years.

The participants would come "prepared (through readings of articles and books) to discuss a number of doctrinal subjects, including the Fall, Atonement, Scripture, Revelation, Grace and Works, Trinity/Godhead, the Corporeality of God, Theosis/Deification, Authority, and Joseph Smith's First Vision."[20] Meetings have been held at Brigham Young University, Fuller Theological Seminary, Wheaton College, the Mormon historical sites of Palmyra, New York and Nauvoo, Illinois, and at meetings of the American Academy of Religion and the Society of Biblical Literature.[21]

After meeting some twenty-four times, it was determined in the summer of 2014 that the dialogue in its current iteration had served its purpose. Convicted civility had become the order of things in the gatherings, trust and respect and empathy had been established, doctrinal clarity on both sides had come to pass, and lasting friendships had been formed. More than two or three had gathered many times in the name of the Lord Jesus Christ, and it was the consensus of the dialogue team that his Spirit and his approbation had been felt again and again.

2

Reflections After Fifteen Years

Robert L. Millet

In 1991, not long after I was appointed dean of religious education at Brigham Young University, one of the senior leaders of the LDS Church counseled me, "Bob, you must find ways to reach out. Find ways to build bridges of friendship and understanding with persons of other faiths." That charge has weighed on my mind since then.

To be able to articulate your faith to someone who is not of your faith is a good discipline, one that requires you to check carefully your own vocabulary, your own terminology, and make sure that people not only understand you but also could not misunderstand you. Mormons and evangelicals have a similar vocabulary but often have different definitions and meanings for those words. Consequently, effective communication is a strenuous endeavor. To some degree, we have been forced to reexamine our paradigms, our theological foundations, our own understanding of things in a way that enables us to talk and listen and digest and proceed.

The Dialogue Begins

Derek Bowen has just provided a useful historical background for the dialogue. Let me begin by suggesting that in the early sessions, it was not uncommon to sense a bit of tension, a subtle uncertainty as to where this was going, a slight uneasiness among the participants. As the dialogue began to take shape, it was apparent that we were searching for an identity—was this to be a confrontation? A debate? Was it to produce a winner and a loser? Just how candid and

earnest were we expected to be? Some of the Latter-day Saints wondered: Do
the "other guys" see this encounter as a grand effort to set Mormonism straight,
to make it more traditionally Christian, more acceptable to skeptical on-
lookers? Some of the evangelicals wondered: Is what they are saying an accurate expression of LDS belief? Can a person be a genuine Christian and yet
not be a part of the larger body of Christ? A question that continues to come
up is, just how much "bad theology" can the grace of God compensate for?
Before too long, those kinds of issues became part of the dialogue itself, and
in the process, much of the tension began to dissipate.

These meetings have been more than conversations. We have visited key
historical sites, eaten and socialized, sung hymns and prayed, mourned together over the passing of members of our group, and shared ideas, books
and articles throughout the year. The initial feeling of formality has given
way to a sweet informality, a brother-and-sisterhood, a kindness in disagreement, a respect for opposing views, and a feeling of responsibility
toward those not of our faith—a responsibility to represent their doctrines
and practices accurately to folks of our own faith. No one has compromised
or diluted his or her own theological convictions, but everyone has sought
to demonstrate the kind of civility that ought to characterize a mature exchange of ideas among a body of believers who have discarded defensiveness.
No dialogue of this type is worth its salt unless the participants gradually
begin to realize that there is much to be learned from the others.

ENGAGING CHALLENGES

Progress has not come about easily. True dialogue is tough sledding, hard
work. In my own life it has entailed, first, a tremendous amount of reading
of Christian history, Christian theology and, more particularly, evangelical
thought. I cannot very well enter into their world and their way of thinking
unless I immerse myself in their literature. This is particularly difficult when
such efforts come out of your own hide, that is, when you must do it above
and beyond everything else you are required to do. It takes a significant
investment of time, energy and money.

Second, while we have sought from the beginning to ensure that the
proper balance of academic backgrounds in history, philosophy and theology are represented in the dialogue, it soon became clear that perhaps

more critical than intellectual acumen was a nondefensive, clearheaded, thick-skinned, persistent but pleasant personality. Kindness works really well also. Those steeped in apologetics, whether LDS or evangelical, face a special hurdle, an uphill battle, in this regard. We agreed early on, for example, that we would not take the time to address every anti-Mormon polemic, any more than a Christian-Muslim dialogue would spend appreciable time evaluating proofs of whether Muhammad actually entertained the angel Gabriel. Furthermore, and this is much more difficult, we agreed as a larger team to a rather high standard of loyalty—that we would not say anything privately about the other guys that we would not say in public.

Third, as close as we have become, as warm and congenial as the dialogues have proven to be, there is still an underlying premise that guides most of the evangelical participants: that Mormonism is the tradition that needs to do the changing if progress is to be forthcoming. To be sure, the LDS dialogists have become well aware that we are not well understood and that many of our theological positions need clarifying. Too often, however, the implication is that if the Mormons can only alter this or drop that, then we will be getting somewhere. As LDS participant Spencer Fluhman noted, sometimes we seem to be holding "tryouts for Christianity" with the Latter-day Saints. A number of the LDS cohort have voiced this concern and suggested that it just might be a healthy exercise for the evangelicals to do a bit more introspection, to consider that this enterprise is in fact a dialogue, a mutual conversation, one where long-term progress will come only as both sides are convinced that there is much to be learned from one another, including doctrine.

A fourth challenge is one we did not anticipate. In evangelicalism, on the one hand, there is no organizational structure, no priestly hierarchy, no living prophet or magisterium to proclaim the "final word" on doctrine or practice, although there are supporting organizations like the National Association of Evangelicals and the Evangelical Theological Society. On the other hand, Mormonism is clearly a top-down organization, the final word resting with the First Presidency and the Quorum of the Twelve Apostles. Thus our dialogue team might very well make phenomenal progress toward a shared understanding on doctrine, but evangelicals around the world will not see our conclusions as in any way binding or perhaps even relevant.

DIALOGUE TOPICS

The first dialogue, held at Brigham Young University in the spring of 2000, was as much an effort to test the waters as to dialogue on a specific topic. But the group did agree to do some reading prior to the gathering. The evangelicals asked that we all read or reread John Stott's classic work *Basic Christianity* (Downers Grove, IL: InterVarsity Press; Grand Rapids: Eerdmans, 1958), and some of my LDS colleagues recommended that we read a book I had written titled *The Mormon Faith* (Salt Lake City: Shadow Mountain, 1998). We spent much of a day discussing *The Mormon Faith*, concluding that there were a number of theological topics deserving extended conversation in the future.

When it came time to discuss *Basic Christianity*, we had a most unusual and unexpected experience. Richard Mouw asked, "Well, what concerns or questions do you have about this book?" There was a long and somewhat uncomfortable silence. Rich followed up after about a minute: "Isn't there anything you have to say? Did we all read the book?" Everyone nodded affirmatively that they had indeed read it, but no one seemed to have any questions. Finally, one of the LDS participants responded: "Stott is essentially writing of New Testament Christianity, with which we have no quarrel. He does not wander into the creedal formulations that came from Nicaea, Constantinople or Chalcedon. We agree with his assessment of Jesus Christ and his gospel as presented in the New Testament. Good book." That comment was an important one, as it signaled where we would eventually lock our theological horns.

In the second dialogue, located at Fuller Seminary, we chose to discuss the matter of soteriology, and much of the conversation was taken up with where divine grace and faithful obedience (good works) fit into the equation of salvation. The evangelicals insisted that Mormon theology did not seem to contain a provision for the unmerited divine favor of God and that Mormons sometimes appeared to be obsessed with a kind of works righteousness. The LDS crowd retorted that what they had observed quite often among evangelicals was what Bonhoeffer had described as "cheap grace," a kind of easy believism that frequently resulted in spiritually unfazed and unchanged people. Toward the end of the discussion, one of the Mormons, Stephen Robinson, asked the group to turn in their copies of the Book of Mormon (each participant came prepared with a Bible and the LDS books of Scripture, what is called the "triple combination") to several passages in which the text stressed the fact that we are saved only through the merits and mercy and grace of the Holy Messiah. After an extended silence, I remember hearing one of the evangelicals say, almost in a whisper, "Sounds pretty Christian to me." Over the years, most of us have concluded that in regard to this particular topic, our two traditions are far closer than we had anticipated.

One of the most memorable of all our discussions centered on the concept of *theosis*, or divinization, the doctrine espoused by Latter-day Saints and also a vital facet of Eastern Orthodoxy. For this dialogue we invited Veli-Matti Kärkkäinen, professor of theology at Fuller Seminary, to lead our discussion. In preparation for the dialogue we read his book *One with God: Salvation as Deification and Justification* (Collegeville, MN: Liturgical Press, 2004), as well as LDS writings on the topic. It seemed to me that in this particular exchange there was much less effort on the part of evangelicals to "fix Mormonism." Instead, the conversation generated much reflection and introspection among the entire group. Mormons commented on how little work they had done on this subject beyond the bounds of Mormonism, and they found themselves fascinated with such expressions as participation in God, union with God, assimilation into God, receiving of God's energies and not his essence, and divine-human synergy. More than one of the evangelicals asked how they could essentially have ignored a matter that was a part of the discourse of Athanasius, Augustine, Irenaeus, Gregory of Nazianzus and even Martin Luther. There was much less said about "you and your faith" and far more emphasis on "we" as professing Christians in this setting.

Not long after our dialogue on deification, Rich Mouw suggested that we not meet next time in Provo but rather in Nauvoo, Illinois. Nauvoo was of course a major historical moment (1839–1846) within Mormonism, the place where the Mormons were able to establish a significant presence, where some of Joseph Smith's deepest (and most controversial) doctrines were delivered to the Saints and the site from which Brigham Young and the Mormon pioneers began the long exodus to the Salt Lake Basin in February 1846. Because a large percentage of the original dwellings, meetinghouses, places of business and even the temple have been restored in modern Nauvoo, our dialogue was framed by the historical setting and resulted in perhaps the greatest blending of hearts of any dialogue we have had.

Two years later we met in Palmyra, New York, and once again focused much of our attention on historical sites, from the Sacred Grove (where Joseph Smith claimed to have received his first vision) to Fayette, where the Church was formally organized on April 6, 1830. We had reaffirmed what we had come to know quite well in Nauvoo—that there is in fact something special about "sacred space." (Professor Richard Bennett will address "sacred space" in a subsequent essay in this book.) Probing discussions of authority, Scripture/revelation, the possibility of modern prophets and the nature of God and the Godhead (Trinity) have also taken place.

As we began our second decade in 2011, it was suggested that we start over and make our way slowly through Christian history until we came to Nicaea (A.D. 325), at which point we could discuss in more depth the theological developments that now divide us. Consequently, we have now held three additional sessions on the doctrine of the Trinity/Godhead, probing conversations that have been both intellectually stretching and spiritually uplifting. The articles by Craig Blomberg, Chris Hall and Brian Birch later in this volume address our dialogues on these topics.

Looking Ahead

In pondering the future, there are certain developments I would love to see take place in the next decade. I would hope that the Church of Jesus Christ of Latter-day Saints would become a bit more confident and secure in its distinctive theological perspectives and thus less prone to be thin-skinned, easily offended and reactionary when those perspectives are questioned or challenged. In that light, I sense that we Mormons have to decide what we want to be when we grow up; that is, do we want to be known as a separate and distinct manifestation of Christianity (restored Christianity), or do we want to have traditional Christians conclude that we are just like they are? You can't have it both ways. And if you insist that you are different, you can't very well pout about being placed in a different category! In addition, it would be wonderful if LDS interfaith efforts of the future would receive the kind of institutional encouragement for which some of the early participants of this endeavor have yearned so often. Often this interreligious effort has been a lot like walking the plank alone. It gets pretty lonely out there sometimes.

On the other hand, I long for a kinder, gentler brand of evangelicalism, one that is less prone to consign to perdition anyone who sees things differently; one that holds tightly to its doctrinal tenets but is more concerned with welcoming and including than with dismissing and excluding; one that is more eager to delight people with the glories of heaven than with terrifying and threatening them with the fires of hell. Rob Bell's book *Love Wins* (San Francisco: HarperOne, 2011) may cause some evangelicals to believe the author is a universalist (which I do not) and others to cry heresy, but it seems to me that he is asking all the right questions. The image of Christianity is at stake, and some outside the fold may well be justified in wondering where the "good news" is to be found.

Well, now that I have offended both sides, let me try to be a bit prescient. Looking ahead, I see two professing Christian bodies who, in spite of their differences (which are significant, to be sure), have learned to talk and listen and digest, have learned to communicate respectfully about those differences and celebrate their similarities. I see two groups who have learned to work together as cobelligerents in stemming the tide of creeping secularism, standing united in proclaiming absolute truths and moral values, and fighting courageously in defense of the family and traditional marriage. We have a society to rescue, and frankly there is something more fundamental and basic than theology, and that is our shared humanity. We are, first and foremost, sons and daughters of Almighty God, and we have been charged to let our light shine in a world that is becoming ever darker, a world that hungers for the only lasting solution to the world's problems—the person and powers of Jesus Christ. Only through him will society be fully transformed and renewed.

What Drew Me to Dialogue . . . and Why I'm Still Talking

J. Spencer Fluhman

I DID NOT EXPECT TO SPEND YEARS in theological conversation with evangelicals. My autobiographical details, in fact, might have predicted something else entirely. Growing up in a densely Mormon Utah neighborhood, I viewed non-Mormons with suspicion. My parents were big-hearted Latter-day Saints who never taught anything but love, but, somehow, I was wary of the Protestant church across the street from my boyhood home. As kids, we would gallop down its hallway on hot summer days, buy our cold 7-Up (we could scarcely believe they put a vending machine in a church) and sprint out as if the devil himself was on our heels. I was scared of the pastor and sensed that some chasm separated us from his congregants. These negative perceptions were reinforced during my years as an LDS missionary in Virginia and Maryland, where the "born-agains"—we turned the phrase into a pejorative noun—unquestionably hated us most. At one point, I found myself staring down the barrel of a rifle wielded by a good Christian, we learned later, who apparently had little interest in Mormonism. (We didn't stop to ask.) I left those two years sure that evangelicals were the *least* Christian people on earth.

My views started to change in graduate school. Training in American religious history provided new understandings of my church's past and the ways it had been shaped by mistrust and violence on all sides. I also had to reckon with a memorable evangelical cast of historical characters (John

Calvin, Jonathan Edwards, Charles G. Finney, etc.) and their gifted evangelical chroniclers (Mark Noll, George Marsden, Nathan Hatch, etc.). These academic experiences blunted much of my contempt, but it was a series of relational developments that drew me into sustained conversation with evangelicals. Shortly after my appointment to the faculty at Brigham Young University, a colleague invited me to meet with evangelical students visiting campus. After spending an exhilarating few hours with them, it was clear to me that I'd happened onto an altogether different set of evangelicals. Indeed, after accepting another invitation to meet with the LDS-evangelical scholarly dialogue group in 2007, I was convinced that my youthful appraisals of evangelicalism had been woefully one-sided. Having become acquainted with the history of American ecumenism, it also struck me that this dialogue was rather unique—even strange in many ways. Even so, I came to believe that it offered hope for a better kind of conversation between our two communities.

Even as I strain against some of what I take to be its pitfalls, the dialogue has fed both mind and heart. I confess to somewhat selfish motives at first: I was sure I was watching something historically significant that would simultaneously bolster my pedagogy. (I teach courses on American religious history and hunger for insight into evangelicalism.) This intellectual curiosity continues to fuel my involvement, frankly. And in the end, I hope to offer evangelicals what I seek from them: I want to represent their faith in a way that does justice to its richness and complexity. I am by no means an apologist for evangelicalism, but I would hope that evangelicals could recognize themselves in my descriptions. I certainly would not want to misrepresent them in any way, and I credit the dialogue for providing me more nuanced understandings. I once joked with Richard Mouw that he's "earned the right," after countless hours with us, to comment on Mormonism. I hope I've done my part with evangelicalism.

The dialogue has also provided countless opportunities to sharpen understanding of my own faith, historically and theologically. Comparative projects force these kinds of insights, I've learned. I wondered when joining the dialogue—and still do—how two communities without institutionally driven systematic theologies can even presume a theological dialogue, but it turns out that our conversations never fail to interest me. They help me see more clearly where we might intersect and where we can emphatically disagree. But for me, even the disagreements have been productive rather than destructive (as I often experienced them as an LDS missionary). By locating rigorous, academic conversations in relationships of trust that have been cultivated over time, we find ourselves able to articulate differences without recourse to derision, stereotyping or dismissal. For instance, I am willing to take Calvinism seriously—not something I was historically inclined to do—in part because of my admiration for the Calvinists I now count as friends! .

I sensed early on that some dialogue members approached it as a kind of Mormon audition for "authentic Christian" status. Such a thing has never interested me. In fact, I spent my first year in the dialogue complaining that it seemed to implicitly interrogate Mormonism only. I felt, and still feel, that to do so would only inhibit real communication. I was touched when the evangelical members not only heard my complaint about power dynamics but also took pains to ensure that the conversations evolved to place the two traditions on more even footing. Even so, we struggle with fundamental questions. Why are we still talking? Where are our conversations going? *Should* they be going somewhere? While we sort through these and other questions, each side seems genuinely to appreciate knowing the other's theology better. Similarly, both sides want warmer personal connections for our communities. Both sense that the past offers a host of examples of *what not to do*. At the same time, no one is interested in doctrinal compromise. No one seems even remotely interested in conversion to the other perspective. For now, most seem content in a rather rich middle ground—we've acclimated to conversations that avoid polemic dismissal on the one hand and relativizing soft-headedness on the other. Neither side can legitimately speak for its community in an official way—because the Mormon scholars have no general ecclesiastical authority and because the evangelicals recognize none!—so we joke that nothing we say matters much anyway.

Our conversations exist as academic exercises at the core, but we've found our religious lives intruding at almost every turn. The dialogue clearly intersects with my intellectual interests, but it has also provided some memorable moments for my LDS soul. I crave candor and openness, and this particular group not only tolerates my spirited accounts of Mormonism's distinctive richness but also patiently tries to assimilate our Mormon variety

of inconclusiveness on various theological points. Our LDS group represents a cross-section of Mormon intellectual life, after all, from "neo-
orthodox" religion professors firmly committed to the Book of Mormon's
soteriology of Christ's graceful justification to historians and philosophers
who are equally at home with Joseph Smith's more radical utterances relating
to anthropomorphic gods and infinite humans. Especially given the "gotcha"
style of "countercult" approaches to Mormonism, I am profoundly grateful
for evangelical partners who are less interested in marking every Mormon
slip-up or idiosyncrasy than they are in truly comprehending what makes a
Latter-day Saint "tick" religiously. They compliment us by actually hearing
us. LDS apostle Boyd K. Packer noted years ago that over time he's cared less
about being agreed with and more about being understood.[1] For me, the
dialogue has provided just that: understanding. And along the way we've
forged rather tight bonds of love and trust around such a worthy goal. We've
all found it much more difficult to dismiss or deride a theology when it is
embodied. Perhaps some of our evangelical counterparts are even less convinced we're *real* Christians, but I doubt it. I am sure of this: I would be
perfectly comfortable with Richard Mouw or Craig Blomberg or Dennis
Okholm answering questions about Mormonism in the press or in print. I
would expect them to be clear about positions they disagree with—heaven
knows they've been clear with us—but I know that my name or my faith is
safe in their hands. The dialogue has been demanding and it has forced some
tough questions, but for the most part I have been moved by the displays of
generosity and humility on both sides.

Early on as a graduate student, I noticed that one could pay a heavy price
for identifying as a person of faith. Not everyone reacted negatively, but my
LDS faith cost me more than one friendship at my secular university.
Probably partly as a result, I developed multiple modes of discourse:
Mormon "talk" with my LDS ward members, academic talk with history
colleagues, Mormon studies talk with LDS academics and so on. The LDS-
evangelical dialogue has proved wonderfully destabilizing for that pattern
of compartmentalization. In the dialogue, all the talk comes together in a
rather raucous commingling of religious and academic discourse. It was
jarring at first, but I've come to value it as a site of real personal synthesis,
where my academic instincts and my religious sensibilities are both firing at

full tilt. Perhaps both are always at work in me, but the juxtaposition is certainly more explicit in the dialogue. When in one instant I quote the Book
of Mormon to underscore contemporary LDS Christocentrism, my academic training then prompts a rehearsal of the nineteenth-century LDS
sermonic tradition that checked and sometimes seemed to ignore those
texts. And when I discourse on the robustness of Progressive-era Mormon
theologizing, I'm in the next moment sharing how the New Testament has
figured in my personal devotional life. The university that employs me is
self-consciously dedicated to the life of the mind and spirit, and I'm struck
by the ways the dialogue forces a kind of correlating education in me, one
shaped "by study and also by faith," as an early LDS revelation had it.[2]

If the early question animating the dialogue was, are Mormons
Christian?—and I think there is evidence that such was the case—I suspect
the question now has become, Can Mormons and evangelicals live up to
their highest ideals, preserving their distinctive witnesses while comprehending the other more charitably? From what I have seen, the answer is *yes*.
No evangelical in our group has backed away from his or her witness to the
truth, as they understand it. But with that, each has offered friendship and
understanding to us who have felt very much targeted in other contexts. For
my part, not only am I more deeply Mormon because of our conversations,
but I suspect I'm a better Mormon, too, in the sense that I can offer love and
generosity, without reservation, to those I once deemed "enemy." Surely, the
God of reconciliation must approve.

4

Looking Ahead

My Dreams for Mormon-Evangelical Dialogues

Craig L. Blomberg

In 1992 Greg Johnson, then the president of the Denver Seminary student council, and an ex-Mormon, introduced me to the writings of Stephen Robinson, professor of New Testament at Brigham Young University, whom I met that fall at the meetings of the American Academy of Religion and the Society of Biblical Literature (AAR/SBL). We struck up a friendship, which led to the idea of a writing project that finally saw the light of day in 1997 as *How Wide the Divide? A Mormon and an Evangelical in Conversation.*[1] About the same time, Johnson, now in ministry in Utah, was developing a friendship and having similar conversations with Robert Millet, also a prominent scholar on the BYU Religious Education faculty. Independently of each other, we two pairs of friends were talking about how to extend such dialogues to involve a wider swath of scholars from both communities.

Many collateral events have been spawned, directly or indirectly related to our dialogue group. These include separate, public conferences at both Fuller and BYU and dozens of public presentations by Millet and Johnson around the country and occasionally overseas, modeling the "convicted civility"[2] that characterizes our gatherings.[3] Well-known Christian pastors and leaders, not in academic positions, have had a chance to meet with some of the Mormon participants in our conversations in various more-informal gatherings, and several Church authorities among the LDS leadership have met with some of us academics and some of those same pastors and leaders. In a historic gathering in March of 2011, Elder Jeffrey Holland of the Quorum of the Twelve addressed the board of the National Association of Evangelicals (NAE) and fielded questions from them afterward at a reception hosted by the governor of the state of Utah in his mansion in Salt Lake City.[4]

By now it is fair to say that the dialogue group has discussed in some detail every major theological issue of interest to our respective communities and probably the most important historical ones as well. We have come to a far better mutual understanding, and we have grasped much more than before where we agree and where we disagree and where there is diversity in perspective among our communities. We have recognized where language usage appears to divide us but where in fact we are really saying much the same thing in different ways. We have also understood that sometimes we appear to be saying the same thing when we are not, because of different definitions given to key terms.

We have never proposed to draft a document like "Evangelicals and Catholics Together,"[5] only between "Evangelicals and Mormons." We have never sought any kind of joint ministry venture, for that matter, other than that some of us have published essays with each other in edited anthologies, co-authored books together in a "point-counterpoint" format or participated in conferences together where a diversity of religious opinions are discussed.[6] We *have* recognized that the most effective forum for mutual understanding comes when we agree that none of us in our joint gatherings will try to proselytize the other, though what two of us might decide to do in some entirely private conversation elsewhere is entirely up to us. At the same time, we have all expected that our communities would continue to proselytize each other actively, but that they need to do so with much greater awareness of each other's beliefs, misunderstandings, stereotypes, "red-flag" issues and the like.

We have hoped (and indeed seen occur sporadically) that in local contexts Mormon bishops and evangelical pastors might model similar dialogues, that select members of wards and parishes would gather for friendly interchange, and that other ecclesiastical and academic leaders could practice and teach about similar interfaith dialogue in college, university and seminary settings. En route, even without explicit evangelism, we have left no topics off limits and have shared from our hearts our deepest personal convictions about our respective faiths.[7] In this respect our dialogue is very unlike the vast majority of conversations at AAR/SBL, where the unwritten rule is never to risk offending anyone by discussing personal theological convictions, except perhaps very much in passing.

As of this writing we have had a Mormon candidate for the presidency of the United States for the first time in history. It is probably fair to say that as a result of the Mitt Romney campaign there is unprecedented public awareness and understanding of who Mormons are, in the same way that evangelicals have had unprecedented notoriety in the public square since *Time* dubbed 1976 the "year of the Evangelical,"[8] when Jimmy Carter was elected president.[9] What then is left for us to accomplish? Have our dialogues served their purpose and run their course? Should they be disbanded or at least radically reconfigured, lest we run the risk of ossifying ourselves, as has so often happened in the history of religion, when an *ad hoc* gathering of people institutionalized itself into something that never needed to be perpetuated in the first place? What are my personal dreams for the future in this arena?

This book represents the realization of one of my greatest hopes, namely, that we could produce a publication of some sort reflecting the past fifteen years of conversations and some of the most important lessons and concepts we have learned, both about each others' beliefs and about methods for healthy interreligious dialogue. Too much useful information has been shared and insights gleaned that have not appeared in print anywhere to let it all disappear now.[10]

My second hope is that we can pass the torch to the next generation. It is one thing to produce publications, but friendships and trust develop best in the context of extended, live, face-to-face conversations and give-and-take. Several of our participants are retired or of retirement age; one has passed away. Most of the rest of us are less than a decade from retirement age. Our longest-time participants are incredibly busy and could easily delegate their leadership to others.

A third hope would be that many more people throughout evangelicalism would hear about what we have done in a context that would spur them on to similar conversations. It is time, for example, for evangelicals to learn why it would be best to lay the "cult" label for Mormonism to rest once and for all. Evangelicals seldom stop to think that we have an idiosyncratic use of the term that refers to new religious movements that are offshoots of larger parent religions but with heterodox beliefs at various points. To the rest of the world, however, *cult* conjures up the notion of a tiny cluster of individuals following a charismatic leader into bizarre behavior, including possibly violent or destructive actions. These are people who are virtually brainwashed and antisocial, such as Jim Jones and his poison-Kool-Aid-drinking followers in Guyana, David Koresh and the Branch Davidians in Waco, or Heaven's Gate in Southern California.[11]

It is also time for people to stop learning only secondhand about people whose religious views at times differ from theirs. In a global village, there is no reason not to engage members of other religions or denominations directly.[12] So much evangelical literature on these topics is overly simplified, historically dated, not representative of the entire movements depicted and/or downright inaccurate. Short introductions to complex belief systems almost inevitably distort, especially when the author has a particular dislike for a given movement. The biases may be semiconscious, but they affect the results nevertheless. Recently I read a collection of John Wesley's fifty most important or famous sermons and realized how much my own theological education, mostly Lutheran and Calvinist, had skewed my understanding of Wesley's theology!

Mormons likewise need to engage evangelicals in far less confrontational settings than the classic door-to-door evangelism they are known for. They should invite evangelical friends and leaders to fireside chats and similar forums, as I have occasionally experienced. They need to get to know the "silent majority" of us who are not nearly as "mean-spirited" (to use their preferred term for the most combative or polemical of us) as the anti-Mormons they are more used to encountering. They need to learn the breadth of evangelicalism, so that we are not all tarnished with the same two brushes of "easy believism" and rigid Calvinism. Many LDS think they are rejecting evangelical theology when in fact they are objecting only to the famous Calvinist "TULIP" of total depravity, unconditional election, limited atonement, irresistible grace and the perseverance of the saints. They too need to read the works of Wesley. Or they find fault with the notion that one can accept Christ as Savior but not as Lord and therefore not begin living a transformed life.[13] This latter view is common in certain dispensationalist circles but actually characterizes only a small percentage of evangelicals. And many of *us* would reject it as thoroughly unbiblical!

Finally, at some point we will need at least an unofficial "imprimatur" of some kind from the most influential and important leaders in our movements. Identifying those people is straightforward in Mormonism, because it is hierarchically structured. It is much more difficult in evangelicalism, but it would not be hard to develop a list of names of people whose endorsements would provide credibility in the eyes of a majority of people in our midst. To date, the responses of individuals among those two groups of leaders has been very much a mixed bag and has left some of us feeling very precarious about our involvement in the dialogue, at least over a certain stretch of time. So many people in our world imagine and even report on things happening in our midst that are simply untrue and impute motives to participants that they cannot possibly know.[14] This needs to be labeled explicitly for what it is—sinful, to be repented of and replaced with trust and good will.

If not a single one of my dreams comes true, the good that has been accomplished in our dialogue thus far will still have surpassed my wildest dreams and probably those of all of the initial participants. But because so much of what some of us dared to dream for *has* come true, often with an amazing working of God's Spirit after a period of time when it appeared that doors had been closed to us for good, perhaps it is not too audacious to keep dreaming for an even greater future for the dialogue in whatever period of time God is pleased to find it useful, constructive and fruitful for furthering his purposes for his world.

Responding to Millet and Fluhman

James E. Bradley

MY OWN EXPERIENCE OF THE Mormon-evangelical dialogue is similar to that expressed by Robert Millet and Spencer Fluhman, but from the other side of the table, as it were. The early mutual suspicion turning gradually to trust and abiding friendships; the serious study of Mormon doctrine, wonderfully enhanced and made infinitely more fascinating by the guidance of Mormon experts in the field; the new insights that emerged concerning one's own faith while learning the faith of others; the challenge of navigating the question of which side will change and how much change is desired (or required) for real Christian fellowship—all of these realities have made for a remarkable and exhilarating experience over the past fifteen years. Like Bob Millet, I have a vivid memory of the second dialogue at Fuller Seminary in the fall of 2000, when Stephen Robinson opened to us the Book of Mormon and displayed in text after text the emphatic stress on the unmerited grace of God found uniquely in the cross and atoning work of Christ. What was very familiar to Stephen, Bob and the other Latter-day Saints who were present seemed utterly new and almost shocking to me and the evangelicals there, not just because of what we found in the Book of Mormon, but also because of what was obviously a personal statement of faith and hope in the finished work of Christ by our new Mormon friends.

I wish to comment briefly on two remarks made in the essays by Bob and Spencer. Bob mentioned the dialogue held at Nauvoo, Illinois, and its powerful and positive impact on our relationships "across the table." For the evangelicals (and Mormons), Nauvoo was hardly "neutral" territory in that it is the site where Joseph Smith's teachings turned far more radical and where, in nearby Carthage, Joseph and his older brother Hyrum were murdered in 1844. But Nauvoo is truly noteworthy for revealing the "peoplehood" and sufferings of the Latter-day Saints. As we stood together on the banks of the Mississippi River (which is about two miles wide at Nauvoo), Richard Bennett and Paul Peterson regaled us with the remarkable narrative of a persecuted people who courageously turned their faces westward, aiming ultimately for the Great Salt Lake and Utah. Quite apart from whether one believes the stories told in the Book of Mormon, here is a story that leads one to appreciate the common memories and corporate meanings of Mormonism in a fresh way. Latter-day Saints are a "people group," and their unique history means that the Mormon faith cannot be easily separated from that story. The question that this experience posed anew for me (and in a way, the question that it poses for all evangelicals) is, must a Mormon deny his or her own peoplehood in order to be a Christian? The question is particularly difficult because the Nauvoo period (the period that gives Mormons part of their identity) reveals Mormon teachings that are impossible to reconcile with traditional Christianity. Evangelicals in the dialogue have come to appreciate the orthodox convictions of our Mormon dialogue partners on the unique nature of Christ's divine person and work. Can these doctrines be sustained over the long haul, *along with* the other distinctive (and from an evangelical perspective, distinctively heterodox) teachings of the faith?

Second, Spencer observed the importance of an academic, scholarly setting for the dialogue, and I would like to briefly expand on his point. The context of relative detachment in the dialogue and the commitment scholars have (when at their best) to fairness, patient research and careful expression have been essential for our mutual understanding. But for the Christian scholar, as Spencer notes, detachment does not entail the absence of religious conviction, and our convictions are closely related to our individual consciences and what we personally hold as sacred. When the Protestant Reformation first championed the necessity that individuals interpret Scripture for themselves, the Reformers established the right of private judgment and thereby laid the foundation for religious toleration in the

Western world. Sadly, in the long history of Protestantism, this respect for others' consciences has not always been honored, and in the case of Mormonism, Protestant evangelicals have failed miserably. In the dialogue we have learned afresh the importance of respecting others' consciences and convictions. But this respect has not meant that we stop making our own convictions known, and we have advanced them with the best arguments we can possibly marshal, recalling that St. Paul *reasoned* with the Athenian philosophers, and he *reasoned* with the Jews at Rome. The dialogue has not contributed to a relativistic indifference to doctrine on either side, and we have all been newly impressed with the importance of "owning" our faith. I believe that the combination of an open, tolerant and more-or-less objective atmosphere with a recognition of serious differences of conviction is what has given the dialogue its integrity. In a sense, then, the dialogue illustrates one way that convicted Christian scholars can help lead and influence the church in an era that desperately needs both more interreligious understanding and, at the same time, true Christian conviction.

A Serious Call to Devout and Holy Dialogue

Going Deeper in Interfaith Discussions

Gerald R. McDermott

WILLIAM LAW (1686–1761) WAS A RARE BIRD—an academic with guts. Because his conscience would not allow him to swear an oath of allegiance to George I, he lost his position at Emmanuel College at Cambridge. The title of this chapter is a riff on his most famous book,[1] not only because of its three useful adjectives and influence on eighteenth-century evangelicalism, but also because his own approach to the religious differences of his day exemplifies the spirit I recommend in this essay. Such evangelical stars as the Wesley brothers, William Wilberforce and George Whitefield went to Law for advice and were moved by what he wrote.[2] He was called a "controversialist" because he wrote serious intellectual critiques of alternative religious movements such as deism[3] and antinomianism.[4]

Unfortunately for those who claim Law for orthodoxy, Law was also an admirer of German theosophist Jakob Böhme, whose work eventually persuaded Law to embrace universalism. But his determination to discuss theological difference with both cordial civility and *serious* rigor was admirable. His polemical context was different from ours, of course. Deists and antinomians were vastly distant from the Christian orthodox, while Mormons and orthodox Christians have many more points of contact, Barth's protests notwithstanding. But we can learn from his recognition of the need for theological seriousness. He knew it was not enough to concentrate on points of contact while skipping lightly over points of difference. For the sake of true understanding, which both sides of most dialogues usually profess to want, he knew it was necessary to explore the points of deepest difference. Only by going to those depths, his works seem to suggest, could any dialogue partner understand either difference *or* similarity. Without such serious intellectual work, recognition of even similarities could be superficial and misleading.

Law's work also reminds us of the difference that devotion ("devout") makes in interfaith dialogue. As my Orthodox Jewish friends said years ago when they started serious dialogues with a number of us orthodox Christian theologians, "This is so much better than our dialogues in the 1970s and after, when most participants, both Jewish and Christian, believed very little and were happy to agree on what they did *not* believe." The example of Law reminds us that the best interfaith dialogue takes place *not*—as the Enlightenment would have us believe—among those who are uncommitted to a faith tradition, but among serious believers who are observant and devoted.

Law's third adjective ("holy") suggests the proper goal of interfaith dialogue: to know the living God. This of course is similar to the need for *devout* minds to get the best work done. But while devotion speaks of the depth from which good dialogue emerges, *holiness* points to its goal—the union of holy souls with the holy God. The best dialogue wants not merely acceptance of the other as religiously legitimate, but also growth in knowledge of God by intensive grappling with the depths of the theological other. Therefore, even though dialogue is primarily intellectual, it will involve to some degree the deepest affections of all participants. These affections, according to Jonathan Edwards, are the most fundamental loves that drive not only feelings and choices but also thoughts of the mind. The human person is unified. Hence we should never separate theology from practice, or doctrine from ethics, by saying one is more important than the other. That is akin to proclaiming the body to be more important than the soul, or the head more important than the body to which it is attached. Similarly, we cannot assume that we can understand religious practices without comprehending the theological framework that gives shape to those practices. Nor should we think that attention to theology is sufficient without consideration of religious practice. Such assumptions falsely compartmentalize the human being, misunderstand religion and avoid the depths to which good interfaith dialogue should plunge.

PRODUCTIVE TENSION

Many of us shy away from these dialogical depths because they might create tension. Can we still affirm one another as good persons and friends while at the same time disagreeing over fundamental points of theology? We can and we must. Let me share some of my experience with this.

Several years ago I gave a paper on Jewish-Christian dialogue at the Van Leer Institute in Jerusalem.[5] The conference was the culmination of four years of intense theological dialogue between Orthodox Jewish theologians and orthodox Christian theologians. The meetings of the previous years had often been punctuated by moments of tension when one or another scholar would charge that another was "dead wrong" or "fundamentally misinformed" or "misrepresenting the tradition." We Christians learned that this was customary for most of our Jewish friends, who had grown up debating one another—often with raised voices in the yeshiva and synagogues and beyond—but usually concluding with words of affection or at least cordiality.

I remember the tension when an esteemed Jewish scholar, famous around the world for his many books and lectures in major world capitals, told us all—Christians and Jews included—that Christians could not be included in the Abrahamic covenant. And the equally uncomfortable moment when a world-class Jewish philosopher said that it was his duty to warn us Christians that we were guilty of idolatry because we were worshiping a man. I also remember the tension I felt while delivering my paper in Jerusalem when I said that the four issues that historically have divided Jews and Christians—law, resurrection, Trinity and incarnation—were all based on Jewish principles, so that only the identity of Jesus divides us. I was surprised to see that these arguments were greeted with smiles and warmth by my Jewish auditors, but their smiles disappeared and everything got quiet when I finished my paper by pleading with them to accept messianic Jews as genuine Jews.

But even more surprising was what happened after all these moments of tension. Our dialogue went deeper and became more serious. Jews learned things about Christians they did not previously know, and we Christians learned things about Jews we did not previously know. And miracle of miracles, we learned *from* one another. Christians learned something about the distinctively Jewish character of the covenant, even while it admitted Gentiles (or so we Christians and some of our Jewish friends believed) by adoption or associate membership. Jews learned that Jesus and Paul were observant Jews—something most Jews had never considered.

My point is that the best interreligious dialogue emerges from respectful but honest exploration of deepest differences. This exploration is in the context of friendship and shared lives and mutual respect, and it never confronts with a confrontational or hostile style. It does not assign bad motives to the other, nor does it assume eternal perdition for those on the other side of the theological divide. But neither does it avoid discussing in depth the points of the most dramatic differences, which are usually doctrinal and the discussion of which sometimes creates tension. That tension can be productive without diminishing shared respect. Oddly, it can enhance mutual respect.

Interfaith Friendship Versus Interfaith Dialogue

For the sake of clarity, it is important to distinguish interfaith dialogue on the one hand from interfaith friendship on the other. The latter is usually private, one-on-one, the stuff of some of our most interesting relationships. We try to learn about each other and enjoy hearing from a different perspective about topics of mutual interest. Sometimes we challenge each other gently, using our own perspective to shed light where we think it might help in the perspective of another. For example, I have had a warm friendship of some years with Bob Millet, one of the editors of this volume. I remember having lunch with him in Salem, Virginia, some years ago at a restaurant, when we were discussing evangelicalism's lack of a *magisterium,* or central authority. I don't think he was trying to change my mind, but his observation that Mormonism's central authorities help provide unity and coherence to Mormons got me thinking for months and years after about the dangers of not having such authority in evangelicalism.

I think of interfaith dialogue as something more structured and purposeful. It is almost always conducted by groups. Or, if it involves one-on-one dialogue, it is usually public and sponsored by a group. Bob and I, for example, have had three public dialogues sponsored by Roanoke College. All were packed-house affairs. In the first two, Bob and I were the sole speakers before a live audience; each of us discussed where our two faith traditions overlapped, but then we placed more emphasis on where we differed, and why. The first was on Mormonism generally; the second focused on Jesus; the third brought in two other speakers, and the four of us discussed the possibility of a Mormon in the White House.

So interfaith dialogue is a different animal from interfaith friendship. One feels free to use a kind of intellectual rigor in the first that would not be as appropriate or welcome in the second. Both kinds of discussion, however, need to be conducted with civility and respect and in a spirit of friendship. One must always assume the best of the other, refraining from presumptions about unstated motives or eternal destinies.

First Level of Interfaith Dialogue: Getting to Know You

If interfaith friendship is different from interfaith dialogue, there are two kinds of this latter dialogue. The first I will call "getting to know you" dialogue. It is an initial phase where representatives of different faith communities spend months and sometimes years learning *about* one another. They focus more on similarities than differences. Their aim is to correct distortions, prejudices and stereotypes. Each side in the dialogue tries to correct both its own distortions of the other, and the other's distortions of itself. For example, as I entered these evangelical-Mormon dialogues, and especially as I did research for a book-length dialogue I held with Bob, I learned that the Mormon tradition was far more Christ-centered than I had imagined. This was contrary to what I had heard and read from various evangelical sources.

I have also learned from my dialogues with Muslims that not all Muslims want *sharia* law. Nor do all endorse what happened on 9/11, as many Americans fear. Some believe passionately in religious pluralism, despite contrary emphases in various strands of Islamic tradition. Another example of learning *about* the religious other takes place in both formal and informal dialogues between Catholics and Protestants. Many Protestants, especially evangelicals, are surprised to learn that salvation by works is not taught by the *Catholic Catechism* or the most representative Catholic theologians such as Augustine, Aquinas and Benedict XVI.

SECOND LEVEL OF INTERFAITH DIALOGUE:
EXPLORING DEEPEST DIFFERENCES

The second level builds on the first. Indeed, the second *requires* the first. If there are not mutual respect and at least a degree of friendship, then any probing of deepest differences, which is the matter for the second phase, will not get very far, and will be unpleasant at that. But *if* one can build this second level on the first, then the second phase is where the most important work of religious dialogue takes place. For it is only at this second level that one side can learn *from* the other.

Jon Levenson has made this point recently in his important book *Inheriting Abraham: The Legacy of the Patriarch in Judaism, Christianity, and Islam*.[6] Many of us talk about the three great monotheisms as three religions that have common elements. Often it is said that their *most* common feature is their shared reverence for Abraham as a father of faith. Levenson cites the Global Negotiation Project at Harvard University as typical of this assumption that these three great religions share Abraham. The project has begun developing a dramatic initiative—a modern, interfaith and intercultural pilgrimage called Abraham's Path, which follows the supposed footsteps of the biblical patriarch. Levenson argues that this project is based on shallow interfaith efforts. By restricting itself to similarities and ignoring deepest differences, it has found a kind of sharing that is actually disrespectful to the particularities of each religion.

> In brief, the Abraham's Path document mixes the theologies of the various Abrahamic religions together in a way that does not adequately respect the distinctive claims of any of them. With its mention of monotheism, it favors Islam and perhaps Judaism above Christianity [because of Christianity's assertion of plurality within God]. With its mention of faith, it favors Christianity (and perhaps Islam) over Judaism [because Jews consider observance more important than belief]. With its mention of fatherhood, it favors Judaism and Christianity over Islam, though the absence of any acknowledgement of lineage alongside history and faith is problematic for Judaism.[7]

Levenson suggests that we can learn from religious others only if we take time and effort to explore our deepest differences. Only then will we find similarities that are true all the way down, as it were. And only then can we learn something truly new that might help us deepen our own faith.

For example, only if we let Mormons challenge Protestantism's tendency toward easy believism and antinomianism can we evangelicals learn something that might guard against those dangers. But that will happen only if we invite Mormons to push us evangelicals at the level of moral theology, and then its necessary connection to dogmatic theology. Islam might teach us about the necessity of faith in the public square, against our tradition of strict separation of church and state—but only if we are willing to tangle in a rigorous way with Muslim thinkers. We might learn something about the Pauline concept of dying to self if we struggle rigorously in intellectual dialogues with Buddhists and their notion of *anatta,* or no self. Just getting to know Buddhists at the first stage will probably not get us there. And we evangelicals might understand better the relationship between faith and works if we are willing to engage in serious theological dialogue with Catholic theologians. Just getting to know them at the first stage will probably not achieve this result—not unless we struggle with them over biblical texts and theological traditions.

THE GOAL OF INTERFAITH DIALOGUE: TRUTH

Remaining at the first stage of interfaith dialogue—getting to know you—we will find more truth *about* the other, but probably not make much headway in what ought to be the goal of all authentic dialogue—Truth with a capital *T.* By this I don't mean to imagine naively that we will all agree if we talk hard enough and long enough. What I mean is that hard wrestling with texts and traditions is necessary to succeed at finding where we really differ. To know that is an accomplishment that is usually missed at the first phase. If it is achieved at all, it is only at superficial levels, which usually simply reinforce stereotypes.

But if we are successful at disagreeing on what is fundamental—and often that lies at more than one point—we have achieved something worth achieving. It is good in itself because it represents true understanding. But it is good for another reason: only at this point are we able to learn something about what really is. In other words, only here can we grow in our vision of God.

Ellen Charry has written an excellent book about theology as an exercise in finding truth with the object of loving and worshiping God.[8] In other words, the purpose of all theology is to know and love God as he really is. The converse is also true: bad theology will lead to faulty vision. As Stanley Hauerwas has put it recently, the purpose of theology is to give us confidence that we are worshiping the true God.[9] Interfaith dialogue is usually between people who are worshiping who or what they consider to be God, or in the case of Zen and Theravada Buddhists, devoted to what they consider to be the truest vision of ultimate reality. For all these communities, it makes a difference to get Truth right. Without seeing the Truth as it really is, we won't get what we want. Or even if we are saved (in Christian terms) with faulty theology, our worship and experience of God will fall short of what Jesus prescribed—to "worship in spirit and truth" (John 4:23).

I am arguing, then, that the goal of all interfaith dialogue ought to be truth, and nothing short of that. We will probably not agree with our interlocutors on everything, but the exercise of theological exploration and argument together should, at best, draw us closer to the true God. This is why Hauerwas criticizes those religious traditions that never give serious attention to heresy and apostasy. They labor, he writes, under the illusion that to investigate such things would violate catholicity. Not so, he insists: true catholicity is "to be ready to challenge as well as be challenged by other Christian traditions."[10] I would add, in the context of interfaith dialogue more generally, "by other *religious* traditions." But Hauerwas's point is particularly apt for dialogue between two traditions such as the LDS and evangelical communities. Both claim to be Christian and the best way to see and follow Jesus Christ. Can both be right? Where they agree, certainly. But where they disagree, no. Let us challenge each other, with respect and in friendship, and seek to grow in knowledge and love of God in Christ.

IS IT WRONG TO TRY TO PERSUADE?

There was a time when it was thought that all attempts to persuade the religious other were illegitimate and disrespectful. For a while most of the Orthodox Jews in our Jewish-Christian dialogues were of this opinion. But then as we argued about this very question, all eventually came to agree, in part or in whole, that it is the very nature of human discourse to persuade. If nothing else, every interlocutor seeks to persuade the other of the coherence of his or her own position. Otherwise he would not make the effort, in conversation or writing, to disagree with others.[11]

Most of us came to realize that all committed believers think their faith is the best—not only for them but for everyone. Even Orthodox Jews who don't believe in converting others believe their worship of the God of Israel is as close as it gets to what is finally real. I would guess that all but the most postmodern evangelicals and Mormons believe this about their own faith. Even those who would argue that their faith does not have to be held by everyone— for they think all will find their own way eventually or all will be saved— would also believe that those who disagree with *these* very ideas are wrong.

We also came to see that to fail to engage the religious other at the point of our deepest differences is to fail to respect that other. For then we are suggesting that we do not consider those differences significant. Yet our religious interlocutors probably do. Our refusal to engage sends the message that that other religion is not worth engaging—especially at the points where it is most distinctive. So the attempt to persuade our interlocutors of the cogency of our position is actually a way to respect our interlocutors and our common search for Truth.

Not Conversion but Bearing Witness

I am not suggesting we can convert our interlocutors in interfaith dialogue. As I argued above, we always already try to persuade others of the cogency of our positions when we argue for them with those who don't hold those positions. To say that we should not is to be unaware of the structure of human discourse—that we already do this whether we know it or not. But just as it is naive to think we do not try to persuade others in interfaith dialogue, it is also presumptuous to think we can convert others to our positions. That is something only God can do.

But if we are foolish to think we can convert others, we are reminded by Scripture that we are called to bear witness to the vision of God we have been given. This is different from proselytization, which is often coercive and dishonest. It is also light years from the Walter Martin approach, of which Richard Mouw has spoken eloquently, that would accuse the religious other of dissimulation if insiders do not agree with outsiders. It is the humbled attempt to share the light we have been given, in the hope that it will enlighten others. It is also the humble awareness that we have seen only a refracted beam from a blinding sun, so we need to see infinitely more. It is faith that the very exchange of vision with the religious other, and the laborious testing of conflicting visions, will help us see more.

THE DANGER OF IDOLATRY

The author of 1 John tells us that the purpose of theology, and I would add interfaith dialogue, is to sharpen our vision of the living God by testing the spirits: "Beloved, don't trust every spirit, but test the spirits to determine what is of God, because many false prophets have gone out into the world" (1 John 4:1, my translation). Mormons and classical Christians agree that this is a warning given by the inspiration of the Holy Spirit. We have different visions of God, and both of our communities are warned here to distinguish truth from error, so that we might sift what is of God from what is not. The exercise of interfaith dialogue can help both of our communities do this, as long as we conduct our dialogue with mutual respect and in a spirit of friendship.

For the stakes are high. Sometimes we forget that a preeminent burden of the Old Testament authors is to shun idolatry, which all of us would agree is the worship of anything other than the God presented by biblical revelation. This God is a "jealous" God (Exodus 20:5), who likens idolatry to "rebellion" (1 Samuel 15:23). This burden reappears in the New Testament, where Jesus admonishes the Samaritan woman that she must worship "in spirit and in truth" (John 4:23), and Paul is revolted by the idolatry at Athens (Acts 17) and distinguishes idolatry from "truth," which God has revealed (Romans 1:18-25).

Because of our finitude and sin, we all possess faith that is partly idolatrous and partly true. Let us not be hesitant to press into the depths of true dialogue. For it holds the promise of both shining the light on idolatrous misperceptions and bringing us a bit closer to knowledge of the living God.

Apologetics as if People Mattered

Dennis Okholm

WHEN I WAS IN SEMINARY I took a course in apologetics that trained me in a two-step strategy. First we proved that God exists, then we proved that Jesus is who he said he is. If our interlocutor disagreed with us at any point it was because he or she was "irrational."

I have since learned that that was just one of many approaches in apologetics—an approach I have chosen not to espouse to the students who have taken *my* apologetics course over the past few years. In fact, I opted for what some might call a "postliberal" approach and subtitled my course, "Winning Disciples Rather Than Arguments" or "Apologetics as if People Mattered."

When we covered the "cults" in my seminary course, Mormonism was in the mix. We were absolutely certain that Mormons were going to hell, but then I had always been taught the same fate for Roman Catholics, and I wasn't sure about Presbyterians, and Anglicans were not even on my radar. Though my assessments have radically changed—I later became an ordained Presbyterian, am now an Anglican priest and have been associated with Roman Catholic Benedictine monks for over two decades—I still embrace one very valuable lesson I learned in our unit on cults. Our professor told us that when we engaged a member of such a religious group we should focus on just one question: "Who is Jesus Christ?" Ironically, it is that question that has also radically changed my assessment of those members of the Church of Jesus Christ of Latter-day Saints (LDS) who have become some of my cherished friends, though I am fairly certain that that is not at all what my seminary professor intended.

How I got to that point requires a narrative that begins in April of 2007.

With some hesitation I agreed to be the faculty advisor for Azusa Pacific University's (APU) spring break student mission trip to Utah. The team's mission was to learn about Mormonism for several months before making the trek to dialogue with Mormon students at various universities in Utah and Idaho. The agenda was not to proselytize (though all the students quietly hoped that the LDS students would come over to our side), but to engage in friendly dialogue that recognized our differences and sought better understanding of each other, practicing what Rich Mouw calls "convicted civility." I would be with the students for a full three days, flying in and flying out.

The agenda was set by Greg Johnson, founder of the ministry Standing Together. Greg is an ex-Mormon (now an ordained Baptist minister) who had developed a close relationship with Brigham Young University (BYU) professor Bob Millet. Though Greg was a new acquaintance, strangely Bob was not. Years before when I taught at Wheaton College, my colleague Tim Phillips and I had initiated the Wheaton Theology Conference (now in its third decade). One year the topic was C. S. Lewis. In response to our call for papers, we received a proposal from a Robert Millet of BYU; his topic had to do with what Mormons found helpful in C. S. Lewis. The college administration was not happy about our acceptance of this paper, but Bob turned out to be delightful, and I learned, among other things, that the BYU library devoted more space to Lewis than to any other single author. My perception of Mormons was ever so slightly beginning to change.

During this foray into LDS territory with my students I was asked to link up with Spencer Fluhman, a church historian at BYU. In front of a classroom full of APU and BYU students I presented a historical sketch of Protestant evangelicalism, after which Spencer did something of the same thing with Mormonism. I was immediately impressed by Spencer's knowledge of American church history and his lighthearted admission of what he found strange or amusing about his own tribe while still clearly committed to his identity as an LDS churchman and scholar.

During this short trip I made more new friends among LDS professors and church leaders. Greg also arranged a visit with one of the LDS Church general authorities over lunch, who addressed any and all questions with gracious and forthright answers.

I have since joined the students each year but one. I always look forward to reunions with my LDS acquaintances in Utah and to the time with my students. I have never seen more intensity among students than I have witnessed on this trip. During the week some students establish lasting relationships with their LDS counterparts, and they learn along the way that they can differ on what they consider the most important element of their lives—their faith—yet respect and enjoy the company of the "other" who is learning the same lesson. Over against the ideological deafness and blindness that is rife in our world today, what my students are learning gives hope.

But the trip is also intense because my students take their beliefs so seriously as they are challenged in dialogue. They question what *they* have always held in such a way that they discern the chaff from the grain and deepen their commitment to what really matters. At the same time, they learn to listen to those who differ and graciously challenge their dialogue partners to do similar questioning and sifting.

What my students are engaged in is a bit of character formation. They are learning to identify "nonnegotiables" but to hold on to them with humility. This requires some elaboration that engages the postliberal approach to apologetics I mentioned at the beginning.

Before the students head for Utah they usually come to our house for a meal, and I share with them what I consider the nonnegotiables of Nicene orthodoxy: that something exists rather than nothing because God created all that is; that Jesus Christ is fully divine and fully human (entailing a commitment to the doctrines of the Trinity—over against Arianism and modalism, and the incarnation—over against adoptionism and docetism); that it is only by the life, death and resurrection of Jesus that we are saved; and that the Bible is *the* unique, reliable, authoritative, inspired witness to Jesus Christ (as it is illumined by the Holy Spirit).

But they learn to hold these convictions with humility. They *must* for this reason: our knowledge of Christian truth is neither completely objective nor radically relative (i.e., totally incommensurable with any other claims to religious truth). In fact, our knowledge of Christian truth is subjective, but it is not for that reason untrue. In fact, all of our knowledge is subjective. There is no view from nowhere and no Archimedean standpoint from which to adjudicate all religious claims. We all are shaped by a tradition (Alasdair

MacIntyre). We stand on the horizon that affects what we see (Hans-Georg Gadamer). But in our conversations there is a "fusion of horizons": sharing enough in common that we can talk and understand each other, we are confronted with a different point of view that may even cause our own horizon to shift a bit. If we do not approach our conversations in this manner then, as James K. A. Smith warns, to engage in dialogue with the assumption that our nonnegotiables are *objectively* true "often translates into the worst kinds of imperial and colonial agendas."[1] But that need not compromise our conviction that the nonnegotiables are in fact true. In his book on apologetics William Placher wisely remarks: "Those who admit they argue out of a tradition . . . can nevertheless believe in the truth of their claims: truth not just for them but for everyone."[2] And so we can be realists and hold convictions that we believe are absolutely true while still confessing our lack of objectivity and practicing epistemic humility.

This is a far cry from the apologetic approach I was taught by my seminary professor and his rather limited concept of "rationality" (which failed to take into account tradition and other pragmatic considerations), and I have tried to instill in my students the attitude that simply because their LDS counterparts hold convictions that are at odds with those held by evangelicals, the LDS position is not for that reason necessarily "irrational."

Returning to my narrative, it was the initial trip with these students that led to my involvement with peers in academia. Twice (during my inclusion in the group of scholars represented by this book) we have taken trips to our respective "Meccas"—hosted by the LDS in Palmyra, New York, and hosted by the evangelicals in Wheaton, Illinois. In each case we have seen the iconic places and heard past and present accounts of our traditions. This has led to greater understanding of each other and, along the way, some intense discussions about everything from sources of revelation (on our Palymyra trip) to how concerned the church should be about "relevance" to this culture (at Willow Creek Church on our Wheaton trip). And we evangelicals have walked away from these deliberations puzzled as to how our Mormon friends can buy into the gold plates, for example, while we realize that on Christmas Eve it should be equally difficult for any outsider to buy into the idea that one person of an undivided triune God can, from that time on, forever assume a human body now resurrected.

Such puzzlements demonstrate what W. V. O. Quine referred to as our webs of belief. It is not the case that our belief systems are constructed on a foundation of some indubitable truth—a starting point that is firmly established on its own. That Cartesian ship has sailed. Descartes didn't get anywhere beyond his dictum "I think, therefore I am" without smuggling in assumptions to prove God's existence and the general reliability of sense perceptions. Our belief systems—whether Mormon or evangelical in this case—are webs that are woven of unchallengeable elements in the center (such as the nonnegotiables) with entailments and more tentative convictions that spin out to the edges where our experiences impinge. As Ludwig Wittgenstein insisted, the foundations are held up by the rest of the house.

Another way of saying all of this is to admit that each of our traditions has an internal logic from which we speak in our own voice, even though we can make connections with those whose voice emanates from *their* system's internal logic. So, for instance, Christians are adamant that Jesus was raised from the dead. It is a conviction that nests in the center of the web. It is unchallengeable in dialogue with those whose plausibility structure simply does not allow for dead people to get up and walk about after three days in a grave. But it is not unchallengeable in the sense that nothing could *conceivably* alter this conviction about Jesus' resurrection. Still, using an analogy that Placher suggested, until there is some empirical evidence of infidelity, a spouse does not *expect* her partner to be unfaithful; in the same way, though it is possible that something *could* count against belief in Jesus' resurrection, the Christian does not *expect* that her faith in this event could or will be undercut.[3] (And, in fact, if something like a sarcophagus of Jesus' bones were "discovered," it is likely that the web will be adjusted to fit the empirical evidence rather than that the center will be replaced.) This is how I understand the commitment taken by my LDS peers to the story of the gold plates, which I would consider, at best, only a legend.

All of this is to say that in our dialogues evangelicals and Mormons have to be aware of relatively unchallengeable centers that hold the threads of the webs together; and while it may be hoped by both sides that the other's center will be replaced (i.e., that there would be a conversion or "paradigm shift"), it is highly unlikely. Still, it may explain why in our dialogues there are edges of our webs that are more easily adjusted than the weave that lies farther within (such as differing conceptions of divine ontology).

These "webs" are discussed in our semiannual academic discussions about theology. As already mentioned, they focus on specific theological issues that have divided us, such as pre-Nicene conceptions of the Trinity. Intense dialogue often ensues around a book or papers written by group members. There have been moments when one or more of us will have an "aha" moment—an insight into the other's position that helps to clarify or surprise, a realization that what we thought we meant is perhaps not exactly what we have been saying, or a recognition that we are in closer agreement on some points of doctrine than we at first realized. In the process of coming to understand LDS teachings better, I have a deeper, more sophisticated understanding of my own Nicene Christianity, while discovering other aspects of my long-held beliefs that need further clarification.

Examples of this include the conversation we had about the evangelical (Nicene) conception of the three trinitarian "persons" who are not three separate "beings." I think it was an "aha" moment for our LDS friends when we appealed to the fourth-century Cappadocian notion of *perichoresis* (co-inherence), which entails such a relation between the three that if one is taken away the other two disappear—a notion that would not be entailed in LDS beliefs about the Godhead.

Another instance occurred when I was in a public dialogue with respected LDS scholar Richard Bushman about our differing views of revelation and authority. I surprised him by articulating what might be a point of confluence between the two of us—namely, John Calvin's insistence in the *Institutes* (1.7.4–5) that "the testimony of the Spirit is more excellent than all reason" and is "the highest proof of Scripture" when it is a matter of establishing Scripture's divine origin; in other words, "Scripture is self-authenticated." (Calvin *did* teach that rational arguments are helpful *after* one has been convinced by the Spirit that the Bible is *God's* word.) The difference between us would be that I would apply Calvin's insistence only to the Old and New Testaments, while Bushman would apply it as well to the Book of Mormon.

Yet again, when I was debating with Spencer Fluhman whether the Christian church had required a restoration (as LDS doctrine teaches that it did), Spencer surprised me when he clarified his position using the analogy of a demolished building that needed complete reconstruction vis-à-vis a damaged building that only needed repairs. The surprise came because, while I expected him to opt for the former, he opted for the latter.

In all these cases (and more), the latter two of which were before "live" audiences, interlocutors were exceedingly gracious, even as we held the line with respect to our positions. That said, reactions from the audience have not always been positive. On yet another occasion when Spencer and I dialogued at a megachurch in Orange County, California, I was subsequently attacked on a website in a vitriolic tirade that accused me of being in bed with the devil. Even some of the parishioners at the Presbyterian church I used to attend found it difficult to understand how I could engage in friendly dialogue with members of the LDS Church, let alone how I could find anything in common doctrinally. But I understand why they are dumbfounded and at times upset with my reports, since I mentioned at the outset that I once shared their judgment.

Reinforcing my commitment to "apologetics as if people mattered" is one of the most significant memories of my interaction with LDS acquaintances. It comes from the day that four of us dialogued at that Orange County megachurch (emceed by Biola's Craig Hazen). Greg Johnson was paired with Bob Millet, and, as mentioned, I was paired with Spencer. Since the dialogue was to take place on a Sunday evening and since the crew had flown in from Utah the day before, they worshiped at the Presbyterian church where I happened to be preaching that Sunday morning, followed by a Sunday noon dinner at the Okholm residence. At this writing we have lived in our house for nearly a decade, and there have been many dear friends and family members who have gathered at our table for a meal and conversation, yet, still, the most memorable and enjoyable gathering we have ever had at our table was the dinner shared with Bob, Spencer and Greg. The irony (and perhaps the shame) is that in the past I would not even have answered the door when, through the peephole, I would spy two young men wearing white shirts and ties. Since then I have indeed learned to hold my convictions as if people, not arguments, mattered.

There will be some who will chide me for being naive (or worse) to savor the company of Mormons in my house without trying to proselytize them, and they may fear that I am wandering off into some relativistic fog. Yet the opposite has occurred: I have learned more about my own orthodox faith and how to articulate it with greater accuracy and sophistication—and love. And by practicing the hospitality that Jesus commends and that the Rule of Benedict insists on (to welcome each guest as Christ), I have discovered that, just as American evangelicals do not agree on all matters of faith and practice, there are "grace Mormons" and "works Mormons" (as one of our discussants, Jerry Root, puts it). This is something I never would have discovered if my only source of information about Mormons had come from the polemicists.

I may never be able to understand why some LDS peers whom I now consider close friends believe what they say they believe. And, frankly, I would not encourage a person to become deeply committed to the LDS Church. Does that mean that I still harbor my early conviction that all Mormons are damned to hell? Not at all. And here is one reason why: this dialogue has forced me to keep central the question that my seminary professor insisted on: Who is Jesus Christ? And I have become convinced that my LDS dialogue partners have more in common with the answer we evangelicals give to that question than I had previously thought.

In addition, our dialogue has forced me to ponder this: How much theology did Jesus' disciples have to articulate with the orthodox accuracy that evangelical (Nicene) Christians now rightly insist on in order for these early disciples to be "saved"? At the end of Luke's Gospel we are told that when the resurrected Jesus appeared bodily, some doubted even as they rejoiced at his presence among them. It would take another three centuries of church disputes to express the church's understanding of the Trinity, and another century to clarify boundaries (the four "withouts" in the Definition of Chalcedon) when articulating the relation of Jesus' humanity to his divinity. In the meantime, many disciples whom we would label "heretics" today declared their loyalty to the Lord Jesus and their conviction that they were saved by his atoning work on the cross, just as the LDS members of our dialogue profess. Perhaps the irony is that most of the people who sit in the pews of the evangelical churches in which I have worshiped cannot articulate with orthodox accuracy the doctrine of the Trinity, let alone a whole host of orthodox doctrines about which they accuse Mormons of being misguided. In fact, many slip into heretical language, yet I have never questioned their salvation precisely because they declare that they are followers of Jesus and that they are saved by his atoning work on the cross—that Jesus is their Lord and Savior.

And there lies the irony of what I was taught in my seminary apologetics course about refuting Mormons.

Maybe the best way to describe what I am learning from our dialogue—why it is good for my soul to continue in it, and why apologetics can be entered into as if people mattered—is to pray with St. Francis, "Lord, make me an instrument of your peace. Where there is hatred, let me sow love; . . . grant that I may not so much seek to be understood, as to understand."

From Calvary to Cumorah

The Significance of "Sacred Space"

Richard E. Bennett

FIFTY YEARS AGO, WHEN AS A YOUNG BOY I first visited Nauvoo and other Latter-day Saint (LDS) historical sites, I wrote in my little diary such fleeting comments as "Arrived at Independence, Missouri, today. Saw the place where the Missouri Temple will be built"; "Went to Palmyra [New York] and slept on the Hill Cumorah"; and finally, "Saw the old Carthage Jail where the Prophet Joseph Smith was martyred. Also we saw other historic sites of the Mormons in Nauvoo" (July–August 1956).[1] Nauvoo was then a far cry from what it is today. There was no Nauvoo Restoration, Incorporated. There were no beautifully restored buildings, no Williamsburg-like effort to manicure and professionally preserve and restore the past, no missionary-oriented visitors' center and certainly no temple restoration as we see today. Rather, Nauvoo slumbered on the banks of the Mississippi—dusty, unkempt and not at all sure if it had a future. Thanks to the work of a few farsighted Latter-day Saints, some efforts were made to resurrect the past. And, of course, families like mine kept coming in ever-increasing numbers to connect with and revere the history of what Mormons call the Restoration.

In awakening to the city's future, the leadership of the Church of Jesus Christ of Latter-day Saints changed its policy and determined to invest in the future of Nauvoo by professionally restoring this site. Elder Delbert L. Stapley, a modern LDS apostle, stated during the early days of the Nauvoo restoration,

Many thousands in the Church today have no real understanding of the personality, power, and mission of the Prophet Joseph Smith and other Church leaders. By developing our understanding and appreciation of Church history, we gain perspective and strengthened sense of purpose. It will aid us in making present-day choices and in obtaining present-day testimonies. . . . History carries the torch of light from the past into the present and illuminates the future. . . . This approach to Church history at Nauvoo demonstrates that Church pioneers were real people, living in the real world of America. History can enable us to ease the transition from one type of living to another and increase our effectiveness in the work of the Kingdom of God. . . . [It] would allow the student to vicariously relive the lives and experiences of these faithful pioneers and to point the way toward increased devotion and perspective. . . . To appreciate the fruits of Mormonism, one must understand its roots.[2]

Also since that time, the intellectualization of Church history and the rise of what many term the "New Mormon History"[3] have changed the intellectual landscape of our past and have invigorated the faith of some while sorely testing it in others.

A place of history such as Nauvoo provides us a timeout from our busy lives and hectic schedules to ponder on the gospel of Jesus Christ and the meaning of history. Nauvoo is a tangible, physical expression of the spiritual reality of the restoration of the gospel, which in turn is the modern, downstream reiteration of the resurrection of the Lord Jesus Christ. It has power as a sacred place because it reminds members of the LDS Church of the importance of their heritage, bringing the past to the present. Behind the buildings and the structures, beyond the pioneers and their families, and before the temple and the Red Brick Store is the First Vision of Joseph Smith, which is a revelation anew of our risen Lord and Savior, Jesus Christ. Fundamentally, if Nauvoo does not mean Christ, then it means very little.

Perhaps the best starting point to understand what sacred space can mean to all of us is to remember the imprint of the divine in our individual lives. From my experience, there are three essential elements to the sacred moments in my personal life: time, place and person. I look back at the YMCA hall on Elm Street in the hard-rock, heavy-drinking mining town of Sudbury, Ontario, where I was baptized on May 23, 1954. Although the building has been razed and the swimming pool, changing rooms and doorways no longer exist, the memory remains, and thankfully the record attests that on that day my life changed forever. It will ever remain a sacred time to me.

So too, the Sudbury Moose Hall on Pine Street, hardly a sacred place, with its moose head, beer hall and dancing floor—an established secularity in an irreverent setting—became a sacred spot for me. It was the place where church meetings were held, where my testimony of the living gospel of Jesus Christ began to take root and where I began to feel those "swelling motions," as the Book of Mormon describes them, and the power of conversion and testimony (Alma 32:28). Richard Mouw recalls something similar in the "gospel tent meetings" of his youth. "I can still smell the sawdust, and this aroma carries with it spiritual associations that have shaped my understanding of what it means to be a Christian human being. And I think it is important—not only for myself but for the evangelical movement in general—to keep smelling the sawdust."[4] This will ever remain a sacred space to me. I am sure that to all of us there are such sacred moments, hallowed places in each of our individual lives that still stir our devotions and recollections.

And as for my person, I came to know the Savior most intimately through my study of the Scriptures. I remember reading Jesse Lyman Hurlbut's *Story of the Bible for Young and Old* with its helpful illustrations.[5] I was given my first Bible when I was ten. I can remember the smell of the leather, the cool crispness of the pages and the warm invitation to read from them. I recall the many stories of Jesus taught to me in Sunday school and Primary (the LDS children's organization) by loving teachers. The Holy Bible, in my very early life, became the anchor of my faith, the authority of my life, my illuminated passageway to Christ, a companion with prayer to personal divine guidance. The Bible made Christ the living person of my life. Not a collection of ethics, not a mere standard for living a good moral life, it was a call to Christ and what we believed to be to the restoration of the gospel.

When I was eighteen, one of my greatest religious experiences came in my own grove of trees while working one day for the railroad in the wilds of Canada. That spiritual experience, with the Book of Mormon in hand, remains forever engraved in my heart not only as a witness of the book's truthfulness but also of my heavenly Father's personal love and concern for me and his "tender mercies." To me, the Bible and the Book of Mormon are far more than mere publications: they are living water from a living Christ. As one passage in the Book of Mormon says of Scripture: "They [the plates of brass] have *enlarged the memory of this people*, yea, and convinced many of the error of their ways, and brought them to the knowledge of their God unto the salvation of their souls" (Alma 37:8).

There are no physical barriers to the operations of the Spirit of the Lord. Just as Paul could never disassociate his conversion from the road to Damascus, so we, as members of the LDS Church who have been touched by the grace of Christ and by the enticings of the Holy Spirit, can never disconnect ourselves from our own history in these sacred places. We find meaning for our living in the history of our lives, those times and places where God has entered in.

So, too, there is a compelling sense of Christian history that should reverence our collective experiences. From the accounts of the New Testament, such places as Calvary, Gethsemane, the garden tomb, Mars Hill and the Isle of Patmos are of lasting importance to us. We remember them for what happened there, what historically transpired. For those of us who have been converted, such locations mean more by the very infusion of our own experience. Places such as these teach us the mighty truth that Christianity, as the great Protestant scholar J. Gresham Machen has so well stated, "is more than just a way of life but a historical fact." Faced with a growing opposition intent on socializing and secularizing the faith, Machen continued:

> The great weapon with which the disciples of Jesus set out to conquer the world was not a mere comprehension of eternal principles; it was an historical message, an account of something that had recently happened, it was the message, "He is risen."
>
> The world was not to be evangelized by the spread of a wonderful new philosophy but would be redeemed through the proclamation of an event. . . . Christianity is based, then, upon an account of something that happened. . . . Christianity is based on a real person and a real series of historical events in that Person's life which, if He or they did not exist or happen, means the end of Christianity.[6]

In more recent times, Adolf Koberle has likewise argued against what he calls the "nonhistorical trend of thought which, as our present age discloses all too clearly, constantly seeks to dominate not only philosophy but also theology. Today it is popular to say that faith is the historical event per se." He continued, "The proud spirit will always maintain that he can grasp the Absolute with equal immediacy at all points of history and that he is in no way dependent on any particular historical events for the appreciation of truth."[7] Koberle rejects such views with this argument:

> If Jesus did not live, if He did not die on Golgotha, if the crucified one was not resurrected, then all existential appropriation of these things is left hanging in air. How is it possible, therefore, to disparage the "facts of salvation," to totally compress the objective occurrence into its subjective consummation in the life of the believer, when everything depends upon the fact that faith has firm ground beneath it because God has acted in Christ as the Saviour.[8]

So, too, Charles Colson has written: "What we need to understand about our faith is that it is not based on wise writings or philosophies or books written in so-called prophetic trances. It is not based on ideologies, which come and go. It is based on the facts of history, real events. . . . That's what Christianity is: history."[9] Once again I quote from Machen:

> Give up history and you can retain some things. You can retain a belief in God. But philosophical theism has never been a powerful force in the world. You can retain a lofty ethical ideal. But be perfectly clear about one point—you can never retain a gospel. For gospel means "good news," tidings, information about something that has happened. In other words, it means history. A gospel independent of history is simply a contradiction in terms.[10]

Latter-day Saints share this view of seeing Christianity historically—that Christ actually lived, died and was resurrected, that the glad tidings of his resurrection spawned a movement and a doctrine that continue to change lives. If there is one recurring theological constancy of the Book of Mormon, it is that Christ was born, that he lived and died in Jerusalem, that he was bodily resurrected and that his atoning sacrifice for sin happened to real people in a real time and place. Abinadi, a Book of Mormon prophet, prophesied some 150 years before Christ:

> And now if Christ had not come into the world, speaking of things to come as though they had already come, there could have been no redemption.
> And if Christ had not risen from the dead, or have broken the bands of

death that the grave should have no victory, and that death should have no sting, there could have been no resurrection.

But there is a resurrection, therefore the grave hath no victory, and the sting of death is swallowed up in Christ. He is the light and the life of the world; yea, a light that is endless, that can never be darkened; yea, and also a life which is endless, that there can be no more death. (Mosiah 16:6-9)

LDS apostle LeGrand Richards wrote of the Latter-day Saint understanding of the historicity of the risen Christ in the following Easter address given in 1955:

The resurrection which we celebrate today has lost all its significance if Jesus did not retain his body following the resurrection. Why should some assume that he is now but a personage of spirit, while he declared so emphatically to the apostles: "For a spirit hath not flesh and bones as ye see me have"? Why did he take up his body from the tomb at all if the work he had to do following his crucifixion could have been done better while in the spirit only? Why did he not leave his body lying in the tomb? Where in the scriptures is there justification for the belief that he has laid his body down again since he took it up from the tomb. . . . Is it possible that our Lord has died a second time, that he can be but a personage of spirit? If so, why do we celebrate Easter in commemoration of his resurrection?[11]

The Latter-day Saint view on the historicity of biblical Christianity is similar to the way we view the restoration. Just as Machen argues that without Christianity's history there is no real Christianity, so in similar fashion Latter-day Saints argue that without the factual literalness of our history, there is no restoration. The First Vision—the appearance of the Father and Son to Joseph Smith in a very real grove of trees near Palmyra in upstate New York in the spring of 1820—actually happened or Mormonism is a fraud. "Every claim that we make concerning divine authority, every truth that we offer concerning the validity of the work, all finds its root in the First Vision of the boy prophet,"[12] President Gordon B. Hinckley said.

That becomes the hinge pin on which this whole cause turns. If the First Vision was true, if it actually happened, then the Book of Mormon is true. Then we have the priesthood. Then we have the Church organization and all of the other keys and blessings of authority which we say we have. If the First Vision did not occur, then we are involved in a great sham. It is just that simple.[13]

Such tangibles in Latter-day Saint history include a book of Scripture written on actual plates of gold, the restoration of priesthood (apostolic) authority by heavenly messengers on "the banks of the Susquehanna River" in 1829, the laying of heavenly hands on earthly bodies. Just as the liberal mind recoils at having to see Christ as the center of history—that "the accent of eternity should be placed upon this one point of history"—so, too, many take offense at the Mormon emphasis on the literality of the restoration as what we might call the "second point" of history.

Of course, the theology of Christian history, as Machen later said, was not merely that Christ died—a historical fact—but that he died *for our sins.* This becomes the doctrinal expression of the historical reality—the personal appropriation of a long-ago event, the spiritual capturing of a physical happening. Latter-day Saints agree with such doctrine but take it one vital step further. The restoration of the fullness of the gospel is not merely a historical fact but a doctrinal necessity as well—that it happened for the *endowment of our eternal life.* The fullness of Christ, the fullness of the gospel, its complete teachings and ordinances, the supernal gift of the Holy Ghost made possible through the restoration of divine authority—these constitute much of the doctrine of our history. These doctrinal truths make our historical facts invaluable, memorable and tangible reminders of modern revelation and its supremacy in our restored faith. This is why we collectively seek to remember and keep sacred such places as Palmyra, New York; Kirtland, Ohio; Independence, Missouri; and, of course, Nauvoo, Illinois. To separate these places, to disconnect the Sacred Grove or the Hill Cumorah from the Christ of the Bible is to build a historical memory that will inevitably fade. Ultimately, this place (Nauvoo) is sacred not just because of the pioneers, not merely because of Joseph Smith or his martyrdom, but because of the Christ of the restoration, who for us is the same as the Christ of the resurrection. They are a continuum in one, from Calvary to Cumorah, from the River Jordan to the Mississippi.

There are, however, other compelling reasons why we Latter-day Saints revere these sacred sites. One of these surely must be that they point to the importance of *the institution* and the establishment of an actual organization, a church, a very corporeal expression of the gospel message. The restoration of the church is of signal importance, for with it came authority and the multiplicity of rules and policies, levels of government and jurisdictions, hierarchies and bureaucracies—the very things that many who wish to humanize religion despise and cast away as irrelevant and obstructionist to the individual freedom of worship. Yet this has given weight and structure to the restoration at a time when many other religions were downplaying the place of the ecclesiastical and the structures of Christian religion. Leonard I. Sweet spoke clearly of such modern trends when he wrote of the anti-institutionalism of the late 1960s: "For the first time in American religion, the authority of the church was widely discredited. Many Christians abandoned an understanding of the church as an institution that sets standards for society in favor of an institution that meets the needs of society, a change in definition that had shuddering consequences for the formation of religious and personal identity."[14]

Likewise the restoration of such sites, and in particular the city of Joseph (or Nauvoo), points to the importance of *community* to the Latter-day Saints. Every careful reader of Latter-day Saint history and doctrine will recognize that although salvation is essentially an individual affair, much is accomplished collectively. The Saints did not come out west in individual migrations; rather, they came as a group or they did not come at all. As William Clayton, for a time secretary to Joseph Smith, penned in his famous hymn "Come, Come Ye Saints," it was always a sense of the collective, that "*we'll* find the place." Nauvoo represented to the Mormons a gathering to Zion of converts in great numbers, the building of a new city of believers. Nauvoo, then, represents a *community* of Saints who shared common beliefs and values. Even in temple worship, Latter-day Saints participate in companies, in groups, not by themselves. Thus while Mormonism preaches individual salvation, it advocates interdependency on one another. Its emphasis on marriage, particularly eternal marriage and the family, speaks of family exaltation as much if not more than of individual salvation. It is this community of believers, this family of support, that means so much to the modern Mormon perspective. And with it has come a strong sense of tradition, family history, even legacy. Some Latter-day Saints see more of this than anything else when visiting such places as Nauvoo. Many who have ancestry who lived and were persecuted there see in this the establishment of lasting family values, if not characteristics.

This emphasis on heritage, on preserving our legacy, has spared the

Church of Jesus Christ of Latter-day Saints from a loss of identity, what Sweet calls "culturalist Christianity" in an age when promoting social causes has come to mean more than preserving historical consciousness. He says:

> What a religious tradition does with its past has everything to do with the establishment of a distinctive identity. The preservation and transmission of the tradition is an ineluctable obligation of the church. But culturalist Christianity discarded the cultivation of religious belief and the preservation of the heritage for social engagements in changing national and international society. . . . In the 1960s . . . the goal was not to prepare a new generation for the church but to promote social and personal values among the young and to translate religious symbols into ethical and political imperatives among the adults. . . . Thus Protestantism raised a generation of kids who were robbed of their history and without inheritance. . . . A tradition cannot long survive without a living memory. By failing to generate among church members a sense of living out their past, much of Protestantism cut the cords of community in the present and endangered its survival.[15]

No more sacred space exists in Mormonism than the holy temple. Such are sacred not only as monuments to our history, our sense of Christ and the restoration and our sense of working together as a consecrated people, but also as place for personal illumination, covenant making, sanctification, and personal holiness and purity. Though the inscriptions on such buildings invariably say "Holiness to the Lord," they are invitations to personal holiness, consecration and sacrifice that no ordinary church history site can ever afford.

The reconstruction of the Nauvoo Temple, its perfect restoration on the very historical site on which the original building once stood, is a combination of collective and individual memory. More than any other site in the old city, it blends the present and the historical and gives embodiment to what it all means spiritually. So too the temples in Palmyra, New York, and certainly at Winter Quarters (Council Bluffs, Iowa) are attempts to capture our history for present spiritual commitment.

Not that such reconstruction came without discussion among those in the highest councils of the Church. Even with the work of President Joseph F. Smith in the late nineteenth and early twentieth centuries to purchase historical properties, many modern LDS Church leaders could not support such expenditures. Considered by some to be a nonintegral part of the mission of the church, the preservation of such places as Nauvoo by the institution of the church was slow in coming. Brigham Young tried desperately to sell the Nauvoo Temple to the Roman Catholic Church, and the temple lot in Independence and the Kirtland Temple were not retained in the desire to establish the Church in the West. Restoration of Church history sites would have to wait until the salvation of the Church was assured. All would come in order. Thanks to the vision, tireless efforts and financial sacrifices of such modern preservation pioneers as Wilford Wood and Dr. LeRoy Kimball, Nauvoo is the classic expression of the inspiration of the rank-and-file membership who have insisted on remembering this place.

There are, of course, problems and pitfalls for a church that insists on preserving its history. I mention but two. The first is in the very selectivity of what the institution chooses to remember and celebrate—that is, in de-emphasizing some things that happened there. Here in Nauvoo, there is little in the corporate remembering, and even less in the missionary rendering, that will ever speak to such practices as plural marriage. It is as if such a practice never happened and was never part of the prophet's teachings. Such selectivity of what to remember and honor and what to discard may lead to a sense of misunderstanding, if not suspicion, for some followers of the faith. For when some of these truths come out—as they invariably have done and will continue to do—some members inevitably feel let down. In recent published attempts to engage the many critical interpretations of the motives and personality of the prophet Joseph Smith in candid, professional and even faith-supporting ways, several modern Latter-day Saint scholars have broached topics that the rank-and-file members know little about. What was best left unsaid by those wanting to project a modern image on our past has become for some an issue of honesty.

The point is, if we believe in literal history and the power of sacred place, excessive selectivity for corporate public-image purposes may lead to a disservice in the long run. The reaction, for instance, to Richard L. Bushman's biography of Joseph Smith, *Rough Stone Rolling*, by several Latter-day Saint readers is not one of objection but suspicion. Why has so little of this been told? If the restoration is, like the gospel of the New Testament, history, then what history are we remembering? One of Bushman's contributions is to show that we take everything, warts and all.

The second problem is somewhat the reverse: seeing what was never there. Some time ago, a colleague of mine approached me with a question. He had just read a chapter in one of my books dealing with the succession of Brigham Young to the presidency of the church in the Kanesville (Iowa) Log Tabernacle in December 1847. "Why didn't you tell about the earthquake?" he wondered. "What earthquake?" I asked. "The one some later said happened on that day in that place. Surely it was a sign of God's benediction." I could only respond that there may have been a retrospective account somewhere that spoke of such things, but from my research into scores of contemporary letters, diaries and sermons, the Spirit of the Lord was in abundance without any earthquake occurring. "But it's such a faith-building story," he argued. "It had to have happened!"

None of us appreciates being purposely misled. Bearing false witness is both a crime and a sin. I believe that in doing so, we not only twist the truth but also destroy our faith for the simple reason that faith is based on truth. As the author of the epistle to the Hebrews said, "Faith is the substance of things hoped for, the evidence of things not seen" (Hebrews 11:1 KJV). The Book of Mormon adds, "Faith is not to have a perfect knowledge of things; therefore if ye have faith ye hope for things which are not seen, which are true" (Alma 32:21). Truth, not deception, is the bulwark of faith.

Yet these pitfalls and problems are the price we are willing to pay for remembering our history and traditions. Much better we have these problems than those of the more serious kind: the loss of the sense of our history and heritage altogether. We can afford and must encourage differing interpretations, but we cannot afford relegating the glad tidings of Cumorah to moral relativism.

In the end, one thing unites Latter-day Saints and believing Christians of all other faiths. That is a mutual recognition of what Timothy George calls "a true bottomless pit," what Machen described as "the abyss between belief and unbelief," namely, "those who believe in something, and the others who don't."[16] As professing Christians, we all believe in our Lord and Savior, Jesus Christ; we all share an "unflinching allegiance to the Holy Scriptures"; we all share in a mutual desire to aspire after holiness; we all seek to oppose secularizing influences rampant in modern society, in protecting the sanctity of human life, in opposing the destruction of family values and in spreading the good word of the gospel of Jesus Christ.

MORMON-EVANGELICAL DIALOGUE

Embracing a Hermeneutic of Generosity

Rachel Cope

ONE AFTERNOON MY HIGH SCHOOL choir teacher announced that we would be singing "In This Very Room."[1] Because the lyrics to this song highlight the presence and power of Jesus Christ in daily life, it could be considered a rather unusual selection for a choir teacher within the public school system. In my hometown of Spanish Fork, Utah, however, which has a predominantly Latter-day Saints (LDS) population, singing about Jesus— in any context—seemed quite natural. In our community, Mormonism entailed more than theology and practice; it had a cultural influence as well. Both wittingly and unwittingly it seeped into various spheres.

As my classmates and I sang "In This Very Room," no one seemed disconcerted by the explicitly Christian message conveyed through the lyrics. After class, however, my friend Alisa turned to me and said, "I can't believe Mr. Smith had us sing that song."[2] Rather startled by her uncharacteristic reaction, I asked why.

"Well," Alisa declared, "Sam Jones is in this class."[3] I wondered where she was going with this comment. I knew Sam was not LDS, but I also knew he was a devout Christian who would embrace the song's message. "Why would that matter?" I asked. "That song is about Jesus," she said. "It must be offensive to him. Sam's not a Mormon. He's Catholic." Although I knew Alisa had minimal exposure to other faiths, I was still baffled by her ignorance.

Her attempt to be sensitive and even inclusive was actually alarmingly narrow-minded. "Alisa," I explained, "Catholics believe in Jesus. My mom was raised a Catholic, and all of her family is still Catholic. They would not have a problem singing 'In This Very Room'; it is not even a Mormon song. Lots of Christians sing it." The expression on her face made it clear to me that she did not agree. In Alisa's mind, only Mormons *really* believed in and experienced the power of the Savior.

Although a young high school student, I recognized the irony woven into Alisa's comment. I knew Mormons felt offended when people of other faiths misunderstood us (particularly when they declared us "not Christian"). And yet, as Alisa demonstrated, Latter-day Saints were also prone to misunderstand. Too often, Mormons failed to recognize or even accept the meaningfulness people found in their own traditions. We too dismissed the role Christ played in the lives of those outside our faith. We made assumptions about beliefs rather than seeking understanding and establishing respect. The former approach, I concluded—one that, I later realized, stemmed from a hermeneutic of doubt rather than a hermeneutic of generosity—disabled rather than enabled the possibility of meaningful dialogue across and within faiths.

HERMENEUTIC OF GENEROSITY

Upon deciding to become a history major in college, I found myself immersed in historiographical conversations that both augmented and challenged Alisa's perspective; myopic views too often dominated conversations. The complexities inherent in discussions about religion became increasingly apparent to me as I became familiar with the different angles from which Mormon history has been written. Polemicists, hagiographers and historians had each embraced strikingly different approaches to the past, and as a result, had reached distinct, and often dogmatic, conclusions. Rather than engaging in conversation with each other, they dismissed perspectives that differed from their own. Consequently, they spoke past one another; argument rather than discussion commonly ensued.

The complexities inherent in misunderstanding are particularly apparent in historical works about Joseph Smith. Apologists have attempted to promote and protect his role as prophet, whereas polemicists have described him as either a liar or a lunatic.[4] Their historiographical objectives do not center on understanding why he "lives on in the faith of Mormons, like Abraham in Judaism or Muhammad in Islam," but rather focus on proving or disproving that he was a prophet—conclusions the historical method simply does not permit.[5]

Over time, as Mormonism became a topic of inquiry broached by professionally trained historians, its historiography became more nuanced and contextualized. And yet, similar divisions have continued to plague conversations about this faith's history. Whereas some rejoice at a more methodologically sophisticated approach to the past, others fear that the accompanying hermeneutic of suspicion will eliminate the spiritual power that they believe should be woven throughout a story about faith. Apologist and polemicist threads thus remain a central part of Mormon history.

There are, however, scholars who employ a more creative model when approaching Mormon history, an approach that Stuart Parker calls a "hermeneutic of generosity."[6] Those who consider the past from this angle proceed from the "conviction that historical actors possess, if anything, a privileged perspective on their motivations and actions, though hardly an infallible one."[7] Historian Richard Bushman, for example, has encouraged greater understanding of Mormonism more generally, and Joseph Smith more specifically. Although a believing member of the LDS Church, Bushman's work still attempts to consider every angle of Smith's past. The biography he authored both engages with the work of skeptics and deals with incongruities in Joseph Smith's life—an approach that Stuart considers both "critical and intellectually courageous"—while also attempting to "think of Smith as the early Mormons thought of him and as he thought of himself—as a revelator."[8]

Although Bushman's work on Smith has received mixed reviews from the apologist and polemicist communities, it has also served as a model for fruitful religious dialogue, both historical and contemporary. It has influenced how scholars of religion and religious scholars think about and approach topics of faith, whether discussing the history of a faith they embrace, or the history of a faith that is not their own. A hermeneutic of generosity has also benefited and guided the Mormon-evangelical dialogues discussed in this book.

Interfaith Dialogue

For over a decade, a group of Latter-day Saint and evangelical scholars have met twice a year to engage in meaningful dialogue with one another. During one of these sessions, Richard Bushman posed an "intriguing question" to the evangelicals in attendance.[9] He asked if Joseph Smith was *possible* for them. In making this query, Bushman was not only encouraging the group to consider the broad implications of Smith's work in historical and contemporary contexts but also implicitly hinting at the importance of pushing and probing the boundaries of scholarship by employing a hermeneutic of generosity. In essence, he was providing a different framework from which to approach religious dialogue.

After reflecting thoughtfully on the implications of Bushman's provocative question, Richard Mouw, then president of Fuller Seminary, responded by writing an article titled, "The Possibility of Joseph Smith: Some Evangelical Probings." In this work Mouw acknowledges that evangelicals have often approached Smith from two angles, both of which discount how his life and teachings have influenced millions of people: Smith has, he explains, been described as either a liar or a lunatic—a "pious deceiver" or a "sincere fraud."[10] While Mouw rejects "the key claims that Smith made," he makes it clear that he wants to move beyond these overly simplified "liar-or-lunatic options."[11] In making this proposition, it becomes clear that his goal is not to solve the mystery of Joseph Smith, but rather to "define more clearly the outlines of the mystery."[12] In other words, Mouw explains, he hopes to create some space that allows evangelicals to consider a more nuanced Smith; he wants to "diminish . . . unqualified hostility" without sacrificing the "theological convictions that have fed that hostility in the past."[13]

Mouw's attempt to tackle the "prophet puzzle" mirrors the approach Richard Bushman has taken when studying Smith's life—both men highlight the importance of considering carefully the content of Smith's teachings, indeed, the meaningfulness of his revelations to his followers and to himself. By embracing a hermeneutic of generosity, these scholars shift away from the traditional attempts to prove that Smith was or was not a prophet, and instead shed light on the historical and theological development of Mormonism by considering how it shaped and was shaped by its surrounding culture, religious and otherwise.

This attention to culture, or historical context, also reveals "interesting experiential parallels" between early Mormon origins and experiences woven throughout the Christian community in the nineteenth century—a detail that both Latter-day Saints and evangelicals need to consider more seriously.[14] Indeed, to dismiss the miraculous on either side is to eliminate spiritual possibilities within one's own faith; it is to promote, albeit unwittingly, a "methodological atheism" that can seep into all interpretations of religion. It is, then, to suggest the impossibility of the divine working in human lives.

Aware of the ever-pressing need to take religious belief seriously, both Mouw and Bushman make it clear that one cannot embrace a hermeneutic of doubt when considering the faith of another, but then expect others to approach one's own faith with a hermeneutic of generosity. Otherwise, all miraculous, mystical or ethereal experiences could be defined as lunacy. Mouw illustrates this point well by reminding readers that Cotton Mather, a respected figure in evangelical history, described an angelic visitation that had a powerful impact on his spiritual life. To dismiss Mather as a liar or a lunatic because of this supernatural experience would be to dismiss the larger contributions he made—it would erase an important part of American evangelical history.

Just as evangelicals should consider the possibility of a Joseph Smith, Mormons need to consider the possibility of Cotton Mather—they need to be more open to the broad visionary culture in which early evangelicalism emerged. For some, this is a challenge. Because Mormons believe that Smith learned, through his First Vision, that all churches were "wrong," they sometimes assume (as demonstrated in the story about Alisa at the beginning of this chapter) that they alone have access to truth, spiritual power, miracles and experiences with the divine. In other words, such individuals may conclude, rather arrogantly, that they have a monopoly on the divine. Consequently, when they hear of spiritual experiences and visions in other faiths, they have a tendency to question their validity. This type of response suggests implicitly that only Smith could communicate with the divine. Such a perspective echoes the dismissal and misunderstanding they feel from those of other faiths when Smith is declared a liar. It is thus important, Richard Bushman has explained, for Latter-day Saints to "leave open the possibility of others besides Joseph Smith hearing from the heavens."[15]

As the work of Bushman and Mouw demonstrates, both Mormons and evangelicals need to engage in more generous, indeed in more empathetic conversations. They need to push and probe boundaries, consider possibilities and rethink myopic conclusions, while also remaining committed to theological differences. A dialogic discussion that centers on theological critique, rather than historical dismissal, certainly allows for a hermeneutic of generosity and thus results in more fruitful and more meaningful conversation.

EMPATHY THROUGH DIALOGIC DISCUSSION

Perhaps the conversational divide that has so often separated Mormons and evangelicals has more to do with a lack of listening or reading than a lack of speaking or writing. Rather than paying heed to what the other says or expresses, both sides have more typically made and acted on often unfair assumptions, almost as if they feared that a genuine dialogue with one another would somehow mitigate differences and legitimate beliefs each found uncomfortable. And yet, as our Mormon-evangelical dialogues have demonstrated over the past decade or so, it is possible to stand in the shoes of another while also maintaining a clear sense of one's own identity.[16]

In order to engage in dialogue that centers on careful listening as well as thoughtful presentation, one can employ two distinctive types of conversation: dialectic or dialogic.[17] In our modern society, we often think of dialogue in terms of dialectic conversation—a conversation that is characterized by sympathy, or feeling what the other person is feeling. Sympathetic listeners often seek to resolve disagreement; they want to achieve synthesis or common understanding. Although appealing at first glance, such an approach can make religious dialogue relative by conflating differences and overemphasizing similarities. The fear of promoting theological sameness has certainly hindered Mormon-evangelical conversations across time and space.

On the other hand, dialogic conversation, which focuses on making people aware of our own views while also expanding our understanding of the perspectives held by others, creates space for differences.[18] Since this type of conversation hinges on empathy (conveying sincere curiosity in and committed attention to others) over sympathy, it challenges participants to both listen and imagine. In other words, those engaged in dialogic conversation step outside of themselves without feeling the need to become the other. Rather than seeking agreement, then, dialogic conversation pushes the listener to be both open-minded and skeptical.[19] This approach to dialogue, conversation that includes thoughtful talking and listening, allows the participants to maintain healthy disagreement. Mouw, for example, has discovered imaginative ways to consider the possibility of Joseph Smith, and the reality of his visions and revelations to Mormons, without having to surrender fundamental theological differences that matter to him.[20] He has stepped into the life of the other while simultaneously remaining on his own side of Christianity.[21]

Richard Bushman has likewise modeled dialogic conversation in his attempt to understand the many worlds of Joseph Smith, as well as through his focus on helping other scholars, both Mormons and otherwise, to employ a more generous hermeneutical approach.[22] Smith was, Bushman proposes, both a product of his culture and an individual who transcended his culture.[23] Understanding this, whether one believes in Smith's experiences and theology or not, is fundamental to understanding the Mormon past and present. Similarly, understanding and being open to the legitimacy of the religious culture in which Smith emerged is key to making sense of historical and contemporary Mormonism.

I have found that our Mormon-evangelical dialogues have been most fruitful when both groups willingly consider the experiences of a Cotton Mather or a Joseph Smith. They are particularly productive when we acknowledge incongruence as well as cohesion. We prosper intellectually and spiritually as we challenge one another, while simultaneously seeking greater understanding of the theologies that are being challenged. We are enriched as we imagine possibilities rather than simply dismissing what seems impossible. We think differently, respond differently, teach differently and converse differently because of the dialogic conversations we have participated in. Generosity has certainly enriched our understanding of self and expanded our understanding of others, even though theological agreement is only occasionally reached.[24] Genuine dialogue, then, "is open-ended" since "neither party knows at the outset what the outcome . . . will be . . . [as it] is a common search for understanding, empathy, or appreciation" but not an agreement to embrace the same theology or worldview.[25]

CONCLUSION

At the age of fifteen, I encountered Alisa's misconceptions about Catholicism—misconceptions that bothered me, since my mother had been raised Catholic, and her family remained members of that faith. Although I grew up within a predominantly Mormon community, one that felt comfortable singing "In This Very Room" in a public high school, I had also been raised to recognize differences while also valuing and respecting beliefs that differed from my own. My mother had taught me, although I certainly did not recognize it at the time, the value of dialogic conversation; she had taught me to look through different lenses, to consider various angles and to think creatively. She had also taught me to remain committed to a faith and way of life I considered true, even while appreciating and respecting different perspectives. She had, albeit unwittingly, prepared me to be a historian of religion who would devote her life to studying conversion, a topic that underscores the need for a hermeneutic of generosity and the power of dialogic conversation.

College history courses, which exposed me to the complexities of religious historiography, modeled the various methodologies from which religious discussion could be approached. Becoming familiar with the different interpretations of my own faith's history proved particularly important. I had to think deeply about how to approach religious history when writing about Mormonism for other Mormons, when writing about Mormonism for people who were not LDS and when writing about Protestantism for Mormons and for Protestants. I had to consider how I would think and write about groups I considered more radical, such as the Shakers. Could I be as generous with them as I was with Protestants? Could I be as generous with Protestants as I was with Mormons? Richard Bushman taught me that I could—or that I should—at least make the attempt. His work has encouraged many scholars to grapple with religious possibilities.

Involvement with the Mormon-evangelical dialogue has helped me apply the methodological skills I learned as a historian to a contemporary context. I have discovered that a hermeneutic of generosity can reach beyond the eighteenth and nineteenth centuries. It involves more than the possibility of a Cotton Mather or a Joseph Smith; as a group, we also consider the meaning of their legacies. Since 2007, when I first became involved in this discussion,

I have seen men and women engage in acts of imagination while maintaining a firm commitment to their beliefs. We have not surrendered our identities in order to become friends; it is empathy, rather than sympathy, that we strive for. By exploring our differences as well as our similarities, we have gained greater respect and appreciation for one another, as well as a stronger sense of our own identities. Healthy disagreement, rather than dismissive consensus, creates powerful dialogue—a dialogue in which friendships have formed despite and because of different theological perspectives.

Temple Garments

A Case Study in the Lived Religion of Mormons

Cory B. Willson

Introduction: An Apology Long Overdue

In his controversial address at the Mormon Tabernacle in 2004, Richard J. Mouw offered an apology to the Latter-day Saint community on behalf of evangelicals for breaking the ninth commandment—bearing false witness against them: "There are very real issues of [theological] disagreement between us . . . matters of eternal significance," said Mouw, "[and yet] we have often seriously misrepresented the beliefs and practices of the Mormon community. . . . We have sinned against you."[1] The common habit of telling Mormons what they believe without bothering to ask them, Mouw noted, has often led to misrepresenting and even demonizing their beliefs and practices—a form of bearing false witness against our Latter-day Saint neighbors.[2] This presumptive witness is misled in many ways, and Mouw's apology was an important step in confronting the acrimonious ways in which evangelicals have treated Mormons. Not only does telling another person what they believe assume that, as an outsider, one already knows the internal religious landscape of their faith, but it also imposes on Mormonism a view that doctrine stands at the center of the other tradition in a privileged place over rituals and practices.

A similar cognitive approach to interfaith dialogue can be found in academic circles where comparative study of sacred texts is undertaken to the neglect of lived religious experience. Drawing on the work of Talal Asad and Roberto Goizueta, William Dyrness has recently argued that insisting on a text-based approach to the study of religions not only mischaracterizes the nature of religion but also rests on a misguided philosophical anthropology that privileges the understanding mind over the affective and embodied nature of humans. Based on this Enlightenment view of the human person that centers on the rational mind, the central aim of religion is construed as teaching adherents to think rather than to train them to adore.[3]

A basic assumption of biblical faith is that religion addresses the whole person with all their cognitive and affective qualities. In Christian terms, the gospel must always be incarnated in the lives of people by addressing their concrete needs and desires, even as it redirects them into paths of righteousness.[4] In this light, it is important for evangelicals to break out of this "intellectualist" view of the human person and recover a holistic philosophical anthropology that situates the intellect within the context of human desire and imagination.[5] Evangelicals must entertain the possibility that in our preoccupation with analyzing doctrinal texts our dialogue with Latter-day Saints may in fact be missing the heart of their experience of faith. We must find ways of discussing the lived faith that animates the lives of Mormons if we hope to understand their faith in light of the gospel of Jesus Christ.

The thesis of this chapter is that following through on Mouw's apology to the Latter-day Saint community should lead evangelicals to explore a mode of interfaith engagement that is attentive to the theology displayed in official doctrines as well as lived religion. A holistic account of another religion must hold together cult, conduct and creed without imposing a hierarchical structure on them.[6] Bearing a truthful witness about our Latter-day Saint neighbors requires exploring the heart of their religion, which entails inquiring into their ritual experiences.

This chapter begins with an exploration of the lived religion of Latter-day Saints through a study of the ritual practices surrounding temple garments.[7] Tools from anthropologists and missiologists will be employed to help discern the needs, hopes and fears underlying the garment rituals. Such knowledge of ritual practices, it will be argued, is essential for understanding the heart of the Mormon faith and the ways these rituals satisfy the affective as well as cognitive needs of the human person. This opens the door for evangelicals to offer a culturally sensitized account of the gospel in their interactions with Mormons. The conclusion reinforces the central theme of this chapter that through understanding the landscape of lived religion for Mormons, evangelicals are better equipped to embody a faithful *witness to* their Latter-day Saint neighbors by bearing a *truthful witness about them*.

TEMPLE GARMENTS AND THE LANDSCAPE OF MORMON LIVED RELIGION

The garment: Secret or sacred? Mormon temple garments have been a source of particular fascination and misunderstanding within American society ever since Joseph Smith's administration of the first temple endowment ceremony in 1842.[8] In subsequent decades the ritual practices surrounding these garments have provided useful fuel for propagandists and journalistic *exposés*, especially in the past two presidential elections.[9]

The American public's misunderstanding of temple garments is exacerbated by the connection to temple practices that are off limits to the public. For many Americans, Latter-day Saint *sacredness* is interpreted as *secrecy*, and ritual privacy is conflated with cultic practices.[10] Given the sacredness that Mormons ascribe to temple life, full disclosure of these religious rituals would profane what they consider sacred. But these challenges need not prove to be a dead end for dialogue.[11]

While access to temple rituals is not afforded to those outside of the Mormon community, there are varying degrees of accessibility to daily rituals—like the wearing of sacred undergarments—that bear the mark (literally and symbolically) of the temple. To properly understand the significance of the garment we must first grasp a sense of the central role the temple plays in Mormonism.

Temple-conscious spirituality from the cradle to the grave. To say that Mormonism centers on the temple would not be an overstatement—for Mormons, the temple is the focal point for the atoning work of Jesus in the world.[12] According to Richard Bushman, temples "represent the culmination of Mormon life as well as Mormon worship"—a fact attested to by former president Gordon B. Hinckley, who said that temples "represent the ultimate in our worship" and are "the most profound expressions of our theology."[13] Deeply embedded in the Latter-day Saint religious life is a focus on the atoning work of Jesus, from which temple life is inseparable.[14]

While the centrality of Christ in the work of the temple is not always fully understood by all Mormons, a thoroughgoing temple-conscious spirituality is fostered in Mormons from an early age. For example, former president Spencer Kimball even recommended that a picture of a temple be placed in children's rooms to cultivate anticipation for temple work,[15] a value captured in this well-known children's hymn, "I Love to See the Temple":

> I love to see the temple.
> I'm going there someday.
> To feel the Holy Spirit,
> To listen and to pray.
> For the temple is a house of God,
> A place of love and beauty.
> I'll prepare myself while I am young;
> This is my sacred duty.
>
> I love to see the temple.
> I'll go inside someday.
> I'll cov'nant with my Father;
> I'll promise to obey.
> For the temple is a holy place
> Where we are sealed together.
> As a child of God, I've learned this truth:
> A fam'ly is forever.[16]

The visceral response evoked by these lyrics touches on the child's need for God and family and inscribes in them a sense of beauty, mystery and sacred awe that all point toward the temple. This temple-centered spirituality is carefully cultivated in Latter-day Saints and endures throughout their life.

The temple also provides strength and refreshment for Mormons in the midst of their mortal life. "I know of no work in the Church more conducive to spiritual refinement and communication," writes Boyd Packer, "than temple and genealogical work. In this work our hearts and our minds are turned to those beyond the veil."[17] As the twilight of mortal existence approaches, temple work provides a comforting preparation for those passing beyond the veil into immortality.[18] Thus to properly understand Mormon religious life, one must explore the ways the sacred space of the temple operates as an organizing center for the spiritual aspirations and imaginations of Mormons.

(Temple) work matters: reenacting the cosmic story for all humankind. A primary function of Mormon temples is to enable the performing of priestly duties on behalf of all humankind. This vicarious work, in church teachings, provides all humanity—both living and dead—the opportunity to receive the fullness of the gospel and to enter into the kingdom of heaven. Because admittance into the kingdom requires that every person pass through these temple ceremonies and receive baptism on this mortal earth, ordinances must take place by proxy for those now deceased.[19]

In the temple-endowment ceremony, participants reenact the cosmic story of humanity's premortal existence, fall and redemption in Christ. During the ceremony, temple-worthy Mormons assume the name of a dead person and take part in the redemption story on behalf of the deceased (by proxy). In so doing the deceased vicariously receive baptism, the gift of the Holy Ghost, washings, annointings, and marriage and family sealings—all of which are required to enter the kingdom of heaven.

Temple work is fundamentally participatory rather than passive, and the eternal significance of this work is reinforced with each temple visit. What is communicated again and again through these rituals is the belief that each person, dead or alive, has a place in God's redemption story if they will only receive the benefits of Jesus' atoning work made available through the priestly work performed in temples.[20] Temple garments fit within this temple consciousness and serve to reinforce a distinctive Latter-day Saint spirituality.

Personal meaning and the heart of faith. Members of the Latter-day Saint Church begin wearing the temple garment following the endowment ceremony in the temple. During this initiation ceremony, instructions are offered concerning God's plans for peopling the earth and his path for human exaltation. Washing and anointing also take place, symbolizing promises and blessing given to the person during the ceremony, following the pattern of Exodus 40:12-13. In addition to these blessings, the person being endowed makes covenants with God and promises to obey his instructions. It is during these initiatory ordinances that the person is first clothed with the temple garment.[21] From that time forth, the garment is to be worn day and night, even outside of the temple, for "the garment provides a reminder of the covenants made in the temple."[22]

The Church *Handbook* provides instructions on upholding the sacredness of the garment, including never altering it, keeping it off the ground and not displaying it openly for others to see. The functions of the garment are explained in this passage from the *Handbook*: "The garment *provides a constant reminder of the covenants made in a temple*. When properly worn, it *provides protection against temptation and evil*. Wearing the garment is also an *outward expression of an inward commitment* to follow the Savior."[23]

The threefold functions of the garment (reminder, protector and symbolic expression) cultivate an ethical lifestyle outside the temple based on the sacred covenant (commitments) made within the temple. The tactile reminder of the garment worn directly against the skin mediates an intimate sense of the temple's sacredness and evokes modesty and righteous living. The physical and spiritual connection of the garment with temple ceremonies transmits blessings, power and ethical instructions amid the day-to-day challenges of living in the world.[24]

Little has been written from Church authorities on the theological meaning of the temple garment, and its significance is by no means exhausted by the handbook's instructions. Church authorities, in fact, assume as much when they instruct faithful believers that those "who have made covenant commitments in the temple should be guided by the Holy Spirit to answer for themselves personal questions about wearing the garment."[25] The challenge this presents to evangelicals is to explore how these personal meanings configure into the larger temple-centered spirituality of the Mormon faith.

Direct observation of garment rituals is not afforded to outsiders, nor does a doctrinal statement exist regarding the official meaning of the garment rituals.[26] But this need not shut down inquiry into the meaning of this practice for Mormons who are, to use Colleen McDannell's term, "silent theologians," constructing their own personalized meanings of this ritual.[27] The task for evangelicals is to respectfully inquire of their Mormon friends as to the personal significance of the garment and the effect its associated rituals have on their life.

Shall we live by doctrine alone? *The role of ritual in the Mormon faith.*
Up to this point it has been argued that interfaith dialogue between Mormons

and evangelicals must attend to the intersection of doctrine and lived experience in order to understand the heart of each other's religion. Studying lived religion requires focusing on the implicit theology embedded in the rituals that compose daily life. For this reason, the polyvalent nature of rituals must be explored at the grassroots level of religion from the perspective of dialogue partners.[28]

Though religious traditions offer resources that guide practitioners toward finding wholeness, happiness, meaning and security, there is no uniform method by which practitioners personalize these resources. The diversity displayed in the ritual expression of lived religion poses significant challenges to theological analysis.[29] Attending to the multivalent nature of rituals helps us inquire as to how people internalize the significance of their faith and to unearth the implicit theologies that govern their lives. Strengthening our ability to understand lived religion through rituals plays a vital role in bearing faithful witness to our neighbor's religion and prepares us to faithfully witness to our own faith.

What we talk about when we talk about religion: formal and folk religion. In anthropology the term *formal religion* refers to the recognized official religious scriptures, creeds, institutions and persons. Wherever the parameters of orthodoxy and orthopraxy are set, therein lies the center of formal religion. The official teachings and rituals of formal religions tend to address issues that are universal in scope, such as questions of human origins, purpose and destiny. In so doing, formal religions make claim to "universal cosmic truth about the ultimate nature of reality."[30] Comparative theology and scriptural reasoning are two approaches to interfaith dialogue that focus on matters of formal religion.

Folk religion, in contrast, is an anthropological term used to describe localized expressions of religion. Most often folk religions combine formal religious teachings and practices with cultural elements (or elements from other religions) in order to address everyday problems, needs and anxieties that formal religions fail to alleviate. Wherever the cosmic truths of formal religion fail to touch down in practical human needs, folk religions fill the gap providing rituals, meaning and hope.[31] Interfaith approaches such as worship and peace-building are forms of engagement that provide exposure to folk religion.

Interfaith dialogue that takes as its subject matter only formal religion and official creeds misses entire worlds of religious experience as practitioners particularize their religious tradition. Likewise, studying folk religion apart from formal religious institutions cuts off inquiry into the communal source of teachings and practices and to the formational influence that religious traditions exercise on their adherents. The authoritative teachings and rituals of the Church are important but are not always determinative of how the meanings are personalized and appropriated in the lives of people.[32] The distinction between formal and folk religions help identify the surplus of meanings operative in rituals and lived religion. But how do we make sense of these overlapping and diverse meanings?

The surplus of meaning in personalizing the faith. In his essay "How Ritual Means: Ritual Circumcision in Rabbinic Culture and Today," Rabbi Lawrence Hoffmann discusses four types of meaning found in ritual practices: official, public, private and normative. Hoffman describes official meanings as those sanctioned and propagated by experts—religious scholars, leaders and institutions of formal religion. For Mormons, this would be the official teachings of Church leaders and their interpretation of sacred texts. Public meanings are those agreed on by a segment of participants but may or may not be officially sanctioned by church authorities. These meanings are often constructed by groups of people at the grassroots level of religion (e.g., the garment is a means of expressing solidarity with the Latter-day Saint community). Private meanings account for the personal interpretations and significance attributed to a particular ritual. These personal and public meanings exist regardless of their congruence with the official meanings or authoritative sanctioning of Church leaders.[33]

Interfaith discussions focused on official meanings of the Church can help identify some of the doctrinal distinctives of the Latter-day Saint tradition but on their own afford no way of accessing the multiple layers of meaning that become attached to the beliefs and practices of the tradition as it makes its way into the lives of Mormons. Hoffman's contribution to this discussion encourages us to explore the process by which specific Mormons create meanings out of the authorized rituals and official meanings offered by the Church. This shifts the discussion from Mormonism in the abstract to a personal conversation about the ways the tradition is personalized in their life.[34]

How do these anthropological tools yield insight into the lived religion of Latter-day Saints? What do these ritual practices tell us about the basic human needs and desires that garments satisfy? And from the evangelical standpoint, how can the historic Christian understanding of the gospel be communicated as good news that satisfies these deep human needs?

TOWARD A HOLY ENVY: AN EVANGELICAL APPRAISAL OF TEMPLE GARMENTS

From what we have learned by stepping into the religious landscape of the Mormon faith through a study of garment rituals, we can see that this peculiar practice addresses universal human needs and challenges evangelicals to show how the gospel offers an equally holistic experience of lived religion. A communication of the gospel that is contextually sensitized to Latter-day Saints will need to (1) address the basic human desire to locate one's place within a larger cosmic story; (2) provide rituals that enlist them to play a vital part in this redemptive story; (3) offer tangible means of blessing, protection and community; and (4) provide symbols that serve as daily reminders of the covenant promises that were made with God in worship.

This approach to dialogue through lived religion respects the integrity of the Latter-day Saint religious system on its own terms while also placing it, as well as the evangelical understanding of Christianity, under the ultimate examining authority of the gospel of Jesus Christ as revealed in the Old and New Testament Scriptures.[35] This highlights the essential shortcoming of the text-based and cognitive approaches to interfaith dialogue: never bothering to step inside the world of our neighbor to identify its logic and governing center will lead to a witness to Jesus who is a stranger to the questions, needs and desires of Mormon neighbors. The good news will only sound like good news to evangelicals, for it will fail to speak the word of life and truth to our neighbor in their circumstance.

The divine origins of the Book of Mormon, the proclamation that the "fullness of the gospel" was restored through Joseph Smith and the Latter-day Saint plot line of the cosmic story—particularly the "fortunate fall"—remain important topics for dialogue between Mormons and evangelicals. Yet it should be apparent now that alongside these discussions on doctrinal matters of formal religion there also needs to be a study of the gravitational pull of lived religion and its power to satisfy universal human desires. If the gospel is to be clearly communicated, inquiry must be made into the religious world of our dialogue partners by attending to the intersections between official and personal meanings, beliefs and rituals, as well as formal and folk religious practices. This entails nothing less than looking for the work of the Holy Spirit in the hopes, fears and desires manifested in the lived religion of Latter-day Saints without loosening our conviction that somehow all of these basic human needs will only find their lasting fulfillment in a dynamic trusting relationship with the triune God through the person Jesus and intimate fellowship of the Holy Spirit (2 Corinthians 13:14).[36]

Conclusion: Making Good on the Apology

The argument set forth in this chapter is that if evangelicals are to make good on Richard Mouw's apology and bear truthful witness about their Mormon neighbors, then they must find ways of taking into account the complexities of lived religion. Underneath the mixture of beliefs and practices, formal teachings, and personal interpretations, we can be confident that the Spirit of God is actively stirring up a seed of religion and a sense of restlessness for God.[37] Remaining in the security of relating to our neighbor on the basis of formal religion and doctrinal statements will prove insufficient for the tasks required of an embodied communication of the gospel.[38] Failure to consider the multivalent nature of rituals and varieties of folk religion will perpetuate truncated views of our neighbor's religion and undermine a robust communication of the gospel of Jesus Christ that addresses all of human experience.

Respecting the ways Mormonism addresses human needs for meaning and salvation need not lead to an epistemological relativism or religious pluralism that would dilute the authority of Scripture or undermine the uniqueness of the gospel of Jesus Christ. The path to bearing faithful witness to our Mormon neighbors begins with bearing truthful and informed witness about their faith. A commitment to the Great Commission requires nothing less than a clear communication of Jesus Christ as Lord in forms and terms that speak to our neighbors at their point of need.

Mormons and Evangelicals in the Public Square

J. B. Haws

FOR A CHILD OF THE 1980S, the photo of the World War II–era Yalta conference was always one of those history textbook surprises. Here sat the United States' Franklin D. Roosevelt and the USSR's Joseph Stalin *together*, as allies in war. It was hard for my classmates and me to imagine that Americans and Russians had ever been allies, yet there they were. When the stakes were high enough, mutual animosities seemed less divisive.

It's probably hyperbole to say that Mormons and evangelicals have had their Cold War periods—but not by much. What this chapter suggests, though, is that we may be witnessing a Yalta moment, a détente of religious exigency. This analogy could definitely be taken too far, since more than the sheer necessity of confronting a common enemy seems to be at work in recent evangelical-Mormon cooperative ventures (though some believers from both traditions might frame the situation that way). The suggestion here is that public-square engagement also signals a mutual recognition that there may be greater common philosophical and theological underpinnings than have been recognized in the past, and this might be a chief byproduct of the interfaith dialogue that this book highlights.

This is not a pattern without precedent. Not long after evangelical ministers led the nationwide petition campaign favoring the removal of LDS apostle and US senator-elect Reed Smoot from government office, Mormons and conservative Christians found some common ground in the push for Prohibition. The early twentieth century found Mormon leaders emphasizing their faith's "Word of Wisdom" tenets with renewed vigor, and this no-alcohol, no-tobacco, no-tea-and-coffee lifestyle became an indelible marker of Mormon identity from then on. This lifestyle resonated with the views of Christian temperance advocates, some of whom acknowledged and appreciated Mormon morality in this new postpolygamy era.[1]

After that public-policy convergence, however, the middle decades of the twentieth century were relatively quiet in terms of evangelical and Mormon interaction. This is not to say that there was no interaction; authors and leaders from both camps occasionally regarded the other (mostly suspiciously) and offered commentary emphasizing the distinctiveness of their respective traditions. But geography and relative national political insignificance seemed to mute these interactions. Through mid-century, Mormons were predominantly found in the intermountain West and California— though that began to change after World War II—rather than in the evangelical heartland of the United States. So while the countercult movement against Mormonism was reenergized in the late 1950s and 1960s, this was long before such attention to the Latter-day Saints registered on the wider public's radar.[2] It would take politics to change that.

The so-called new evangelicals, with Billy Graham as their chief face, were prominent in public life throughout the 1950s and 1960s, but many evangelical and fundamentalist Christians seemed to have been less engaged in that way. Molly Worthen has recently argued against the "self-imposed exile" thesis, which posits that many Christians retreated from the public square after the Scopes trial–type modernist-fundamentalist debates of the mid-1920s.[3] The corrective that she and others offer is an important one. The story is certainly more complex than that. Still, it's also hard to argue that there was not something new about the way conservative Christians emerged onto the scene in the 1970s—or at least how that emergence was perceived. *Newsweek's* designation of 1976 as the "Year of the Evangelical" is only one case in point, as are polls that suggest that organizers like Jerry Falwell registered four million new evangelical and fundamentalist Christian voters in the late 1970s. Vice-president-elect George Bush in early 1981 even thought it necessary to explain to reporters that no one group could be credited for Ronald Reagan's election, so widespread had been the coverage of the voting power of the new "Religious Right."[4]

To a lesser degree, Mormons had been in the news at about the same time and for a similar reason. The LDS Church's opposition to the Equal Rights Amendment in the late 1970s and early 1980s had proved potent in several states, and media attention reflected that. Mormons had secured a reputation for their family-focused theology, and official LDS opposition to the amendment followed that theology, on the grounds that the amendment was so broad as to pose a potential threat to traditional protections for mothers and children. Some commentators saw Mormons as part of this wave of a conservative religionist voting bloc, and Jerry Falwell explicitly included Mormons when describing the makeup of the membership rolls of the "Moral Majority."[5]

Yet what really happened seemed, to some, unexpected, even counterintuitive. Ironically, just as their positions on social issues seemed to reflect parallel concerns, evangelical-Mormon friction produced more heat than it had for decades. While the explanations behind this phenomenon deserve more nuance than this chapter can give to them, it is not unreasonable to say that the source of this friction was the question of "counterfeit Christianity."[6] At the very time that a Christian voting bloc was coalescing over the express need of preserving America as a Christian nation, many in that same bloc were confronted with evidence of Mormon growth—often, they lamented, at the expense of evangelical congregations. "Mormons are winning over Baptist souls at a rate of '231 every single day'" was what the associate pastor of First Baptist Church in Dallas told *Newsweek* in March of 1985. Arthur Criscoe of the Southern Baptist Sunday School Board in Nashville was likewise distraught that LDS missionaries were "moving across the Southland . . . knocking on doors, penetrating."[7]

Latter-day Saints completed temples in Atlanta in 1983 and in Dallas in 1984. *Newsweek* saw this as a "turf war" right in the nation's religious heartland.[8] To many concerned Christians, this was about more than simple "sheep stealing" and church-membership numbers. To them, the Mormon threat centered on a common Christian worry that because Mormons purportedly believed in the "wrong Jesus," Mormon proselytizing was actually antithetical to Christian evangelism, and no seemingly common political agenda superseded the importance of decrying what they saw as a soul-destroying heresy. To many Christians, the superficial moral similarities between the two traditions meant that better-publicized distinctions were a must.

The depth of those worries was on display in a 1981 *Christianity Today* (*CT*) interview with Jerry Falwell. The issue at hand for the *CT* interviewer was "the deceptive advertising in the *Reader's Digest* by the Mormons"; *CT* asked if Reverend Falwell would ever use his television program to expose Mormonism accordingly. Falwell responded that no, he would not divide his political coalition in that way—even if the number of Mormons who joined the Moral Majority was small. The interviewer came back with this: "Say that in Salt Lake City they took the Moral Majority position right down the line, but because of false doctrine, they would not ultimately go to heaven. . . . I'm concerned that we could get the country morally straight and people would still go to hell." Reverend Falwell's answer showed just how tenuous—and potentially tense—such a coalition still was: "If a nation or a society lives by divine principles, even though the people personally don't know the One who taught and lived those principles, that society will be blessed. An unsaved person will be blessed by tithing to the work of God. He'll still go to hell a tither, but God blesses the principle."[9]

Some joint initiatives did come out of the decade. The LDS Church's Public Communications and Special Affairs director at the time was Richard Lindsay, whose professional background was in the public sector, as both a civil servant and an elected official. His experience in government social services served him well as he worked to involve the LDS Church in community-action coalitions on issues "where there seemed to be some kind of a fit for [LDS] values," most notably in the fights against alcohol and pornography.[10]

The Religious Alliance Against Pornography, for example, honored Mormons for doing more than any other church to combat pornography through media messages. Lindsay was one of four religious leaders invited to testify before a senate subcommittee about the "problems of family breakdowns in the United States." The church's Washington, D.C., Public Communications Bureau hosted an interfaith press conference at which representatives of "Islamic, Jewish, Protestant, Catholic, and Sikh faiths pledged long-term involvement in seeking solutions to drug abuse and drug-related crimes." These types of issue-based alliances built friendships and heralded a potential for improving outside perception of the LDS Church, especially

with like-minded religious leaders. At the same time, though, Mormon participation in these coalitions often brought to the surface the discomfort that
some evangelical partners endured when they associated with Mormons.[11]

One snapshot: Richard Lindsay recalled what he felt was a pleasant encounter with several evangelical Protestant leaders on a trip to Washington,
D.C., to meet with President Reagan. After returning home, Lindsay wrote
to one of the pastors: "Hey, when you come out this way I would really love
to have you meet the Presidency of the [LDS] Church." Lindsay received
what he called a "very quick returned note that said, 'Dear Richard, I love
you, but I hate your theology.'"[12]

Perhaps nothing symbolizes just how fraught with tension the 1980s were
better than *The God Makers*. This film's production team was led by Ed
Decker, a former Mormon whose group "Saints Alive in Jesus" had an express aim to convert Mormons to Christianity. The film found its largest
audiences among evangelical Christian congregations—perhaps as many as
a thousand such screenings a month.[13] The film depicted Latter-day Saint
theology and practice as having ties to pagan and even occult and satanic
traditions. It reinforced for many viewers concerns about the potentially
soul-destroying effects of Mormon proselytizing.

Some Mormons marshaled counteroffensives, even if their responses
never found the size of audiences *The God Makers* did. One Mormon book,
Stephen Robinson's *Are Mormons Christians?* (1991), did, however, find its
way into the hands of several professors at the evangelical Denver Seminary.
Gregory Johnson, a seminary student (and former Latter-day Saint), suggested that the Denver faculty respond to Robinson's book. Stephen Robinson was a religion professor at Brigham Young University (BYU) with a
PhD in biblical studies from Duke. His principal thesis was that for every
so-called non-Christian belief in the Mormon system, one could find a
number of orthodox Christian writers and thinkers who espoused—or at
least allowed for—something very similar. Robinson quoted Irenaeus, Athanasius, Augustine, Martin Luther and others.[14]

Several Denver professors took up Greg Johnson's suggestion to react to
Robinson's book, and they organized a symposium with that aim. It is
telling that Stephen Robinson declined an invitation to attend the symposium and offer a response. He felt that he would be entering a theological

lion's den, so sure was he that the two sides could not meet on amicable terms. Johnson forwarded the Denver Seminary professors' papers to Robinson, however, who was intrigued by the thoughtfulness of one in particular—that of Craig Blomberg.[15] After corresponding, the two agreed to meet at the Society of Biblical Literature convention. Conversations grew into collaboration, and the two cowrote *How Wide the Divide? A Mormon and an Evangelical in Conversation.*[16]

The book's 1997 appearance was something of a watershed moment. Not only did the conversations and interpersonal connections that *How Wide the Divide* spawned lead indirectly to the formal Mormon-evangelical academic dialogue that has resulted in this volume, but *How Wide the Divide* also seemed to create a space where there could be appropriate appreciation for theological parallels in the two traditions. The book offered sound counterevidence against the anathema of saying that Mormons and evangelicals had more in common than the two groups, respectively, might have thought. And without that space, it is likely that recent public-square cooperation would not have been possible, at least on the level that has been recently apparent. That is because these theological conversations made an impact when evangelical Christians wrestled with an important question in 2008 and 2012: Could they vote for a Mormon for president?

In the years before those pivotal elections, Fuller Seminary president Richard Mouw also played an important role in widening that space. One of the moments that demonstrated just how much ground had been covered in evangelical and Mormon conversations was evangelist Ravi Zacharias's appearance at the pulpit of the famed Mormon Tabernacle in Salt Lake City. The occasion was as historic as the building. But what really grabbed headlines that night were Mouw's introductory comments. He apologized for what he saw as evangelicals' bearing false witness against their Mormon neighbors in the way they had typically represented the Latter-day Saint faith. The apology ignited a firestorm of responses from countercultists, but it also signaled a new middle way among some evangelicals and Mormons in dialogue.[17]

That middle way would become especially important when Mormon Mitt Romney, former governor of Massachusetts, emerged as a leading contender for the Republican presidential nomination in 2008. His candidacy indisputably revealed the persistence of deep, religiously based reservations about legitimizing Mormonism among large numbers of conservative Christian voters, but Romney's campaign also resulted in some surprises.

Bob Jones III, for example, endorsed Romney. "Evangelicals for Mitt" drew supporters and media attention. Still, Romney's 2008 presidential aspirations seemed to fall victim to the emergence of an evangelical competitor, Southern Baptist minister and former Arkansas governor Mike Huckabee; Romney withdrew from the campaign after he suffered losses in evangelical-heavy primaries like Iowa and South Carolina, where support for Huckabee surged. But in retrospect, instead of representing a serious setback in the state of Mormon-evangelical relations (which is how many Mormons might have initially perceived conservative Christian opposition to Mitt Romney), the 2008 election became a significant turning point—more because of a ballot initiative in California than because of presidential politics.

Proposition 8 in California emerged as the hot-button topic in the aftermath of the 2008 election season. The ballot question centered on the definition of marriage in California—and proposition supporters aimed to establish marriage as between one man and one woman. Even last-minute, preelection polling portended the proposition's defeat. The shock that reverberated nationwide was that the proposition passed. And Mormons received the lion's share of the credit—or blame.

The opponents to Proposition 8 showed their displeasure by organizing boycotts against business owners that supported the measure. Singled out for special retribution was the Church of Jesus Christ of Latter-day Saints. Many gay rights activists attributed their defeat in the Proposition 8 debate to the organizing capacity and financial contributions of Mormons, even though Mormons were invited to join a preexisting pro-Proposition 8 coalition of evangelical Christian and Catholic groups, among others. And in response to the protests staged at LDS temples and meetinghouses, a number of prominent evangelicals and Catholics came to the Mormons' defense.[18]

For that reason, Michael Otterson, managing director of the LDS Church's Public Affairs Department, sees Proposition 8 as a defining moment for Latter-day Saints in the public square. "What people didn't see," Otterson said,

> was the reaction from the faith community as a whole and how appreciative that faith community was for the role that Latter-day Saints played in pro-

tecting traditional marriage in California. . . . And whether you agree or disagree with same sex marriages isn't the point. Purely as a historical phenomenon, Proposition 8 put the [LDS] church on the map with many other churches and faith communities in this country and we became relevant.[19]

While the cooperation in California also seemed to portend for some an easing of the evangelical discomfort of voting for Mitt Romney the second time around, the 2011–2012 presidential primary-season buildup still featured a number of prominent Christian voices who were, to say the least, undecided. Emblematic of that uncertainty were Pastor Robert Jeffress's comments at the October 2011 Values Voters Summit. He told CNN at the summit that Mitt Romney belonged to a cult—albeit a "theological" rather than a "sociological cult"—and "born-again followers of Jesus Christ should always prefer a competent Christian to a competent non-Christian" (in Jeffress's case, he was endorsing Texas governor Rick Perry).[20] The reaction to Pastor Jeffress's characterization of Mormons, however, showed that the ground had shifted since 2008.

Richard Mouw was only the most prominent evangelical commentator to dispute the "cult" designation before the weekend was out. Mouw's reasoning was that the type of academic exchange and interfaith outreach characteristic of the Latter-day Saints he knew meant that the "cult" label simply did not stick. And Biola University's John Mark Reynolds, in a *Washington Post* blog post, called on his fellow evangelicals to disavow what he saw as "anti-Mormon bigotry."[21]

As it appeared more and more likely that Mitt Romney would secure the Republican nomination, the volume of the "can't-vote-for-a-Mormon" voices dramatically decreased. Part of that was undoubtedly due to the perceived need for party unity—and to what some saw as the cynical lowest common denominator: that even a Mormon was preferable to a second term for President Barack Obama. But there also was something to be said for the number and influence of evangelical thinkers who publicly stated that they saw no inconsistency with their faith and their support of Mitt Romney. The Southern Baptist Theological Seminary, the Southern Baptist Convention's flagship school, hosted a September 2012 forum that took a strongly affirmative stand in response to the "Can Christians vote for a Mormon?" question. Even Pastor Jeffress endorsed Romney almost exactly a year after

his well-known Value Voters Summit comments. His FoxNews.com post
was titled, tellingly, "Romney and the disappearing evangelical dilemma."[22]

This is not to say that religious opposition to Mitt Romney's faith and
candidacy did not affect his election fortunes; some have argued that many
Christian voters simply chose to stay home from the polls rather than make
what they saw as a no-win choice. Utah Valley University president Matt
Holland has made the compelling argument that Mitt Romney's campaign
was forced to spend its way through a brutal primary season—and much of
those primary battles seemed to center on securing the conservative
Christian bloc.[23] What is just as significant, though, is that based on election-
day exit polls, a greater percentage of evangelical votes went to Mitt Romney
than they had four years earlier to John McCain—and at the same rate that
they went to George W. Bush in 2004—and this in an election when "the
evangelical vote was 27 percent of the overall electorate—the highest it's ever
been for an election."[24]

Perhaps even more noteworthy, just a few weeks before the November
2012 election, photos of Mitt Romney meeting with Billy Graham sped
across the newswires. Franklin Graham also released an open letter arguing
that Mormons and Catholics and Jews shared with evangelical Christians
values that were "biblically based." And the Billy Graham Evangelistic Association removed from its website references to Mormonism as a cult. To
be sure, the number of Christians who responded indignantly to that removal showed that the fires of this debate still burned, yet that emendation
to the BGEA website also suggested—as did the decisions of millions of
evangelicals in voting booths across the country—that perhaps some
guards had been lowered, and it would be difficult, even awkward, to raise
them again.[25]

In that post-2012 environment, LDS leaders have embraced opportunities
to join forces on shared values and reach out across what have felt like
former battle lines. In the fall of 2013, a "Faith, Family, and Society" lecture
series brought the Southern Baptist Convention's Richard Land, Assemblies
of God general superintendent George Wood and Southern Baptist Seminary president Albert Mohler to LDS Church–owned Brigham Young University. Ravi Zacharias came to the campus in mid-January 2014. The important symbolism of these visits was not lost on Mohler, who plainly noted

his theological disagreements with Mormonism, but then outlined the contours of a pragmatic friendship over "common concerns and urgencies." Because of what he saw as the dire threat to religious freedom in the American public square, Mohler told his BYU audience, "I do not believe that we are going to heaven together, but I do believe we may go to jail together."[26]

It is on this issue of religious liberty that, at the time of this writing, LDS and evangelical policy collaborations most markedly center. But this also extends beyond just evangelical-Mormon relationships, although the thawing of those relationships described here has been absolutely critical to the attention LDS have garnered and has paved the way for LDS to be in the conversation.[27] Mormons are partnering with Christian and non-Christian faith groups in making their public case for protecting religious freedom, with recent endeavors like the annual International Law and Religion symposium at BYU (which in its October 2013, twentieth-annual iteration included delegates from over forty nations and focused on religion and human rights), friends-of-the-court briefs connected with provisions in the Affordable Care Act and high-level talks between Latter-day Saint apostles and Catholic cardinals.[28]

Because of its centralized, hierarchical organizational structure, the LDS Church is able to speak with a unified corporate voice in a way that a diverse and decentralized group like evangelical Christians cannot. This, of course, can sometimes belie or obscure the real political diversity within Mormon ranks. But at the same time, this institutional framework also allows observers to determine "official" Latter-day Saints positions. And recently, those positions on some issues—immigration reform and nondiscrimination ordinances, for example—have been decidedly moderate.[29] This suggests that Latter-day Saint leaders desire to chart an independent policy course for their church, while at the same time allying with like-minded individuals and groups more than ever before.[30] And all indications are that evangelical Christians are more willing to see Mormons in that same "like-minded" light than ever before.

An Evangelical at Brigham Young University

Sarah Taylor

Moving to Provo felt kind of epic, like entering a parallel universe. Everything seemed Mormon—the emergency supply stores, the cap-sleeved shirts, the married twenty-year-olds, the giant inflatable missionary on University Parkway . . . even the roads were Mormon, with their easily navigable grid system and prophetically inspired street widths. There was not a Starbucks in sight.

I had moved from Minnesota to Utah after meeting both a Utah pastor and Mormon missionaries who talked about the Provo area like it was the second coming. I didn't intend to stay long, in the beginning—I expected it to be a three-month stint in a random place like I had had before. But within weeks of arriving, I wanted to stay longer. There was just something about the place that I liked, and that something seemed like Mormons.

Men opened doors for me, women asked if I was married and people my age played board games and watched edited movies with enthusiasm. The day I moved into my Provo apartment, neighbors brought me homemade cookies and invited me over for a *Gilmore Girls* marathon, and the first time I was caught walking in the rain, three people pulled over to offer me rides. But it was more than just the niceness that endeared me to Provo; it was the way religion seemed to saturate just everything. I liked that a lot—so much that I decided to apply to Brigham Young University (BYU), which I imagined would be like Provo on steroids, religious-saturation-wise. As excited as I was becoming about the idea, it never seemed like a light decision.

It would mean four years of being a religious minority in a missionary culture, for one thing, and also my mostly positive experiences with Provo so far had not, by a long shot, canceled out the preconceptions of Mormons that I brought with me to Utah. For instance, I believed that Mormons would lie to me whenever it served them. I had heard that Mormons had a network of spies who reported the activities of suspected anti-Mormons to church leaders, and that Mormons used evangelical terms but meant something different by them. I needed to keep an eye out for that, people said. Nearly everything I thought I knew about Mormons I had heard from fellow evangelical Christians, and none of it was positive.

But somehow in spite of that, I felt that going to BYU might be genuinely fun. I was enjoying getting to know Mormons and Mormonism so much that I became set on the idea of BYU almost as soon as I had it. Whatever else BYU might end up being, it would be worth it, I felt sure; and when I was notified I had been accepted, I didn't think twice about what to do.

Shortly before classes began that fall, I moved into an apartment south of campus that came with three roommates. It turned out that evangelicals seemed to have nearly as bad a reputation among Latter-day Saints as Latter-day Saints had among evangelicals, and one of my roommates knew of it, or knew some unfortunate evangelicals—I never found out which. Things were awkward between us from the outset. She mostly kept her distance, except to ask why BYU, and did I believe Mormons were Christians, and how did I feel about the church. After a week of my fumbling the responses, her bishop showed up on our doorstep one night and asked point-blank if I had come to Utah to convert Mormons to evangelical Christianity.

Stunned, I didn't know what to say. I wanted to tell him that asking an evangelical if she wants people to convert is like asking a fish if it wants to swim, but that if he could see my heart, I think he would feel that I was no threat. And I wanted to say that I had grown up hearing that his church was a cult, and that I had this inexplicable need to understand why, knowing some people thought so, Mormons still chose it. Nearly all I think about is religions, I wanted to say, and Mormonism more than most. It is because of the way there's this edge in evangelicals' voices when they talk about it, the way I wasn't allowed outside as a kid when missionaries came by, in case I believed something I heard from them, the way they weren't allowed inside, because some Bible verse I've long forgotten seemed to my mom to forbid it—these things make me want to be here, and I don't entirely understand it myself, but it feels right. But instead I replied, "not really."

"I'm not really here to convert people" was not the confident "no" that might have put the issue to rest. The bishop stayed for half an hour asking follow-up questions that to him must have seemed simple and easy but to me did not yet have clear answers. The conversation just went nowhere. It only made things more awkward with my roommate, if more awkward was possible, and I started spending more time on campus to avoid the awkwardness.

Things were better at school. There was a lot I didn't understand, but I liked BYU for its foreignness. It was a continual point of wonder to me how much my classmates, who seemed so much like me in some ways, were privy to a cultural narrative that I wasn't. We had all grown up watching *Full House* and *Boy Meets World*, but I'd never seen *Saturday's Warrior* or heard that Jesus wanted me for a sunbeam, or read the Book of Mormon.

Before I discovered the philosophy department, religion classes were my favorite. It had never occurred to me that there might be diversity of thought among Mormons like there was among evangelicals when it came to interpreting Scripture, and I loved that there seemed to be. Did 2 Nephi 25:23 mean that grace kicked in once one's own efforts have been exhausted, or that in spite of one's own efforts, it was really by grace that one was saved? It hardly mattered that the Book of Mormon was not Scripture to me—what was being discussed, I thought, was the nature of salvation, and I felt as invested in that conversation as the next person.

Gradually, things started to seem less foreign. A class discussion about reconciling Joseph Smith's multiple First Vision accounts did not seem to me entirely unlike evangelical conversations about reconciling the Synoptic Gospels. I read the Book of Mormon and began to understand what people meant when they spoke of the three Nephites or Alma the Younger or holding fast to the iron rod. "Seminary" started to mean religion classes for high schoolers, "testimony" started to mean a spiritual witness from the Holy Ghost and I started to feel more like a student in my classes and less like a spectator.

The things I was learning—and the people I was learning them with— brought up all sorts of questions I had never considered. Was Jesus still embodied, and did it matter if he was? Would Jesus' having been married necessarily change anything, christologically? Did marriages extend past earthly life in any way? I wondered about the theoretical possibility of a universal apostasy and whether the phrase "image of God" could have any physical implications, and whether the finitude of humanity necessarily precluded pre-earth human life. I was reading the Bible in ways I never would have considered and hearing familiar stories with new ears, and I loved it.

I took a class on American Christianity my sophomore year that shattered my assumptions about what was possible in terms of Mormon-evangelical relations. The way Protestantism had been addressed in other classes was similar to how Mormonism was discussed in-house among evangelicals; one came away with the impression that Protestantism was absurd, and that Protestants would jump ship if they would only think through their nonsensical beliefs. Knowing that this kind of thing would be no better (and would probably be worse) for a Mormon who attended an evangelical school did not make me less frustrated with what I felt were serious mischaracterizations; that hypothetical Mormon wasn't around to commiserate with, and no one else seemed to notice it happening.

This class, though, was different. The professor—Spencer Fluhman—talked about Protestantism with such insight and generosity that I found myself tearing up during the first lecture, completely disarmed. He was being fair when he didn't have to be, when no one would have been the wiser. Questions like, "How can Calvinists believe in predestination?" were met with sermon-quality descriptions of Reformed perspectives on God's sovereignty. The most stunning thing about it, to me, was that Dr. Fluhman was not just acting generous; he *was* generous. This was no mere academic posturing. He did not leave the classroom and sing a different tune to his colleagues, I felt certain. Surely, in Dr. Fluhman's estimation, evangelicals were wrong about quite a few things, but I did not get the impression that "wrong" meant "dumb" to him.

It was a turning point for me. I found aspects of my classmates' faith as unreasonable as some of my professors found aspects of mine (and I brought two decades' worth of negative bias against Mormons to the table to boot), and it had never occurred to me that there might be another way to see it. I could continue to view the Church of Jesus Christ of Latter-day Saints as I always had, at some level—as being wrong, and therefore ridiculous—or I could start taking it seriously, as Dr. Fluhman had done with Protestantism. But the door was closing, I felt, on my acting with Mormons as though I respected their beliefs when mostly I did not. Politeness did not seem a worthy goal once I saw what love looked like.

It took about two years for me to really make friends at BYU. It was a lonely two years. I liked the people I knew during that time, but never seemed to quite move past the friendly, curious stage with anyone. About once a month, someone in one of my classes would invite me to attend church with him or her, or to a ward activity, and I usually went and enjoyed it. But I had a hard time with the turnover rate of those relationships; they tended to fizzle out when I said no to meeting with missionaries. It turned out that missionaries were not my thing. I was interested like crazy in discussing religion, but to me the missionary discussions felt less like conversations than like paint-by-number exchanges. I just did not like the feel of them.

My two-year friendlessness might have been due in part to it taking that long for me to declare a major (philosophy) and start seeing the same people every day. Or maybe it was just that I hadn't yet encountered the kinds of people who tended to take philosophy classes, because once I met them, things just clicked.

It began with this guy Billy, who spoke up as much as I did in class but said opposite things. We found that we had more to argue about than we had time in class to do it. So we started meeting to argue at other times too, and then we started inviting other people to argue with us. Pretty soon, a group of about ten people, mostly BYU philosophy students and some evangelical friends of mine, began meeting twice a month to discuss everything from the nature of God to songs and poems we liked. The group—philosophy group, we called it—quickly became my favorite part of being in Provo.

One fall day my junior year, Billy and I paced the lawn behind the library arguing about whether or not God had ever sinned. I was adamant that God had not, and Billy disagreed, at least to the extent that it wouldn't have mattered to him if God had. Jesus' atonement was so profoundly absolute, he said, that it would have completely washed away any past sin that even God committed. I was stunned by Billy's appeal to the total efficacy of Jesus' atonement; I had heard people argue for God's having sinned before, but had never heard someone cite the atonement as a reason why, if God had sinned, it wouldn't matter. In point of fact, Billy was taking Jesus' atonement a step farther than I was willing to, and that gave me pause. I thought for a minute and then told Billy that while I found his conclusion horrifying (diplomacy was not my strong point), his way of reaching it struck a deep chord with me. This wasn't the first time this kind of thing had happened with Billy, but it was the first time I felt like I understood why it was happening.

All at once, it hit me that Billy—Mormon, God-may-have-sinned Billy—was a Christian. Whenever Billy talked about Jesus, he talked like a man in love, and that was just *it* for me.

Billy has the Holy Spirit in him, I kept thinking. *Billy has been born again.* And the act of being born seemed like an all-or-nothing event. In all his Mormonness, Billy was no less born again than I was. *Literally,* I thought, as I sat down next to Billy, *we are the same amount Christian.*

I immediately thought about how in Acts 15, in addressing the phenomenon of Gentile believers, Peter says, "God, who knows the heart, showed that he accepted them by giving the Holy Spirit to them, just as he did to us. He did not discriminate between us and them, for he purified their hearts by faith" (Acts 15:8-9 NIV).

For weeks I was stuck on the thought that God did not discriminate between Billy and me, and for weeks after that on the thought that in the Acts 15 scenario, it made as much sense for me to be the Gentile to Billy's Jew as vice versa. Billy's path to Jesus was necessarily as legitimate as mine, and it had never left Mormon territory—to think otherwise, I would have to consider Mormonism and truth to be mutually exclusive, and to define truth as inherently evangelical. In other words, I could interpret Billy's love for Jesus as being essentially evangelical and un-Mormon, or I could stop equating evangelicalism with truth and Mormonism with untruth, and accept that Jesus, who was the truth, suddenly seemed very distinct from the religious categories with which I was obsessed. Jesus did not belong to evangelical Christians; evangelical Christians belonged to Jesus. I had it all backward.

Billy and I still disagreed plenty after that, but for me our discussions took on a different meaning. Completely gone was my interest in proving Billy wrong in the hopes that his wrongness would be evidence to him of a larger pattern—namely, that he was wrong because he was Mormon. Where I thought Billy was wrong, I sure wanted to persuade him, and I actually felt freer to try, once I could do it without having an agenda. I just didn't feel any more like exploiting his concessions or hiding mine.

Philosophy group lasted for two years and became a place where it seemed that nearly anything was fair game. We covered topics that I previously could not have imagined discussing openly and honestly with Mormons, or with many evangelicals, for that matter. For me, it was also a much-needed coming together of worlds, the only place where the evangelicals and Mormons I knew and liked knew and liked each other. I told the group how I was having this kind of religious identity crisis because of how fuzzy things seemed to me at times, how I felt cornered when Mormons bore their testimonies to me and how I wished we could just have a conversation instead, how being on the receiving end of proselytism was making me fundamentally rethink what I believed about evangelism, how bewildering I found it when Mormons said things like that I wouldn't lose any of my beliefs if I joined the church, how Billy was a Christian, but how this guy I went to church with did not seem like one in the least, and how much of a category-buster that was for me, how I knew a guy who protested at General Conference and I liked him, and how I felt like I had a foot in two worlds but was beginning to wonder if I belonged in either. Nothing seemed to make sense anymore. At least, not in the neat way it had before. But I was starting to enjoy the chaos.

I loved the philosophy department for the way it was anything but paint-by-number. The professors were just amazing, the kinds of teachers who were as interested in the process of having a thought as they were in where the thought ended up. And the philosophers I met in their classes had tackled topics that seemed immediately applicable to my life. Søren Kierkegaard had me questioning my access to objective truth, and William James gave me a framework for responding to a question I never knew how to answer—"Why aren't you Mormon?" *Because Mormonism isn't a live hypothesis for me,* I would think from then on; *it isn't that I'm not choosing your church, it's that given what I already believe, there is no real choice to be made.*

It wasn't that I felt that the church had nothing to offer. The opposite was true. LDS theology had shaped my own in ways that I was just beginning to understand. By the time I graduated from BYU, I resonated more with the experiential way that Mormons approached truth and Scripture than with the rationalistic approach of evangelicals, and I felt like Mormons were on to something in their rejection of the idea that human nature was essentially bad. I did not believe people could become big-G Gods (and neither did many of the Mormons I knew), but talking and thinking about it so much had landed me somewhere close to an Eastern Orthodox perspective of *theosis*. Wrestling with the idea of a Godhead composed of three distinct beings had turned me into a social trinitarian. I heard about free agency so often at BYU that it started to make sense, and I changed from being mostly Reformed to being mostly not. I did not believe God the Father had ever been human, but the idea of a once-human God caused me to grapple with God the Son's humanity in ways that I had not done before.

In some ways, my beliefs hadn't changed much. To me, God was still the Trinity, salvation was still by grace, the Bible was still Scripture and so on. If anything, I believed those things more by the end of four years at BYU than I had at the beginning, for all the talking and thinking I did about them. But I had changed.

I learned something of humility at BYU, and not just from how frequently I turned out to be wrong. I saw humility modeled by Mormons. It made me reconsider the way I thought about wrongness, and the way I defined theology. Did God care more that I believed he had never sinned than that I had believed his character to be congruent with religious pride? Did he care more that I believed him to be a Trinity than that I believed him to be so small, his arm did not extend beyond the borders of my own religious culture? These were all inherently theological issues, it seemed to me, just different kinds. I had placed the former kind so far above the latter in importance that the latter had escaped introspection entirely, but BYU had drawn it out.

There is no denying that for me, being at BYU was downright hard at times. I was not always happy to be there, and I did not view every challenge as an opportunity for growth. Some of the challenges were just problems with no resolution. I did not spend the whole four years, or even the last two, feeling grateful about how much I was learning and marveling at the generosity of strangers. Sometimes I got angry and cranky and felt like transferring to Wheaton, but it would be an understatement to say that I am glad I didn't.

In the end, BYU had become home, and I loved it because it was mine.

PART TWO

Specific
Doctrinal Discussions

How Many Gods?

Mormons and Evangelicals Discussing the Debate

Craig L. Blomberg

Setting the Stage

Put fifteen or sixteen evangelical and Latter-day Saint (LDS) scholars in a conference room at Fuller Seminary in Pasadena, California, in May of 2011. Several of them have been meeting once or twice a year for just over a decade. Most have joined these Mormon-evangelical dialogues somewhere in the decade of the 2000s. One or two are quite new to the conversations. The topic for conversation is Larry W. Hurtado's widely heralded but provocative book *How on Earth Did Jesus Become a God? Historical Questions about Earliest Devotion to Jesus.*[1] How will the various conversation partners react? Will there be consensus on anything significant or only disagreement?

Why choose this book? It's scarcely a *New York Times* bestseller, but responsible works of scholarship representing more than one author's idiosyncratic views seldom turn into blockbusters! Perhaps more than any other New Testament scholar today, Hurtado has researched and written a series of highly acclaimed articles and books on the nature of monotheism in Second Temple Judaism and its significance for the development of early Christian reflection about the person of Jesus.[2] In *One God, One Lord: Early Christian Devotion and Ancient Jewish Monotheism,*[3] Hurtado investigates the features of Second Temple Judaism that made it even possible to conceive of a human being as God. He draws attention to intertestamental

Jewish writings that personify divine Wisdom, or that exalt angels and arch-
angels, along with patriarchs and other heroes from ancient Israelite religion,
in ways that rabbinic Judaism would probably have disallowed. Hurtado
then describes the "mutations" of these exalted figures that led to Christian
devotion to Jesus as God himself. In his major work, *Lord Jesus Christ: Devotion to Jesus in Earliest Christianity*,[4] Hurtado demonstrates in detail how
this devotion cut across all strata of New Testament documents and their
sources. To borrow the language of one of his earlier journal articles, the
high Christology of the New Testament was a "revolutionary" rather than
an "evolutionary" development that happened shockingly early and amaz-
ingly quickly in the first generation of Christian history.[5]

In *How on Earth Did Jesus Become a God?* Hurtado summarizes some of
his previous work and pushes other parts of it further. His eight main
chapters present, in turn, the history and state of the discussion; the reasons
for seeing devotion to Christ as emerging within *Jewish* circles rather than
merely later Greco-Roman ones; the negative social and political consequences for many early Christians for this devotion, showing that they truly
did push the limits of acceptable boundaries between the human and the
divine; a detailed analysis of Philippians 2:6-11 as an early hymn of worship
of Christ; a discussion of how this devotion could have emerged with Jewish
monotheism; a comparison and contrast between this devotion and people's
responses to Jesus already during his lifetime; the significant innovation
represented within Jewish monotheism; and the experiential and revelatory
bases that alone could have caused such significant innovations.

It is instructive to contrast Hurtado's biblical and historical approach with
the approaches so often taken among systematic theologians. It is common-
place for theological students, especially in evangelical traditions, to learn
to cite key biblical texts, especially in the New Testament, that refer to the
Father as God, that show Jesus to be the Son of God and God the Son, and
that equate the Spirit with deity as well. Then they highlight another set of
texts which reiterates that there is only one God. From this, it is argued,
comes the historic Christian conclusion that the Godhead is one God in
three persons, or one essential entity or Being with three centers of personal
consciousness. None of the individual persons constitutes the sum total of
the Godhead, but each is fully God. The unity goes beyond that of the com-

plete cooperation of three distinct persons, agreed on everything they desire to do, because of the *perichoresis* or coinherence of each member of the Godhead with each of the others. The Father is *in* the Son and the Spirit; the Son is *in* the Father and the Spirit; and the Spirit is *in* the Father and the Son. This, then, becomes the biblical foundation for the doctrine of the Trinity, elaborated and clarified in response to various challenges fueled by the insertion of Greek philosophy into Christian thinking, and articulated *in nuce* in the third-century Apostles' Creed and in more detail in the fourth-century Nicene Creed. The conviction remains, however, that these creeds simply elaborate and clarify what is genuinely in the Bible in seed form.[6]

Latter-day Saints, on the other hand, find the disconnect between New Testament teaching and Nicene orthodoxy to be much greater. As they study Christian history, they conclude that Nicaea not only reacted to Greek philosophy but also imbibed it. Athanasian and Arian debates between Christ being of the *same* substance or essence (*homoousios*) as the Father and being merely of a *similar* substance or essence (*homoiousios*) have absorbed a theological atmosphere far removed from the first-century Christian climate. Not only is the word *Trinity* not found in the Bible, but neither is the concept, according to standard Mormon thought.[7] First-century Christianity was so corrupted in successive centuries, even more in Roman Catholic thought than in Eastern Orthodox thought, that a Reformation was not enough. A full restoration of primitive Christianity was needed. This, the LDS believe, occurred with the establishment of their religion by Joseph Smith Jr. in 1830.[8]

It is easy to reach a stalemate when evangelicals point out that the revelations of Joseph Smith, especially in the Doctrine and Covenants and Pearl of Great Price, create an authoritative filter through which Mormons *must* read the New Testament, but then Mormons point out that Nicene orthodoxy puts almost as binding and focused a grid over evangelical reading of the New Testament. Perhaps one of these lenses is a correct lens; perhaps neither is. But when they contradict one another, as they at least occasionally do, they cannot both be correct. And neither group is likely to concede that their lens is the wrong one when such contradiction occurs. But what if we all tried to read the Bible historically rather than systematically? What if, at least temporarily, we bracketed our interpretive grids and filters, and tried our hardest to understand first-century theological developments within a Second

Temple Jewish framework? This is precisely what Hurtado's work calls us to, and why it proved an excellent point of departure for our conversations.

Formal reviews of Hurtado's book, setting forth its main points, along with reviewers' assessments of its strengths and weaknesses, can be found in numerous other sources.[9] The rest of this short paper is designed only to highlight the apparent agreements and disagreements that our extended conversation in 2011 in Pasadena produced. Not every participant in the dialogue would phrase things exactly as I have, but my thoughts here represent the unpacking of an outline of agreements and disagreements that I drafted from the notes I took throughout our sessions, which I then circulated to all the participants for their feedback, and subsequently revised in light of the feedback I received. If someone from our gathering disagrees with what I put forward here, it is not because I have avoided including their input but only because they did not indicate such disagreement at that time or when I later more formally requested input.

AREAS OF ESSENTIAL AGREEMENT

Relatively straightforward agreement among the dialogue participants quickly emerged that Hurtado was correct to stress that the man Jesus of Nazareth, a Jew who lived in the first third of the first century in Israel, was adored by many of his followers already during his ministry in ways that at the very least bordered on worship, and that very quickly after his death he was worshiped in fashions quite reminiscent if not even identical to the worship Jews had previously reserved solely for the God of Israel. The distinctive Mormon belief that equates Jesus with Jehovah (or Yahweh) of the Old Testament probably made this an even easier affirmation for the LDS participants to make than for the evangelicals. As Roger Keller once phrased it, "The unique knowledge that we gain from the incarnation is that Jehovah, the incarnate God of the Old Testament, has a Father who had previously been hidden from us."[10] Instead of the New Testament clarifying that the God of the Old Testament has all along had a preexistent Son who has now taken on human flesh, for the LDS the New Testament clarifies that Jesus, the God of the Old Testament, has himself had a heavenly Father. This discussion occupied portions of earlier Mormon-evangelical dialogues but was not pursued on this occasion.

Analyzing events from the perspective of the history of Second Temple Judaism, all participants in the 2011 dialogue could agree that there was a more flexible form of Jewish monotheism prior to A.D. 70 than what developed afterward. Although her work has always been on the fringe of mainstream biblical scholarship, Margaret Barker with her repeated appeals to the concept of a great angel in ancient Israel functioning very similarly to God even while not identical with him[11] has often found a receptive hearing in LDS circles.[12] So Hurtado's appeals to more mainstream scholars such as Jarl Fossum and Alan Segal[13] make his case for a variegated monotheism even more convincing. Judaism was never ditheist (as Barker has claimed), but there remains that intriguing passage in Daniel 7:9 in which the rare dual form is used for "thrones," when we read that Daniel saw in heaven that "[two] thrones were set in place / and the Ancient of Days took his seat."[14] For whom is the second throne? In Daniel 7:13 "one like a son of man, coming with the clouds of heaven . . . approached the Ancient of Days and was led into his presence." The text never says that he sat on the other throne, but it does go on to elaborate that "he was given authority, glory and sovereign power; all nations and peoples of every language worshiped him. His dominion is an everlasting dominion that will not pass away, and his kingdom is one that will never be destroyed" (Daniel 7:14). If this human being ("a son of man") has an everlasting kingdom, then he must be a king, and kings typically sit on thrones.[15] Of course, "Son of Man" is Jesus' most characteristic and distinct title for himself throughout the Gospels, including in contexts that suggest he is claiming to be more than just a human being.[16]

No disagreement in our dialogue arose over Hurtado's explanations that what facilitated identifying Jesus with deity was the more flexible monotheism prior to A.D. 70 in which even Torah and Logos, in addition to Wisdom, patriarchs and angels, were at times quasi-divinized. We also recognized with Hurtado that these partial precedents stopped short of what early Christians ascribed to Jesus, thus explaining the recurring hostility within Judaism among those who did not accept the first Christians' claims. Roman persecution, already occasional in the first century and more frequently and with greater intensity in the second and third centuries, made one's beliefs about Jesus at times something one might be called on to die for. Clearly more than semantic disputes or conceptual debates were involved. Two early hybrid or syncretistic forms of Christianity came into being that dissolved the tension in affirming Jesus as both fully God and fully human. Ebionism preserved Jesus within the constraints of conventional Judaism by stopping just short of ascribing full deity to Jesus, while Gnosticism denied his full humanity. Neither of these belief systems, however, should be confused with apostolic Christianity, which both evangelicals and LDS claim to represent.

The Mormon emphasis on personal experience of God and a testimony instilled by the Holy Ghost/Spirit in the life of every believer made Hurtado's crucial chapter on revelatory experience a fairly easy one for all of us to accept. With cessationism increasingly occupying a miniscule portion of evangelical scholarship,[17] none in our midst wished to deny the likelihood then or now of God disclosing himself in Jesus and the Spirit through direct, supernatural disclosure. We also agreed that the threeness and oneness of the Godhead originally came into being for the first time neither as a result of the Council of Nicaea nor from the revelations of Joseph Smith but because men and women closely associated with the historical Jesus found themselves unable to speak about his words, deeds and overall significance without using language that transgressed conventional boundaries between the human and the divine. After Pentecost, Jesus' followers were filled with the Spirit and experienced God so powerfully and miraculously that they also attributed to the Spirit attributes once reserved for God himself.

The participants in the dialogue, in addition, all affirmed that they were monotheists. Occasionally Latter-day Saints have self-identified as polytheists or, more precisely, tritheists.[18] More commonly, evangelicals have charged them with being such.[19] At least in this gathering, there was no desire to accept either of these designations. We agreed that we could simultaneously affirm statements like, "There is only one God who is worthy of worship," and "The entire Godhead—Father, Son and Holy Spirit—is worthy of worship." Moreover, human beings are not worthy of worship, and we will forever be vastly subordinate to and dependent on the Godhead. However Godlike or Christlike we may become, however exalted or glorious our resurrected and perfected bodies and spirits will be, we will always and forever worship the members of the Godhead and only the members of the Godhead.[20]

Moreover, we agreed that it is perfectly appropriate to pray to God (the Father), in the name of Jesus Christ, by the power of the Holy Spirit. This is the classic Mormon formulation, which is thoroughly biblical, and which evangelicals can and should likewise affirm. Latter-day Saints may be less comfortable interchanging any of those roles and praying directly to Jesus or the Spirit, as they typically affirm the eternal subordination of the Son and the Spirit to the Father. Evangelicals these days, if for no other reason than the frequent use of analogies between the roles of the members of the Godhead with gender roles in home and church, vigorously debate whether the Son was subordinate to the Father only during the incarnation or also in eternity. Unnecessarily harsh language about the other side in the debate representing heresy or heterodoxy is occasionally thrown about by representatives of each side.[21] Patristic sources on the topic are read and interpreted variously. But most scholars recognize that genuine believers fall on both sides of this debate. One ought never to exclude someone else from Christian orthodoxy simply because they disagree with one over the economic or functional roles of the Trinity throughout eternity.[22] If someone were to say the Son or the Spirit were essentially or ontologically inferior to the Father, then we could have the specter of Arianism (Christ as the first created being) to deal with once again. But that does not appear to be an issue in the current intra-evangelical debate, nor has it emerged in our Mormon-evangelical dialogues, even as our LDS participants have acknowledged that sometimes Mormon thought on this topic has veered in a more Arian direction. Nothing, however, in any official Mormon Scriptures affirms that Christ is *merely* God's initial creation, so there is no reason any Latter-day Saint should feel compelled to move in that direction.[23]

Discussion of the logic of the humanity and deity of Jesus appeared to elicit further agreement that it is crucial for Christ to be fully God so that he can provide an *infinite* or *eternal* salvation for humanity. But it is equally crucial for Christ to be fully human in order to be our adequate *representative* or *substitute*. It is obvious by this time that our conversation did not remain at the first-century historical level. It is almost impossible to have these kinds of conversations without starting to draw out implications for perennial systematic debates, nor is it necessarily desirable to be too historically limited. But it is also important to stress that we did not find our-

selves compelled to debate *homoousios* and *homoiousios*, the precise relationships between the deity and humanity of Christ, or numerous other
age-old issues about the inner workings of the Godhead. Both faith com-
munions may well have at times predicated more than has truly been revealed to us. What often seem like the logical outgrowths or necessary corol-
laries of what *has* been revealed are not always as unambiguous as they first
seem, especially for us as humans who are both finite and fallen, yet trying
to search out the deep things of God.

A classic example of such ambiguity involves the possible corporeality of
God. We agreed that corporeality need not limit a divine being's power or
sovereignty. After all, if Christ could retain every one of his divine attributes,
even while limiting their use during his time on earth to the settings in
which it was the Father's will for him to utilize them, then his mortal existence did not prevent him from still being spiritually omnipresent, omnipotent and omniscient.[24] More importantly, it is standard orthodox theology
that Christ retains his resurrected body in eternity, without it limiting his
deity in any fashion.[25] Analogically, therefore, there is no reason *in principle*
why God the Father could not likewise have a body but not be limited by
that body in the ways that mere human beings are.

The biblical texts relevant to this question can be divided into two groups:
texts that most naturally suggest that God is disembodied and only a spiritual being (e.g., John 1:18; 4:24; 1 Timothy 1:17; 6:15-16) and texts that most
naturally suggest that God has body parts (e.g., Exodus 33:11; Psalm 18:8;
Isaiah 53:1; Luke 11:20). Historic Christianity has by far most commonly
taken the first set of texts literally and understood the latter texts meta-
phorically, as anthropomorphisms. Without prejudging which is exegeti-
cally more likely, however, it is certainly possible that one could take the
latter set of texts more literally and the former set of texts less so. In other
words, to say "God is (a) S/spirit" need not imply that God is *only* or *merely*
(a) S/spirit. He might conceivably have a uniquely omnipresent Spirit while
still having the ability to appear in bodily form, which form is also an essential part of his being.[26] Only patient exegesis of each relevant text, studied
one at a time, can allow one to assess the relative merits of the two approaches (the method that evangelicals prefer) or else further divine revelation has to settle the matter (the Mormon option). Yet even if our two

communities never reach agreement on this matter, belief in the corporeality or incorporeality of God should never be a determiner by itself of whether someone is deemed a true Christian.[27]

AREAS OF POSSIBLE OR ACTUAL DISAGREEMENT

One could scarcely expect a gathering of evangelical and Latter-day Saint scholars to agree on everything emerging from a discussion spawned by the analysis of the high Christology of the early church. Time prevented us from exploring every question that we might have liked to address or to tease out the implications of positions that various people did affirm. Hurtado uses "binitarianism," a term common in the scholarly guild, to affirm early Christian devotion to Jesus as on a par with Judaism's pre-Christian devotion to Yahweh. In other words, before full-fledged trinitarianism, there was binitarianism. On this model, beliefs about the relationships between the Father and the Son do not compromise monotheism any more than classic Christian doctrine about the relationships among the Father, Son and Spirit.

Or do they? One of our LDS participants asked if they might not line up on a trajectory that leads more naturally to ditheism (and hence later to tritheism) than on a trajectory that leads merely to trinitarianism. Then Jesus and his Father would be separate beings, but inextricably united in mind, will and purpose.[28] This is a question we have discussed in previous dialogues, and it still merits further exploration. Social trinitarianism is one model that a few self-identified evangelicals have adopted and promoted[29] and that holds greater attraction for the LDS than classic formulations,[30] but many evangelicals wonder if this pushes the envelope too far.[31]

A fascinating question involves the famous Lorenzo Snow couplet. The fifth president of the LDS Church succinctly summarized what many Mormons before and afterward have believed when he declared, "As man now is, God once was. As God now is, man may be."[32] Pithy, proverbial-type sayings, of course, can be applied in many ways, not always consistent with the intentions of their original authors. In addition, this statement has never been formally canonized by the LDS. But what would happen if one substituted "Christ" for "God" in this couplet: "As man now is, Christ once was. As Christ now is, man may be." Would it be any less objectionable for evangelicals? If the point of the first sentence were to argue that Christ was once a sinful human being, it would be highly objectionable, but that is not the directions Mormons take it. Jesus once was limited by having an incarnate body, just as we do. Humans one day can have resurrected, glorified and perfected bodies, and we will also be sinless, just as Christ now is. And if Christ was and is fully God, can we then put "God" back into the couplet as in the original? Evangelicals would probably still demur, since Christ is not all there is to God and even if what are usually deemed scriptural anthropo-morphisms were taken literally, they do not denote limitations on the part of God, as common interpretations of the couplet have suggested. But at least such a thought experiment suggests that the two groups are not *as* far apart as we might once have imagined.

A related topic involves LDS use of the concept of humans being of "the same species" as God.[33] Most evangelicals recoil when they first hear such language because they have been sensitized to watch for anything that smacks of the idolatry of confusing the creature with the Creator, as outlined so powerfully in Romans 1:18-32. But they equally quickly want to stress that humans alone of all God's creation were fashioned in the *imago Dei* (the "image of God"). Must Mormons necessarily be implying any more than this with their terminology? On one key point they have not distinguished be-tween what classic Christianity has differentiated: God's communicable and his incommunicable attributes. In the former category are character traits such as love, mercy, justice, holiness and so on. In the latter fall especially the three "omnis"—omnipresence, omnipotence and omniscience. Stephen Robinson explicitly stresses that part of our perfected, glorified humanity, united with God in the life to come, will include all the divine attributes.[34] Richard Mouw finds this to be the most serious doctrinal divergence that still significantly divides our two communities.[35] But he later notes that this may have been an understandable even if exaggerated corrective of a lack of intimacy between God and people in early nineteenth-century New England Calvinist theology. He suspects that a coming generation of younger Mormons may yet find a more balanced way to formulate what God and humanity do genuinely have in common.[36]

Another fascinating debate that was left unresolved was how to square the earlier Joseph Smith with the later one. Lutheran historian George Arbaugh understood early Mormonism as just a Campbellite sect,[37] referring to Alexander Campbell, one of the cofounders of the Disciples of Christ Church and part of the broader early nineteenth-century American Restorationist movement. By the time Smith moved to Nauvoo, however, in the last years of his life, one finds new teachings about temple ordinances, more explicit language about humans becoming gods and the practice of polygamy, which stand in potential tension with the earlier period. Mormons typically argue that these developments were present in seed form all along, that we have no contradictions and that we should interpret the earlier Smith in light of the later Smith. But what if we reversed that process and interpreted the later Smith in light of his remarkably orthodox teachings in, for example, his earlier *Lectures on Faith*?[38] What if we saw all of the repeated references in the Book of Mormon to Father, Son and Holy Ghost as one God, in contexts and using language closely reminiscent of the King James Bible (e.g., 2 Nephi 31:31; Alma 11:44; 3 Nephi 11:27; Mormon 7:7),[39] as truly consistent with historic Christian faith and interpreted later teachings as not contradicting those earlier affirmations? What if the repeated emphasis in the Book of Mormon on salvation and sanctification by grace through faith (e.g., 2 Nephi 10:24; Moroni 8:3; 10:32-33; cf. Doctrine and Covenants 138:14)[40] wholly "by the merits, the mercy, and grace of the Holy Messiah" (2 Nephi 2:8)[41] were allowed to govern later teaching on the role of works? Once again the two communities might find themselves not very far apart at all.

One of the most striking statements made by one LDS participant in the 2011 dialogue was that he was convinced that 99-plus percent of the time when Mormons try to articulate what they believe is the classic Christian formulation of the doctrine of the Trinity, which they then reject, they articulate modalism. Modalism is the heresy condemned in the early church of viewing the three persons of the Godhead as merely three different forms of one person.[42] God wears three different masks, as it were, depending on the role he is currently playing. Popular analogies to the Trinity, like H_2O, which can exist as steam, water or ice, unfortunately fit better with the heresy of modalism than with true, biblical teaching. Many evangelicals unwittingly perpetuate this misunderstanding because they have never learned sufficiently precise theological language to faithfully reflect the results of the ancient, protracted Christian debates about how best to describe trinitarian relationships. Would LDS views of "the Trinity" change at all if they realized that what they are probably rejecting is what the church fathers decided *should* be rejected as well? Does the language of one being with three centers of personal consciousness alleviate any of their concerns?[43] Is there some other, as-yet-untried way of formulating the threeness and the oneness of the Godhead that creates a closer relationship among them than mere unity of mind, purpose and will, yet retains the full distinctiveness and personhood of each of the three?

After all, Latter-day Saints appear to practice a trinitarian *spirituality* when they pray to the Father, pursue discipleship by imitating the Son and seek to be guided by the power of the Holy Ghost. In their haste to show the full deity of both Son and Spirit, have evangelicals lost sight of genuine biblical distinctives among the three persons of the Trinity? It may not be wrong to pray to Jesus, but it would be very difficult to imitate God the Father or his Spirit. Jesus is more than a model to follow, but he is not less. Have we lost the dimension of asking "what would Jesus do?" (especially after being trivialized into a bracelet) for fear that we would *only* be imitating him and not also participating with him in new life, achieved for us by his work on the cross and his resurrection from the dead?

For those evangelicals who do not see any eternal subordination in the Godhead, even just functionally, how should John 14:28 be explained when Jesus says "the Father is greater than I"? If the answer is that Christ is referring only to the time of the incarnation, then what do we do with 1 Corinthians 15:28, where Paul insists that at some time after the end of the world as we now know it, "the Son himself will be made subject to him who put everything under him, so that God may be all in all." In context, this refers to a time after everything has been subjected to the Son, so we obviously are not talking about the incarnation.[44] Does this form of eternal subordination reduce the gap between historic Christianity and Latter-day Saints?

What, moreover, are evangelicals to do with John 17:21? Here, in his so-called high priestly prayer, Jesus petitions his Father, "that all of them [his disciples] may be one, Father, just as you are in me and I am in you. May they also be in us so that the world may believe that you have sent me." What kind of oneness or unity is this? Is it unity of mind, will and purpose? We see no ontological oneness that creates one being out of all Christ-followers. But then why would we see a more tightly knit unity in the way the Son is in the Father and vice versa? Or suppose we begin at the outset of the Farewell Discourse. The first reference to coinherence appears in John 14:10-11—"Don't you believe that I am in the Father, and that the Father is in me? The words I say to you I do not speak on my own authority. Rather, it is the Father, living in me, who is doing his work. Believe me when I say that I am in the Father and the Father is in me; or at least believe on the evidence of the works themselves." If we take this to be an essential and not just a functional unity, then how do we exclude believers participating in the same kind of unity with, and even within, the Godhead when we get to John 17:21-23?[45] These were still further unresolved issues.

How do we decide what is anthropomorphic and what is literal in the Scriptures, without presupposing in advance what *must* fall into each category? Is there language anywhere in the Bible that has traditionally been taken anthropomorphically that might have been intended to be taken more literally? By what criteria would we determine the answer to that question? When we see that other Christian thinkers down through the ages have from time to time wrestled with or at least raised the question of divine embodiment, must we immediately reject it out of hand? Even if we do, does belief in divine embodiment automatically disqualify a professing Christian from being a true one? And if so, on what grounds?

One of our evangelical participants, whose expertise is the patristic period, stressed that the ancient creeds were not intended to explicate the mysteries of the Godhead but rather to serve as theological boundary markers. While there will inevitably be disagreements as to where those boundaries should be drawn, does this help to make the creeds any more tolerable to the LDS? Restorationism more generally was very anticreedal, believing that it invariably distorted or overly simplified biblical teaching. Yet even Joseph Smith penned the Articles of Faith, which takes the exact form of a creed or confession of faith, with a series of thirteen verses, all but one beginning with the words, "we believe," followed by the content of that belief. The topics covered readily call to mind the kinds and sequence of topics frequently found in systematic theology: God, sin, salvation, baptism, ordination, ecclesiology, spiritual gifts and so on.

CONCLUSION

While disagreement existed in the provisional answers given to all of these latter questions, nothing drew lines in the sand so firmly that acceptable boundaries of the faith might not be redrawn elsewhere in the future by either community. When one moves behind Nicaea, and when one recognizes the diversity within the teaching of Joseph Smith and the difference between what LDS have officially canonized and what is just widely accepted, more options for legitimate evangelical and legitimate Mormon belief emerge, respectively. Occasionally, that pushes the two faith communities farther apart; more often it draws them closer together. And that is in the areas on which we disagree; we have also highlighted the major areas of agreement. Which trajectory, if either, will prevail in the future? Only God knows. Meanwhile, both groups in our dialogue continue to sense that he is doing something significant in our midst. At the very least, there is greater mutual understanding and the ability to more accurately represent one another. There is the recurring sense that there is absolutely no need to vilify one another and that God's Spirit is working, even mysteriously, in each community, bringing us closer together personally but also doctrinally. We pray these trajectories continue.

THE TRINITY

Christopher A. Hall

AS OUR EVANGELICAL-MORMON DIALOGUE has met over the years, discussions have often been fruitful, kind, honest and transparent. As an atmosphere of trust and friendship has developed among participants, our talks have helped each other to more clearly identify both points of agreement and disagreement among dialogue members. Behind this disagreement exists a significant parting of the ways regarding the nature of God, God's relationship to time and space, whether God is corporeal or incorporeal, whether God was once a human being and, perhaps at the top of the list, the Trinity. Perhaps the greatest difference between evangelical and LDS dialogue members concerns the doctrine of the Trinity. While the triune God—God as one and God as three—has been worshiped and pondered by Christians across almost all denominational lines—Orthodox, Roman Catholic, Anglican and Protestant evangelical—Latter-day Saints openly reject the idea that God could exist as Trinity, for what they believe are cogent and coherent reasons.

Robert Millet, for instance, a valued Latter-day Saint (LDS) dialogue participant and noted Mormon theologian, has gently probed concerning the coherence of trinitarian affirmations. "I simply ask: How can $1 + 1 + 1 = 1$? Again, meaning no irreverence, I ask: If we were to invite the Trinity to dinner, how many settings would I need to set? Three persons are three persons. Three persons cannot be one person, nor can I conceive how three persons can be one being."[1] From the perspective of Latter-day Saints, when evangelicals and other "orthodox" Christians affirm that God is both one and three, they are speaking illogically and incoherently. God cannot be both one and three, *at least if we are all using language in the same way and with the same meaning.* What dialogue members have discovered, of course, is that we are not.

When Latter-day Saints speak of God and God's relationship to the world and to human beings, they generally speak *univocally*, an adverb that has Latin roots meaning to speak with "one voice." So when Millet comments that if God is three persons then there must be three table settings at the dinner table, he is speaking and thinking univocally. When we speak of God as three "persons," we must mean persons in the same sense as humans are persons.

The meaning of human personhood seems clear; we interact with persons every day. Humans, as Millet expresses well, share common characteristics with other persons, and yet human persons are not identical. If three human persons attempted to occupy the same space at a dinner table, confusion and collision would occur. The problem—a key one from an orthodox perspective—is that Millet assumes the same would be true for God. Such is the case only if we define "person" univocally—understanding it to mean the same thing when referring to God as when referring to humans.

By way of contrast, orthodox Christians speak *analogically* when referring to the three persons of the Trinity. That is, there is "a similarity, a relation, an analogy, between what we say about God and what we say about creatures, but the meaning of the terms and concepts we use is not identical in the two cases."[2] Hence, as I have written elsewhere, "The Father, the Son, and the Holy Spirit really are like human persons, and the word 'person' is used in a way that reflects ordinary, nontheological usage. Yet while it *reflects* that usage, it is never simply *identical* to it. God is not a 'person' in any of the obvious, ordinary ways" that a *univocal definition* would demand.[3] The use of analogical language regarding "person" has enabled the church across the centuries to preserve its understanding of God as *one* and *three*; a univocal definition would inevitably drive the church into tritheism, the worship of three gods, an unthinkable option from the perspective of traditional orthodoxy.

Evangelical and LDS theological thinking part paths in other significant ways, many of them related to the constellation of issues surrounding the orthodox affirmation of God as one and three. Again, the question of language and meaning raises its head. Mormons, for instance, believe that God and humans share what we might call the same spectrum of "being." There are surely differences between God the Father and his children, but in terms of "being" itself, there is no ontic divide between God and the children he quite literally has begotten. Indeed, God was once a human being, begot spiritual children through normal means of procreation and has entered into a relationship of love with them that is very much like the relationship between an earthly father and his children. So when LDS Christians speak of God as their Father, they understand God and themselves to be common partakers of a material yet spiritual essence, one shared in a like manner between God and God's children. In a word, Mormon metaphysics is fundamentally materialistic. In fact, as Stephen Webb explains, "Matter is one of the characteristic perfections of the divine. . . . Matter has multiple depths that can be differentiated according to their closeness to the divine."[4]

Mormon exegesis and theology, then, ultimately leads to a multiplicity of gods along an ontic spectrum, with Latter-day Saints increasingly moving into a deeper relationship with God as their literal Father, one that will finally result in the complete transformation of God's spirit children into gods that will inhabit a world much like this one, though rinsed clean of sin and evil.

An evangelical/orthodox perspective is strikingly different. Think, for instance, of the personal distinctions between the Father, Son and Spirit, relational distinctions often described with words such as *unbegotten*, *begotten* and *proceed*. The Father is said to "beget" or to "generate" the Son, while he himself is described in the creeds as "unbegotten" or "ingenerate"; the Son relates to the Father as "begotten"; the Holy Spirit "proceeds" from the Father (or the Father and the Son). As my colleague Steve Boyer and I have written elsewhere:

> Obviously words like these—"generate," "unbegotten," "proceed"—mean something that we can understand. . . . Otherwise we could just as easily and appropriately use *any* words to describe the relations, even nonsensical words, and this would clearly be a mistake. No, says Christian orthodoxy, we know that relationally the Son is different from the Father because the Son, as "begotten," finds his source, his "begetting," from the Father. This is what "Father" and "Son," "begetting" and "begotten," mean.[5]

The minute we express trinitarian relationships in this manner, however, we immediately realize there are "absolutely no adequate categories in the created order" that match how the church is employing this specific trinitarian language. Such would not be the case from an LDS perspective, which consistently employs univocal language and a materialistic metaphysic in its descriptions of God—and in its understanding and rejection of the Trinity.

Orthodox Christian doctrine insists that the begetting of the Son is a "noncorporeal begetting, a generation that has no beginning and no end. It is therefore a begetting or a generation unlike any we could ever imagine. If we were to employ our normal classifications and connotations for the concept of biological generation—that is, if we were to use our words univocally," as our Mormon friends do, we would naturally conclude "that the Father begets the Son as human fathers beget human sons."[6] This was a move the church vigorously rejected, worshiping and thinking against the grain of religious thought and practice in the Greek, Roman and Egyptian world at the time. Though Zeus begat many children through having sexual relations with goddesses, the church firmly believed such an idea was foreign to the Hebrew Scripture and the New Testament. Yes, the Father "begets" the Son, but in an ineffable, mysterious manner that surpasses the limits of human comprehension and language. Gregory of Nyssa puts it this way: "The inspired teaching adopts, in order to set forth the unspeakable power of God, all the forms of generation that human intelligence recognizes, *yet without including the corporeal senses attaching to the words*."[7]

We should not be surprised, then, that more traditional Christian tenets—"God is one and God is three"—with their specific theological, biblical, historical and linguistic underpinning, appear nonsensical to LDS theologians and historians. Orthodox and heterodox Christians such as Mormons clearly disagree at this point, a disagreement based on theological, biblical and historical understandings.

When Joseph Smith received his vision of the Father and the Son in the sacred grove in Palmyra, New York, he saw two distinct persons. Both possessed bodies; both were clearly powerful material beings localized in space and time. Mormons affirm that these embodied, material deities communicated to the prophet—Joseph Smith—who they were and what they were calling him to be in the world they had created. Yes, the message Smith received was replete with Christian words, phrases and symbols. Significantly, though, these words and symbols were given new, fresh, heterodox meaning.

So, when Mormon theologians think of God, they think of God as composed out of a material substance and substrate in which all reality subsists. God is a material, corporeal being. Yes, God is spirit. But in Joseph Smith's thinking, this did not preclude God also being a material being. "There is no such thing as immaterial matter. All spirit is matter, but it is more fine or pure, and can only be discerned by purer eyes; we cannot see it; but when our bodies are purified we shall see that it is all matter."[8] Smith's conclusion is a natural inference from the vision he received. As Webb puts it, "He inferred from his vision that the world consists of levels or layers of matter, rather than two kinds of substance, one material and the other not material at all."[9] This materialistic understanding of God's being lies at the heart and core of LDS teaching and practice. And quite clearly, it poses a major roadblock for an LDS appropriation of the orthodox model of God as fundamentally incorporeal, immaterial, ineffably and irreducibly one God in three persons.

This fundamental difference in perspective came home to me shortly after I met Bob Millet and another member of the evangelical-Mormon dialogue group, Greg Johnson. Greg is a former LDS member and now an evangelical pastor in Utah. I first met Bob and Greg at a Wheaton College theology conference; I had delivered a talk on the importance of understanding the relationship between tradition and the Bible and had just finished the question-and-answer period. Bob and Greg came to the front of the auditorium, introduced themselves and explained their backgrounds, and then let me know they would both be attending a class I was teaching that summer at Regent College in Vancouver, British Columbia, on the spirituality of the church fathers.

Sure enough, when the class began in July, there they were. For much of the two-week class Bob was simply part of the group, asking questions and studying patristic texts with evangelical graduate students. Occasionally Bob would share an insight from his own devotional life. No one had any idea he was a well-known Mormon theologian.

Things continued this way for at least a week and a half. Then the time came for a closer look at the prayers of the Egyptian desert monks. We focused on a festal letter sent out by Theophilus, the bishop of Alexandria and pastor responsible for the orthodoxy of the monastic communities scattered throughout the Egyptian desert. Theophilus's instructions in his letter were quite clear. The monks were not to envision God as having a material body or shape as they prayed to him. Theophilus—at least at this time in this letter—was concerned that the monks were falling into a materialistic understanding of God, with God possessing a body, arms, legs, eyes and so on, and he wanted the monks' praying and thinking this way to cease and desist. It's difficult to trace how at least some monks had learned to pray this way; it is clear that at least some were praying to an image in their mind of a physical, male father, one much like their earthly father but on a much grander scale. We do know of one monk by the name of Serapion who was overcome with grief at Theophilus's command to change how he was praying. "They have taken away my God," Serapion cried, "and I don't know where to find him."

As I explained in class the rhyme and reason of Theophilus's letter and Serapion's response, I launched into a short explanation of God's "simplicity." God is "simple," I explained. "Not 'simple' as in easily understood, but 'simple' as uncomposed. God is not made out of something else; God is not a material being composed out of ontic building blocks. God is incorporeal, immaterial, timeless, immutable and so on, all attributes of God that the orthodox 'great tradition' has consistently affirmed." As I was speaking, things suddenly clicked for me. I stopped writing on the whiteboard, turned around, and said directly to Bob: "I think this is where you and I disagree, isn't it?" Bob smiled and nodded yes.

I proceeded to introduce Bob to the class and shared his Mormon background with students; needless to say, they were shocked. Why? When it came to the words Bob used in class to describe his relationship with God, his love for Jesus his Savior, his personal relationship with Jesus, his desire to grow spiritually and his belief in Christ's atoning sacrifice on the cross, resurrection from the dead and future coming in glory, Bob sounded just like his student evangelical colleagues. Clear differences in perspective and belief had become evident, however, as we more carefully examined the church's exegetical and theological tradition. When we began to explore more thoroughly in class the theological underpinning for our common beliefs in Jesus, the cross, the resurrection and the future, significant disagreements emerged; points of seeming convergence proved to be more difficult to discover and maintain.

Where do we go from here? Bob Millet, for example, is completely comfortable being described as a "heterodox Christian." I think many LDS members would willingly accept this description. What wounds our LDS colleagues, though, is the unwillingness of other more traditional Christians to accept the Latter-day Saints as a legitimate branch of the Christian tree. From the LDS perspective, they affirm a host of traditional Christian beliefs. Key differences, though, emerge when we closely examine the theological/metaphysical substructure of what Mormons attest to be true. Our dialogues have made clear that LDS beliefs concerning the Trinity, the nature of God, Christian anthropology and eschatology are significantly different from Christian orthodoxy. Is the difference so great that we must finally admit that the God and the Christ we worship are indeed fundamentally different?

Divine Investiture

Mormonism and the Concept of Trinity

Brian D. Birch

In 2000, the Society for Christian Philosophers drafted guidelines for hosting regional meetings that excluded institutions "subscribing to doctrinal positions directly contradicting the ecumenical creeds accepted by all branches of the Christian Church, Orthodox, Catholic, and Protestant." The events leading up to this statement involved debates regarding whether to allow Brigham Young University (BYU) to continue to host society meetings given Mormonism's idiosyncratic theology and its explicit rejection of the traditional Christian creeds. Alongside well-known philosophers of religion such as Nicholas Wolterstorff and Marilyn McCord Adams, BYU Professor David Paulsen argued that the creedal exclusion was unnecessarily narrow and would apply to Christian groups that reject the creeds yet maintain a commitment to traditional biblical Christianity. An interesting dimension of these discussions involved Paulsen pressing leadership to clarify the precise ways in which Mormon theology was said to be inconsistent with the Nicene Creed. This kind of engagement is characteristic of a relatively new approach on the part of Latter-day Saint (LDS) thinkers to challenge the boundaries of Mormonism's theology relative to more traditional Christian concepts and categories.

It is in this spirit of comparative analysis that I will examine a handful of issues in understanding how Mormon concepts of God have related to traditional Christian formulations. Though necessarily selective, it is intended to highlight the dynamics of LDS thought on these questions and point toward further possibilities for productive exchange.

THE LANDSCAPE

Since the formulation of the Nicene Creed in A.D. 325, the Christian tradition has affirmed that the Father, Son and Holy Spirit are three divine persons in one substance.[1] The need to formulate a trinitarian conception was informed by the challenge of reconciling how the three divine beings described in the New Testament can be understood to be truly one God. At Nicaea, this was accomplished through the employment of Greek and Latin philosophical concepts that were said to capture the relationship among the three persons of the Trinity while preserving a legitimate form of monotheism.

The Nicene Creed was thus an effort to navigate the straits between heretical positions that came to be known as *modalism* and *tritheism*. Modalism is the idea that God is a single divine person who revealed himself in the forms (or modes) of Father, Son and Holy Spirit. On the other side of the spectrum, tritheism is the position that the Father, Son and Holy Spirit are not only three separate persons but also three individual gods. The creed staked out a position "neither confounding the persons nor dividing the substance."[2]

As a form of restoration Christianity, the Church of Jesus Christ of Latter-day Saints does not recognize the traditional creeds as authoritative formulations. Though they recognize the canonical status of the Bible, Mormons rely on additional Scripture produced through revelations to Joseph Smith during his prophetic ministry. In the adventurous period between 1830 and 1844, Smith expressed a range of ideas that both affirmed and challenged mainstream Christian sensibilities. Neither his revelatory nor his homiletic productions were systematic treatments of doctrines. Rather, they leave the theologically minded to grapple with the implications of his ideas and how they might be brought into a coherent theological whole. This is especially true in the case of the Trinity, or the "Godhead" as Latter-day Saints prefer.

DIVINE INVESTITURE

In 1916, the First Presidency of the LDS Church presented one of the more significant documents in the history of Mormonism. "The Father and the Son: A Doctrinal Exposition" is a rare treatment of Latter-day Saint doctrine presented in an official and unified manner. The document is momentous because it sets the direction for Mormon thought in a time of unease among church leadership on key theological questions.[3] It was during this period that the First Presidency asked apostle James Talmage to compile a series of his lectures into a book that could serve as a definitive text and stabilize doctrinal discourse within the church. This work, *Jesus the Christ*, laid the groundwork for the 1916 statement and instantly became the gold standard of christological interpretation for modern Mormonism.[4]

The statement affirmed that the Father and the Son are two separate, distinct and physically embodied beings. The Holy Sprit was said to possess a "spiritual body" though maintaining his own form of personal distinctiveness. This is a reiteration of an earlier canonical statement that "the Father has a body of flesh and bones as tangible as man's; the Son also; but the Holy Ghost has not a body of flesh and bones, but is a personage of Spirit."[5] The idea of the first two members of the Godhead being separate and physically embodied has been among the distinctive and more provocative features of Latter-day Saint theology.

Among the issues that stood in the background of the statement was the presence of more traditional sounding ideas in the 1830 Book of Mormon as compared, for example, to the teachings of Joseph Smith in Nauvoo, Illinois shortly before his death in 1844. The attempt to reconcile Smith's Nauvoo sermons with earlier teachings has been a challenge for those attempting to defend a consistent conception of God as it was taught in the fifteen intervening years. Evangelical theologian Ronald Huggins puts the matter more bluntly: "The early Joseph Smith falls to the right of traditional Trinitarianism by 'confounding the persons.' The later Joseph Smith falls to the left of it by 'dividing the substance.' In other words, he begins by teaching modalism and ends teaching polytheism, or at least henotheism."[6]

Though many defenders of Mormonism have acknowledged some form of historical refinement on the nature of God, they are anxious to defend against a developmental view that implies any form of doctrinal inconsistency.[7]

FROM "MODALISM" TO "TRITHEISM"?

The identification of Jesus Christ as the Father is found in passages scattered throughout the Book of Mormon. These so-called modalistic passages have been the subject of considerable debate among scholars and critics of Mormonism in light of later dynamics of LDS trinitarian thought. Perhaps the most eloquent example is the sermon of Benjamin, a Book of Mormon prophet-king who prophesied that

> the time cometh, and is not far distant, that with power, the Lord Omnipotent who reigneth, who was, and is from all eternity to all eternity, shall come down from heaven among the children of men, and shall dwell in a tabernacle of clay. . . . And he shall be called Jesus Christ, the Son of God, the Father of heaven and earth, the Creator of all things from the beginning.[8]

Other passages include divine self-descriptions. Later in the book, during a dramatic revelatory encounter with a prophet known as the Brother of Jared, God declares,

> I am he who was prepared from the foundation of the world to redeem my people. Behold, I am Jesus Christ. I am the Father and the Son. In me shall all mankind have life, and that eternally, even they who shall believe on my name; and they shall become my sons and my daughters. . . .
>
> Behold, this body, which ye now behold, is the body of my spirit; and man have I created after the body of my spirit; and even as I appear unto thee to be in the spirit will I appear unto my people in the flesh.[9]

In the early years following the publication of the Book of Mormon, Joseph Smith worked periodically on a "new translation" of the Bible in an attempt to amplify the text and correct scribal and translation errors. A relevant modification was made to Luke 10:22, which reads in the King James as "No man knoweth who the Son is, but the Father; and who the Father is, but the Son, and he to whom the Son will reveal him." Smith altered this verse to read: "No man knoweth that the Son is the Father, and the Father is the Son, but him to whom the Son will reveal it."[10]

A final example is the voice of God in revelations given directly to Joseph Smith. In one of the earliest revelations given to the new church, God begins the revelation by speaking in the person of the Son and then suddenly shifts voices to the Father referring to the Son in the third person.

> Verse 1: Listen to the voice of Jesus Christ, your Redeemer, the Great I Am, whose arm of mercy hath atoned for your sins.

> Verse 46: But behold, I say unto you, that little children are redeemed from the foundation of the world through mine Only Begotten.[11]

For some critics of Mormonism, these passages imply that the early church embraced a form of modalism in which the terms *Father* and the *Son* were used to designate the specific role they were serving rather than as designating two distinct beings. An intriguing passage along these lines is found in the sermon of Abinadi.

> And now Abinadi said unto them: I would that ye should understand that God himself shall come down among the children of men, and shall redeem his people. And because he dwelleth in flesh he shall be called the Son of God, and having subjected the flesh to the will of the Father, being the Father and the Son—The Father, because he was conceived by the power of God; and the Son, because of the flesh; thus becoming the Father and Son—And they are one God, yea, the very Eternal Father of heaven and of earth.[12]

However, not unlike the biblical text, there are numerous passages in the Book of Mormon that suggest a more literal separation of identity. These include the ascension narratives and passages referencing the subjection of the will of the Son to the Father. "Behold verily, verily, I say unto you, I give unto you another commandment, and then I must go unto my Father that I may fulfil other commandments which he hath given me" (3 Nephi 18:27). Given this hermeneutical diversity, it became increasingly clear that some effort was required to clarify and categorize passages in terms of literal versus figurative references to the relationship between the Father and the Son.

In an apparent effort toward clarification, Joseph Smith oversaw subsequent editions of the Book of Mormon, which included modified passages expressive of a more distinct delineation between Father and Son. For example, he changed the passage that read "the virgin which thou seest, is the mother of God" to "the virgin whom thou seest is the mother of the *Son of God*."[13] Interestingly, many of the so-called modalistic passages were not revised in subsequent editions, and there appears to be no overarching criterion that informed which passages were edited and which were left unchanged.[14]

All of this takes us to the later Nauvoo era, which is clearly the most theologically adventurous period in Joseph Smith's career. His descriptions of God and the cosmos took a form that proved especially challenging in both their Christian heterodoxy and their alignment with earlier teachings. For it was during this period that Smith spoke of a "plurality of gods" and gestured toward a beginningless genealogy of gods operating within a broader cosmological framework. Despite these apparent innovations, he resolutely proclaimed just eleven days before his death,

> I have always and in all congregations when I have preached on the subject of the Deity, it has been the plurality of Gods. It has been preached by the Elders for fifteen years.
>
> I have always declared God to be a distinct personage, Jesus Christ a separate and distinct personage from God the Father, and that the Holy Ghost was a distinct personage and a Spirit: and these three constitute three distinct personages and three Gods.[15]

This was the challenge faced by Latter-day Saints interested in synthesizing the enormous body of Smith's work into a coherent and theologically adequate framework.

This background returns us to the 1916 statement, which was specifically designed to (1) clarify passages in which the Son is "designated as the Father" and (2) explain the type of unity that exists among these three "distinct personages" of the Godhead. The document begins by acknowledging that both the Bible and additional LDS Scripture employ the term *Father* with "plainly different meanings." The authors then specify four broad categories to capture the ways this appellation is used. The last of these, titled the "Divine Investiture of Authority," is especially important in addressing questions of doctrinal consistency.

Divine investiture refers to situations in which "the Father placed His name upon the Son" such that "His words and acts were and are those of the Father." In this case, the Son is indeed the Father, not through identity of substance, but in a figurative sense given the Son's ability to take on the name of the Father and represent him in the affairs of humanity. An important functional outcome of this category is that scriptural texts that appear to imply metaphysical or numerical identity of Father and Son can be read as an instance of divine investiture.

THE BEGOTTENNESS OF THE SON

The last paragraph of the 1916 statement adds some crucial language to the issues at hand. "Jesus Christ is not the Father of the spirits who have taken or yet shall take bodies upon this earth, for He is one of them. He is The Son, as they are sons or daughters of Elohim." Latter-day Saints thus understand the second person of the Trinity to be both an eternal god and a spirit child of the Father. This takes us to the question of Jesus Christ as the "only be-gotten Son" of God. To do this, we need to go back to the questions debated in the early centuries of Christianity. Simply put, if Jesus Christ is an eternal divine being, how can he be understood as begotten? Does not begottenness imply createdness?[16] This question was exceptionally important, and hotly debated, at the Council of Nicaea (A.D. 325).

After lengthy and detailed deliberations, the critical distinction that emerged from the council was that the Son was indeed *begotten*, though not *created*. Thus the Nicene Creed reads: "We believe in one Lord, Jesus Christ, the only Son of God, eternally begotten of the Father, God from God, Light from Light, true God from true God, *begotten, not made,* of one Being with the Father."[17] What made this clause especially important was that the eternal status of the Son had not been a universally shared belief leading up to Nicaea, and had been fiercely challenged in certain quarters of the Christian world. The faction that triggered Nicaea was led by an Alexan-drian Presbyter named Arius, who argued that the Son was "created by the will of God before all times and all ages, receiving from the Father his life and his existence."[18] Jesus Christ was the only-begotten Son of God in the sense that he was the "firstborn among the creatures." In support of his ar-gument, Arius utilized biblical passages in Colossians and Romans in which the Son is referenced as the "firstborn of all creation" (Colossians 1:15 NAB) and "firstborn among many brothers" (Romans 8:29 NAB).

By way of comparison, Latter-day Saints believe that Jesus Christ is the firstborn of all the spirit children of the Father. In one of Joseph Smith's key revelations, Christ discloses not only that "I was in the beginning with the Father, and am the Firstborn" but also that "ye were also in the beginning with the Father."[19] Mormonism's distinctive cosmology includes the Son sharing with the rest of humanity a form of createdness that had a be-ginning in time in a premortal realm. The 1916 statement maintains that there is "no impropriety" in referring to Jesus Christ as the "Elder Brother" of humankind. At the same time, it also seeks to preserve the uniqueness of the Son.

Let it not be forgotten, however, that He is essentially greater than any or all others, by reason (1) of His seniority as the oldest or firstborn; (2) of His unique status in the flesh as the offspring of a mortal mother and of an immortal, or resurrected and glorified, Father; (3) of His selection and foreordination as the one and only Redeemer and Savior of the race; and (4) of His transcendent sinlessness.[20]

Though Arians did not profess a common premortal existence, Latter-day Saints are not infrequently accused of perpetuating Arianism by virtue of their shared understanding of the createdness of the Son. A more careful comparison, however, reveals intriguing points of contact with both sides of the Arian debate.

On the one hand, Mormonism shares with Arianism a subordinate relationship of the Son to the Father that involves ontological dependence. However, the *type* of ontological dependence differs between the two. Though Arius taught that the Son is a creature of the Father, he maintained that the Son was created as a *qualitatively* different being from all other creatures. He rejected the idea that the Son graduated to the status of divinity through some kind of developmental process such as adoptionism.[21] Arius's emphasis was to preserve the singular status of the Father as the eternal God from whom all other things come.

Mormon cosmology diverges at this point through its rejection of creation *ex nihilo*. When Joseph Smith reported that "ye were also in the beginning with the Father," this is understood to support the premortal existence not only of human spirits but also of a more primordial and uncreated essence of each individual soul. In this sense, Latter-day Saints "out-Nicene the Nicenes" by positing that in a fundamental sense all human beings, and not just the Son, are coeternal, cobeginningless with the Father. Thus Mormons join orthodox Christianity in rejecting the Arian slogan "there was when he was not"; but by maintaining a shared uncreated essence between the Son and the rest of humanity, Latter-day Saints remain outside the limits of the creedal formulation.[22]

Mormons also diverge in the way they understand eternal Sonship. Though they would maintain with the Nicenes that "Jesus is the Christ, the Eternal God," as stated in the title page of the Book of Mormon, this does not necessarily imply that he has been God from the eternities. Though the

Son is an eternal *being*, as we have seen, Mormon cosmology suggests that he is not eternal *as God*. From an orthodox perspective, this is critical for reasons that take us back to the debates between the Arians and the Nicenes. It was not good enough for the Nicenes to have the Son as the firstborn of all creation as a divine being. They insisted that an eternally divine and ontologically necessary being is indispensable for the salvation of humanity.

Thus a remaining challenge for LDS scholars has been to clearly and articulately navigate the straits between eternal Godhood and the spirit creation of the Son. Talmage's own writings are conscientiously inconclusive. In the opening chapter of *Jesus the Christ*, entitled "Antemortal Godship of Christ," Talmage lays out the nature of premortal life and the critical role of the Son in preparing the way for the salvation of humanity. In the course of his crucial argument that Jesus Christ is the God of Abraham, Isaac and Jacob, he states:

> The central fact connoted by this name *I Am, or Jehovah*, the two having essentially the same meaning, is that of existence or duration that shall have no end, and *which judged by all human standards of reckoning*, could have had no beginning; the name is related to such other titles as *Alpha and Omega*, the first and the last, the beginning and the end.[23]

From the standpoint of the Christian tradition, the qualifying clause (in italics) is not only theologically crippling but also shifts the ground on which the dialogue is being conducted. The extent to which commonly referenced terms (such as *eternal* and *beginning*) have idiosyncratic meanings is the extent to which additional care must be taken to explicate these distinctions and their theological implications. Idiosyncrasies are certainly not a problem in themselves, but they bring with them an extra burden of responsibility.

Similar tendencies can be found in apologetic writings that trace their intellectual roots to Talmage. In his book *A Different Jesus?* Robert Millet shows the challenge by using Bruce R. McConkie's influential writings on the subject.

> As to what existence was like before our birth as spirits, we really do not know. One Church leader Bruce R. McConkie, has written that Christ "*is described as being* 'from everlasting to everlasting' (D&C 61:1), and 'from all eternity to all eternity' (D&C 39:1). . . . He was born, as were all the spirit children of the Father. God was his Father, as he is of all the rest."[24]

As one not prone to qualification, McConkie's words gesture toward the need for further clarification and analysis. Some excellent theological work has been done in refining these ideas, and there are those who have offered alternative readings. Whatever one's approach to LDS Christology, there is a wealth of careful and precise work yet to be completed.

Conclusion

From the earliest days of the movement, Latter-day Saints have proclaimed that Jesus Christ is the eternal God. This has been especially manifest in recent decades throughout church curriculum, public relations and interfaith outreach. In ongoing dialogues with evangelical Christians, Latter-day Saints tend to emphasize language in LDS Scripture that demonstrates commonalities with orthodox formulations. This is a natural and productive mode of engagement. At the same time, Latter-day Saints need not feel obligated to "color within the lines" of Christian orthodoxy. The Arian debate is just one example of the ways in which Latter-day Saints can probe the Christian tradition in all of its variety in articulating its distinctive flavor of Christianity.

Praxis

A Lived Trinitarianism

Bill Heersink

GATHERED ON THE CAMPUS OF Brigham Young University (BYU), we were engaged in a day-long dialogue. Through the large windows inside the Gordon B. Hinckley Alumni and Visitors Center, a lofty view of the Wasatch Range lifted our minds and spirits toward the day's topic: God— God as being both three and one.

At one point in the interfaith interaction, one participant, Camille Fronk Olson, began to recount her life experiences in coming to know God. She talked fondly of relating to God as her Father in heaven, a key influence coming through her biological father's calling his family to prayer each morning. She spoke of a grace-filled relationship with Jesus, much as she had done in previous dialogues. And she became most intense when describing her feelings of the Holy Spirit's presence within her at and following her baptism.

That God to her is three was obvious. But his oneness was equally evident. The Holy Spirit's primary role has been to point her to Jesus; she noted how, at the Last Supper, Jesus said it would be that way. Jesus, in turn, had opened the way for her to trust and adore the Father. In meaningful meditation, she said, her distinct images of three became mostly "meshed" in one—a "lived trinitarianism." Though humbly aware of her limits—"so much about God I do not know"—she heartily affirmed: "But I do know him and know he knows me."

A Disjuncture

Testimony-type accounts like this provide a unique dimension and dilemma for Mormon-evangelical dialogue. In the case above, we had spent most of the day discussing doctrinal developments of the fourth century, much of it focused on theology expressed in the Nicene Creed, which has become a standard of trinitarian faith for most Christian traditions, but for Latter-day Saints (LDS) an unacceptable statement of who God is. In fact, in exploring some of the classical philosophical views that undergird our differences on this, one participant noted that it's "like comparing apples and oranges."

Yet when it comes to hearing one another describe our lived experiences of knowing the God who has revealed himself as Father, Son and Holy Spirit, the contrast quickly shrinks. I dare say that all of us, several evangelicals and several Mormons, resonated with or at least embraced this woman's experience of God. Change a few idioms, leave out certain details about her baptism, limit Scripture quotes to the Bible and it would be difficult to discern her identity as Mormon or evangelical.

Dealing with this disjuncture is what for me has made dialoging with Latter-day Saints both fascinating and challenging. What am I to say when doctrines diverge but personal experiences appear to converge? How am I to relate when shared testimonies cultivate closeness, but shared theologies indicate distance? How am I to think when the praxis that should be informed by theory seems to contradict it?

Attempted Explanations

I have heard (and given) various explanations attempting to resolve this tension. The following are given from an evangelical viewpoint, but Latter-day Saint counterparts are surely available. I have witnessed a similar explanation-demanding bewilderment among them when from my testimony they sense I have had "promptings of the Spirit" I am not supposed to have apart from believing their teaching and receiving their ordinances.

"This has to be a select group of Latter-day Saints with whom you are dialoguing. This woman's testimony is not at all typical for Mormons," might be one explanation, and probably not without some truth. All the Mormon participants at this dialogue were university professors. They are, however, among the more influential teachers in the LDS Church educational system.

Camille is currently chair of the Department of Ancient Scripture at Brigham Young University, and her books have been bestsellers at her church's publishing agency, Deseret Book. She and another member of our group are among four authors of a book about Mormon teaching whose publication coincides (not by mere coincidence) with a decision to terminate printing a previous single-volume work that for decades had functioned as the standard on Mormon doctrine (*Mormon Doctrine* was its title) to many. If space allowed, I would list credentials of other Mormons in the group, many of which put them also in a position of influence. One evening two senior LDS Church leaders, known as General Authorities, attended and encouraged our dialogues.

Furthermore, while this group may be select, their accounts of encountering God as both three and one are not exclusive. Currently, I also participate in another group in which a half-dozen evangelical clergy engage in Bible study with a half-dozen instructors at an LDS institute of religion where LDS university students come to socialize and learn. Here again I am challenged by how honest discussions of doctrinal differences often end up being interwoven with common experiences in how we relate to Christ as the Savior from sin and the Lord we follow.

To these two groups I could add one-on-one interactions with Mormons in which the same disjuncture between theology and testimony emerges. I think of extended conversations with a retired school principal, a carpenter remodeling our kitchen or the friend who has served as LDS church historian. I remember Truman G. Madsen, a BYU philosophy professor (a Harvard Divinity School PhD who studied with Paul Tillich and Krister Stendahl), describing his encounter with Christ in a Mormon Sacrament (Communion) service, and a Relief Society president (women's group in a local congregation) narrating her experience in the LDS temple.

To be sure, I have heard many testimonies from Latter-day Saints with which I did not resonate at all. The same could be said, however, about many coming from evangelical church members.

"*Religious experiences are for the most part feelings, highly subjective, not reliable,*" is another evangelical response to a Mormon's testimony. "Apart from commitment to objective, biblical truth, such feelings are fabrication or counterfeit." I have become increasingly uncomfortable with that explanation, particularly when in the process of relating his story a Mormon friend has trusted me by exposing vulnerable feelings. Besides, are not we evangelicals disingenuous when discounting religious experience? Was it not a subjective encounter with Jesus (a "born-again" experience) that initially brought most of us to faith?

"But the Jesus of Mormonism is different from the Jesus of Christians," is probably the explanation I most frequently hear from evangelicals, and occasionally from Mormons as well. The nature and significance of that difference is probably at the heart of most evangelical-Mormon dialogue. The difference is not about the historical Jesus, the Christ of the New Testament, who was born, lived, died and arose from death in the first century. Nor, as has become increasingly evident to me, is it necessarily about the Jesus we experience today as we receive his forgiveness and become his followers. The difference is in the theological narrative we affirm: Who was Jesus before he came to earth? How is he one with the Father and the Spirit? In what way is he both human and divine? So this explanation does not eliminate our dilemma, but actually highlights it. We are left pondering: Just how significant is theological agreement?

Theological Significance

My evangelical tradition, on the one hand, rooted as it is in the fourth- and fifth-century church councils and the sixteenth-century Protestant Reformation, places a premium on good theology about Jesus. What is at stake is his very power to save us. Mormonism, on the other hand, has bypassed all those centuries, focusing instead on the restoration in the early nineteenth century. What is at stake here is the very authenticity and authority of the church of Jesus Christ, which they say had apostatized in the generations immediately following Christ and his first apostles. Consequently Mormons place a premium on receiving ordinances (sacraments), including baptism and the laying on of hands from those with the authority, now restored in their church, to perform them. Thus theology, at least theology about the church, is also significant to Latter-day Saints.

So here we are, evangelicals and Mormons, both considering doctrine important but often differing in our theologies and even on which doctrines are most important; at the same time we both consider our testimonies of encountering Jesus important, and find (perhaps to our surprise) that often in some essential ways our experiences of this are similar. So what are we to do? Keep searching for a way to explain away the disequilibrium?

CONCLUSION

While respecting those who may differ, I have come to believe this is not what Jesus would have us do. Rather, his desire seems to be that all who claim to have received his forgiveness and become his followers experience a bonding relationship not only with him but also with each other. And for this to happen among Mormons and evangelicals in a place like Utah (or California, or Chile, or the Philippines) requires genuine dialogue—a lot of it.

Genuine dialogue, in my experience, calls for a lot of listening—listening not for the sake of preparing a good rebuttal and not only for the sake of understanding the other better, but also for the sake of allowing our own thoughts and feelings to be challenged and refined. For example, dialogues like the one I described at the beginning have helped me to recognize an imbalance in my own view and experience of the Trinity—an overemphasis on God's oneness at the expense of his threeness.

Genuine dialogue, in my judgment, also calls for interaction not only about the doctrinal propositions we hold to, but also about the way those doctrines become lived experiences. This seldom happens in an atmosphere of mistrust. Who wants to expose their deeper feelings when they fear they will be discounted or explained away? At the same time, sharing feelings as well as thoughts takes a willingness to let go of our defensiveness and venture a measure of risk.

Genuine dialogue between evangelicals and Latter-day Saints, I am convinced, happens best when Jesus is the focus, at the center of our exchange. And this happens best when the Scriptures that bear witness to him are open in front of us. They inform our discussion and also encourage us when we fear our efforts will fail to be fruitful: We are told Jesus prayed on the night he was arrested (John 17:20-26)—and I trust is praying for us even now (Romans 8:34; Hebrews 7:25)—that we will come to a mature unity (not uniformity) of our faith, both in experience and in doctrine.

Theological Anthropology

The Origin and Nature of Human Beings

Grant Underwood

Spirits were high that May morning as the 2013 evangelical-Mormon dialogue group convened on the main campus of Fuller Theological Seminary in Pasadena, California, to discuss the topic of theological anthropology. I had been asked to lead the discussion of Truman G. Madsen's *Eternal Man* (1966), a milestone work in Mormon thought and one anticipated to generate lively conversation among the dialogue participants. Mormonism is widely recognized as holding a high view of human nature, but few have articulated that position more insightfully or elegantly than the twentieth-century philosopher Madsen. Here is just an initial example of both his fundamentally optimistic assessment of humanity and his eloquence: "Modern man has penetrated the self and found much that is shocking and unspeakably dark. . . . But this, for all its professed depth, has been too shallow. For deeper still, in and not just below all in man that needs healing and redeeming, are the remnants and rudiments of glory."[1] Unpacking what Madsen meant by this statement and exploring how representative it is of Mormon thought over time will be the particular focus of this chapter.

Most treatments of theological anthropology begin with a discussion of the *imago Dei* ("image of God"). In the book of Genesis the crowning moment of divine creative activity, in all aspects deemed "good," occurs when God declares, "Let us make man in our image, after our likeness" (Genesis 1:26 KJV). In time, Christian theologians would devote considerable attention to the implications of this terse declaration, but in ancient Israel interpretations were straightforward: *tselem* ("image") and *demut* ("likeness") denoted physical resemblance.[2] The influential Old Testament scholar Gerhard von Rad urged that interpretations "be rejected which proceed from an anthropology strange to the Old Testament and one-sidedly limit God's image to man's spiritual nature, relating it to man's 'dignity,' his 'personality' or 'ability for moral decision,' etc. The marvel of man's bodily appearance is not at all to be excepted from the realm of God's image."[3]

Latter-day Saints (LDS), of course, are well known for not omitting this aspect of the *imago Dei*. Joseph Smith understood his multiple visions of God in a way that led to a robust anthropomorphism rather than the standard "accommodationist" interpretation of biblical accounts of divine appearances.[4] In turn, this influenced his interpretation of the *imago Dei*. In Joseph Smith's amplification of the biblical text, to the declaration in Genesis 5:1—"In the day that God created man, in the likeness of God made he him"—he added "in the image of his own body."[5] This understanding is also embedded in the Book of Mormon, where at one point a prophet sees the finger of Jehovah—"and it was as the finger of a man, like unto flesh and blood." Eventually, the Lord shows himself fully. "Seest thou that ye are created after mine own image?" queries the Lord. "Yea, even all men were created in the beginning after mine own image. Behold, this body, which ye now behold, is the body of my spirit; and man have I created after the body of my spirit" (Ether 3:6, 15-16). Although Latter-day Saint discussion of "image" and "likeness" stresses divine corporeality, it also touches on many of the themes addressed in the long history of Christian reflection on the meaning of the *imago Dei* ("image of God"). LDS church president Joseph F. Smith, for instance, broadened the meaning of the phrase in a way that is common among other Christians: "[Man] is made in the image of God himself, so that he can reason, reflect, pray, exercise faith."[6]

Some Christian theologians have also emphasized a "relational" understanding of the *imago Dei*. From this perspective, humans are created by God to love and serve him and to enter into relationship with him. As Augustine says in the eloquent opening lines of his *Confessions*, "You made us for yourself, and our hearts are restless until they find their rest in you."[7] C. S. Lewis echoed the sentiment in the twentieth century when he spoke of a God-shaped gap in all humans that generates a deep sense of longing, a longing that only God can fill but that fallen humans mistakenly read as a longing for the things of the world. If humans are made for God and God alone, then nothing else will satisfy. Latter-day Saints fully embrace the idea of divine-human relationship and of a yearning that can only be fully satisfied in God, but they ground it in a literal parent-child relationship hardwired into humanity through preexistent procreation rather than *ex nihilo* creation. Human beings are understood to be the literal spirit offspring of God, "born," rather than "made," to have a loving relationship with the heavenly Father. Although Mormons acknowledge with other Christians that human love of God can grow cold through neglect ("sin"), the divine-human relationship, being "genetic" in LDS thought, can never be destroyed. Human "prodigals" may be estranged from their Father, but they are still "sons." In short, the Mormon estimation of humanity, even in its fallen condition, is among the most positive of Christian anthropologies.

If other Christians sometimes discuss in dark and dismal detail human self-desecration of the *imago Dei*, they also hold out hope for its restoration. That hope resides in Christ, the perfect *Imago Dei*, who came to renew it in humankind. Ultimately, the *imago Dei* can only fully be restored in the afterlife, as the culmination of a grace-empowered life of conformity to, and union with, the Son of God. In the words of an oft-quoted New Testament passage: "It doth not yet appear what we shall be: but we know that, when he shall appear, we shall be like him" (1 John 3:2 KJV). This theological schema of human existence from creation to fall to redemption to glorification has been outlined by one Reformed theologian as moving from "original" image to "perverted" image to "renewed" image to "perfected" image.[8] Such a positive depiction of the Christian's final destiny is in line with the optimistic spirit of Mormon thought, which envisions the eventual deification of the redeemed more profoundly even than the Eastern fathers, such as Athanasius, who described human glorification as deification. Early in the twentieth century, the LDS Church's First Presidency officially summarized the Mormon position in these words: "Man is the child of God, formed in the divine image and endowed with divine attributes, and even as the infant son of an earthly father and mother is capable in due time of becoming a man, so the undeveloped offspring of celestial parentage is capable, by experience through ages and aeons, of evolving into a God."[9]

THE HUMAN SOUL AND ITS ORIGIN

The conception that the human being consists of a physical body and a separate and separable immaterial soul, what is often called anthropological "dualism," has a long and venerable history in Christian theology. Scholarly analysis of the Old Testament, however, has yielded a consensus verdict that ancient Israel monistically conceived the human being to be a divinely animated body rather than a body and a soul. Among the Hebrews, "a strict dualism, which feels that flesh and spirit, body and soul, are irreconcilable opposites, is completely unknown."[10] If the Israelite conception of the human being was that of an animated body, the Hellenistic notion, influential in early Christianity, was that of the incarnated soul. Still, the New Testament itself does not provide unambiguous testimony to a dualistic anthropology. The apostle Paul, for instance, deploys all the relevant terms—*psychē* ("soul"), *sōma* ("body"), *pneuma* ("spirit") and *sarx* ("flesh")—when discussing the human being but does so without systematic definition or semantic consistency.[11]

Particularly with regard to Pauline anthropology, a nontraditional, monistic reading of New Testament anthropology was given significant impetus in the 1950s by Rudolf Bultmann in his two-volume *Theology of the New Testament*. Bultmann famously remarked, "Man does not *have* a *soma*; he is *soma*." Yet despite his argument that Paul retained the monistic, animated-body anthropology of his Hebrew upbringing, Bultmann acknowledged that Paul's use of the Platonic term *eso anthropos* ("inner man"—Romans 7:22; 2 Corinthians 4:16) "comes very close to Hellenistic-Gnostic dualism not merely in form of expression, by speaking of the soma under the figure of the 'tent-dwelling' and 'garment' . . . [as] a shell for the self (the 'inner nature' *eso anthropos*)."[12] In conjunction with recent developments in the neurosciences, some Christian scholars have developed a perspective known as "physicalism" or "holistic dualism" that is similar to Bultmann's monism. Holistic dualism, contrary to traditional mind-body dualisms, views the human as a unified, embodied whole consisting of various capacities and characteristics.[13] Still, the persisting popularity of belief that a separable human spirit or soul lives on after death in conscious, personal existence independent of the deceased body acts as a major deterrent to general Christian acceptance of a physicalist anthropology. So does the fact that such views compel reconsideration of other aspects of traditional Christian thought from eschatology and Christology to Christian spirituality.[14]

Mormonism's distinctive metaphysics and cosmogony offer a unique perspective on these matters. Depending on the vantage point, LDS anthropology can be considered either dualist *or* monist. It is dualist in its affirmation that the human being consists of a body and a distinct, separable soul or spirit. It is monist, or better, "materialist" in its claim that souls are not immaterial but composed of "spirit-matter." In words attributed to Joseph Smith that were eventually canonized, "There is no such thing as immaterial [souls]. All spirit is matter, but it is more fine or pure, and . . . when our bodies are purified we shall see that it is all matter" (Doctrines and Covenants, 131:7-8). Madsen puts it this way: "Mind, spirit, and body are all material, in varying degrees of refinement. They have equal status in spatiotemporal existence and are, in their perfected state, of equal worth."[15]

What is more, spiritual corporeality is as freely affirmed as spiritual materiality. Latter-day Saints commonly refer to souls as "spirit *bodies*." Here there are echoes of early Christian theologians such as Tertullian, who also believed that souls are both material and corporeal. Tertullian was influenced by the materialism of Stoicism, which eschewed difference between the material and the immaterial. Similar to how Joseph Smith contrasted refined spirit-matter with denser, visible matter, Tertullian, along with the Stoics, described the soul as an invisible body composed of an ethereal substance, a kind of "thinking gas."[16] Tertullian believed, as Mormons do, that "the soul conforms exactly to the shape of the body that it pervades, containing all the appendages, eyes, ears, mouth and the like, that distinguish the outer contours of the fleshly body."[17] Although such conceptions of spirit were not unknown in the early Christian centuries, after Origen, "the idea that the soul was a refined material substance more or less evaporated from Christian theology."[18]

Mormon anthropology looks most distinctive, however, when comparing

LDS and other Christian ideas about the origin of the soul. Although almost nothing is said about this in the Bible, by the end of the fourth century three basic theories (all bearing relatively modern titles) circulated among Christian thinkers: (1) *creationism* (not to be confused with the current name of a particular understanding of the origin of the earth)—in an on-going process of divine creation, souls are tailor-made by God for each human embryo and infused in the fetus sometime between conception and birth; (2) *traducianism* (from the Latin *traducere*, "to lead across, transport, transmit")—the soul is transmitted biologically from generation to gener-ation; God created only one soul, Adam's, and from that point forward the soul is part of the biological inheritance parents pass on to their children; and (3) *preexistentialism*—all souls were created simultaneously in the be-ginning before the physical creation and kept "in storage" until conferred on individual humans sometime between their conception and birth. One modern scholar has memorably dubbed these theories of the origin of the soul as, respectively, "custom-made," "second-hand" and "ready-made."[19]

"The third option" (preexistence of souls) in Christianity, argues Paula Fredriksen, was "the one most natural to the Greek metaphysics that most of these theologies presupposed."[20] Fredriksen's statement reminds us that the (Greek) metaphysics of an immortal soul presumes a preexistence of some kind. Additionally, the Hellenistic privileging of spirit over matter made it reasonable to believe that the higher spiritual/intellectual realm would have been created before the lesser physical/material universe. In reality, several Christianized versions of the theory of the preexistence of souls were in circulation in early Christianity, but because the one pro-pounded by Origen was eventually anathematized, all became theologically suspect thereafter.[21] In a different time and place, unconcerned with Helle-nistic metaphysical speculations or the constraints of traditional Christian orthodoxy, Mormonism also proclaimed the preexistence of souls. Indeed, in the century or so following its initial articulation by Joseph Smith, the idea became a favorite Mormon topic for doctrinal reflection. By the time Madsen wrote *Eternal Man*, he could say, "not only does awareness of the pre-existence make a difference, but [it makes] a prodigious difference."[22]

The Latter-day Saint doctrine of the preexistence differs from all other preexistentialist theories yet has something in common with each of them.

A key divergence is that souls are understood to be derived from Deity by procreation rather than emanation or *ex nihilo* creation. Latter-day Saints assert that at some point in eternity (Mormons view eternity simply as everlasting time), prior to creation of the physical universe, God "begat" human souls, what Mormons refer to as God's "spirit children." Consistent with this concept, Latter-day Saints interpret the occasional New Testament designation of Christ as "Firstborn" to mean that among these begotten souls Christ the Son was first in terms of birth sequence as well as status. Although Christ is understood to share a "sibling" relationship to the rest of the heavenly Father's spirit children, he is viewed as preeminent, qualitatively superior to his "brothers" and "sisters" in every way. Conceiving all human souls as spiritually begotten requires Latter-day Saints to interpret "Only Begotten" as a reference the fact that only Christ, of all God's spirit children, can claim the Father as *physical* Sire. He is, as Latter-day Saints are wont to say, the Only Begotten "in the flesh."[23]

Although authoritative Mormon sources do not explain *how* spirits were begotten, over time "birth" and "procreation" (or cognates) became the primary vocabulary for discussing the spirit creation. Early on, the inner logic of this language led to contemplation of the existence of a "heavenly Mother." The following words, first published in 1845, are still sung by Latter-day Saints today:

> O my Father, thou that dwellest
> In the high and glorious place;
> When shall I regain thy presence,
> And again behold thy face?
> In thy holy habitation,
> Did my spirit once reside?
> In my first primeval childhood
> Was I nurtur'd near thy side? . . .
> I had learn'd to call thee father
> Through thy spirit from on high,
> But until the key of knowledge
> Was restor'd, I knew not why.
> In the heav'ns are parents single?
> No, the thought makes reason stare;

Truth is reason—truth eternal
Tells me I've a mother there.[24]

In addition to the fact that this hymn is still included in the current LDS hymnbook, an official 1995 statement issued jointly by the church's First Presidency and Quorum of Twelve Apostles reaffirmed LDS belief that "all human beings—male and female—are created in the image of God. Each is a beloved spirit son or daughter of heavenly *parents*, and, as such, each has a divine nature and destiny."[25] Although the doctrine of a heavenly Mother has been consistently affirmed in LDS discourse, detailed discussion is restrained by the fact that nothing is known about her role in the process of spirit birth or about other aspects of her divine nature and activities.[26] With regard to the divine generation of souls, most Latter-day Saints are in fundamental agreement with sentiments expressed by Hilary of Poitiers about the begetting of the Son. Hilary wrote that although God was willing to accommodate finite human understanding by using examples from human birth, believers should not take such analogies so far, or be so literal, as to include such reproductive details as "coition, conception, lapse of time, delivery."[27]

Another divergence from early Christian preexistentialism is that Latter-day Saints envision an eons-long preexistence prior to the physical creation of the universe. Early Christian preexistentialism dramatically foreshortened the period of souls' preexistence, typically placing their creation in conjunction with the temporal creation. No authoritative LDS source identifies *when* the begetting of souls took place, but Mormons commonly assume it was long before the physical creation. Twentieth-century apostle-theologian Joseph Fielding Smith offered his view that the spirit creation took place "untold ages before we were placed on this earth. . . . Man [was] not created in the spirit at the time of the creation of the earth, but long before."[28] Few early Christian fathers posited anything like the lengthy preexistent life of the soul contemplated in Mormonism, and none envisioned it as a "primeval childhood" in which divine spirit children were "nurtured at [Father's] side." Madsen's perspective on the matter is typical.

> In mortal birth, inherent physical and personality traits of the father and mother are transmitted to their son or daughter. . . . It is exactly so with man's

spirit. Long before mortality, in a process of actual transmission, there were forged into man's spirit the embryonic traits, attributes, and powers of God Himself! And in the surroundings of that realm man was nurtured in the Divine image.[29]

One important Mormon convergence with Christian preexistentialism has to do with interest in the preexistence's potential for providing a more satisfying theodicy. Origen described preexistent souls' personal responsibility for their earthly circumstances in these words:

> Because these rational creatures themselves were endowed with the power of free will, this freedom of will either incited each one to progress by imitation of God or reduced him to failure through negligence. And this is the cause of the diversity among rational creatures. . . . Now God, who thought it right to arrange his creatures according to their merit, brought down these different rational creatures into the harmony of one world. . . . And these causes are antecedent to [each soul's] bodily birth.[30]

Mormons sympathize with Origen's interest in relieving God of culpability for the human predicament, although they do not agree with his view that embodiment was a "precosmic fall" or punishment. They have, however, throughout much of their history, used the notion of the preexistent experience of souls to account for diversity in human personality, religiosity (or lack thereof) and even personal talent.[31]

By the third quarter of the twentieth century, LDS speculation about the preexistence had reached its high-water mark. As a period piece, Madsen's *Eternal Man* is an eloquent reminder of an earlier, exuberant enthusiasm for the value of the doctrine of the preexistence. From the perspective of belief in a long preexistence at heavenly Father's side, human religion is viewed as "more involved in *re*covery than discovery" propelled by "revelatory touches with the self that seem to disclose the longer-than-mortal sense" of human existence and point to a destiny that "is not union with Divine realities, but *re*union." For God's mortal children, "the glow of an evanescent past reawakens responses of awesome love" toward their heavenly Father, and faith is "the expression of the inner self in harmony with a whole segment of one's prior experiences." Moreover, although preexistent experiences are "hidden under mortal amnesia," they "are indelible in their effect on our affinities, kinships, and sensitivities." In the end, humans live with a "luminous nostalgia," and their preexistent experiences account for many of life's otherwise inexplicable déjà vu occurrences (Madsen lists nine different types).[32]

Not surprisingly, Madsen also finds Mormon preexistence doctrine consolatory in the face of human suffering. In one passage, he constructs a hypothetical dialogue with a suffering mother who is told:

> You and the child of your bosom counseled intimately with God the Father. Freely, fully, and with a courage that astonishes mortal imagination, you elected and prepared for this estate. The contrasts of the flesh, its risks, its terrific trials were known to you. More than that, you comprehended your actual appointed mission in this world, designed to meet your individual needs, and those who would depend upon you. Perhaps you anticipated these exact circumstances.[33]

Mormons today may be less confident about the explanatory power of the preexistence, particularly as theodicy, than they were fifty years ago when *Eternal Man* was written, but because the key Mormon concept of literal kinship with God the Father is central to LDS preexistentialism, belief in the preexistence is still prominent in the pantheon of Mormon doctrines.

"Man Was Also in the Beginning with God"

The heart of *Eternal Man* and a focus of the 2013 evangelical-Mormon dialogue on theological anthropology was an exploration of the significance of the canonical LDS statement "man was also in the beginning with God" (Doctrines and Covenants, 93:29). This simple declaration has yielded a range of interpretations over the nearly two-hundred-year history of Mormonism, and Madsen's volume represents an able articulation of one of them. Before considering *Eternal Man*'s position, it is worth briefly noting other views. The current student manual for LDS college-level religion classes studying the Doctrine and Covenants includes this statement: "The word *beginning* may refer to the time when we began as the spirit offspring of God or to the time when the earth began as a temporal sphere."[34] LDS Church leaders have given voice to both interpretations. Joseph Fielding Smith, for instance, wrote of the beginning as referring to the physical creation of the universe detailed in Genesis: "Man was in the beginning with

God. In that day, however, man was a spirit unembodied. The beginning was when the [heavenly] councils met and the decision was made to create this earth that the spirits who were intended for this earth, should come here and partake of the mortal conditions and receive bodies of flesh and bones."[35] Church leader-theologian Bruce R. McConkie wrote that "man was also in the beginning with God" meant "that the spirits of men were created, begotten, and organized, that they came into being as spirits at the time of their spirit birth." The expression "simply mean[s] that all the spirit offspring of the Father were with him in pre-existence."[36]

Yet Madsen spoke for an interpretive tradition long in place in Mormon thought that pushed beyond even the spirit creation. The human "autobiographical thread," he wrote, "leads backward through the lineage of Deity and on to the original individual unit called 'intelligence.'"[37] What Madsen means is that the creation of preexistent spirits/souls was no more *ex nihilo* than the physical creation. In the view of Madsen and his interpretive predecessors, self-conscious, individual entities known as "intelligences" subsisted independently and eternally until God "organized" (a Platonic-sounding synonym for "create" first popularized by Joseph Smith) them as spirit beings. The concept of such a *kosmos noētos*—a realm of bodiless, immortal intelligences or minds—might have been palatable to Platonic tradition, but neither there nor in Christianity generally would there have been much resonance for the idea that those incorporeal minds were subsequently advanced to a higher level of development by God procreatively fashioning spirit bodies for them out of "spirit element" and endowing them with his image so that they became his spirit "children." In short, there was a preexistence of intelligences before there was a preexistence of spirits/souls.

These distinctive ideas grow out of reflection on several key passages in LDS Scripture. Immediately after the declaration "man was also in the beginning with God," this statement is made: "Intelligence, or the light of truth, was not created or made, neither indeed can be. All truth is independent in that sphere in which God has placed it, to act for itself, as all intelligence also; otherwise there is no existence" (Doctrines and Covenants, 93:29). Elsewhere it is stated: "Now the Lord had shown unto me, Abraham, the intelligences that were organized before the world was; and among all these there were many of the noble and great ones" (Abraham 3:22). Although noncanonical, another text that serves as the basis for Mormon theological reflection on the origins of humanity is a funeral sermon Joseph Smith preached in April 1844 popularly known as the "King Follett Discourse." As preserved by note takers, Smith reportedly said, "The soul—the immortal spirit—the mind of man. Where did it come from? All doctors of divinity say that God created it in the beginning; but it is not so. . . . The mind of man—the intelligent part—is as immortal as, and is co-equal with, God Himself. . . . Their spirits existed coequal with God. . . . Is it logical to say that a spirit is immortal and yet have a beginning? . . . God never had the power to create the spirit of man at all. . . . Intelligence is eternal and exists upon a self-existent principle. It is a spirit from age to age and there is no creation about it."[38]

Smith's synonymous use of "soul," "spirit" and "intelligence" can be confusing to modern Latter-day Saints accustomed to the distinctive definitions eventually given to these terms, but it seems clear enough that the Mormon prophet's primary intent was to communicate the idea that some essential, irreducible aspect of humanity is eternal and uncreated, preexisting *both* the spiritual and physical creations.[39] Although Madsen admits that "much is left indeterminate," he follows in the footsteps of some earlier commentators who read Smith and the canonical passages cited above as teaching that in the primordial past, before even the creation of preexistent souls, humankind existed as separate "intelligences" with these four fundamental characteristics: individuality, autonomy/freedom (human selves have always had *libero arbitrio* [free choice], not as a divine gift but as an innate condition), consciousness/selfhood ("there is no inanimate intelligence or unconscious mind"; the ego is eternal) and capacity for development/progress (the corollary/consequence of self-existence and freedom).[40]

Not all Latter-day Saints, however, have been comfortable construing these somewhat ambiguous statements in such a fashion. The popularity of such interpretations in the early twentieth century prompted some corrective interventions by the church's First Presidency. The prolific and influential church leader–theologian Brigham H. Roberts was asked in regard to one of his manuscripts to "eliminate his theories in regard to intelligences as conscious self-existing beings or entities before being organized into spirit."[41] Several years later, John A. Widtsoe, president of Utah State University and later a member of the LDS Quorum of Twelve Apostles, was asked to prepare a theological study manual for the church's priesthood. When church president Joseph F. Smith and his counselor Anthon H. Lund reviewed the completed manuscript with Widtsoe, Smith "eliminated from it all that pertained to intelligences before they became begotten spirits as that would only be speculation."[42] When published in 1915, *Rational Theology* included no references to independent "intelligences" preexisting God's procreated spirit children.

Still, Widtsoe (and Roberts) were able to affirm the eternality of humankind in the sense that humanity's constituent components were eternal. As undifferentiated intelligent "matter," not preexisting, autonomous intelligent beings, the cognitive core of the human soul had always existed. Only at spirit birth, however, did individual "intelligences" come into being, fashioned from uncreated "intelligence." This view was summarized several years later by Charles Penrose, then a member of the church's First Presidency:

> Now don't confound, as some of our brethren have done, the expression "intelligences," referring to individual spirits, [with] that intelligence that is an attribute of those spirits, "that never was created, neither indeed can be." What is that uncreated intelligence? Why it is "the light of truth. . . . It always existed and always will persist. . . . Intelligences . . . had a beginning when they were born of God as the sons or daughters of God.[43]

Widtsoe himself would later advise: "In reading Latter-day Saint literature, the two-fold sense in which the terms *an intelligence* or *intelligences* are used—applied to spiritual personages or to pre-spiritual entities—must be carefully kept in mind."[44]

Throughout the remainder of the twentieth century and into the twenty-first, individual LDS church leaders and members alike continued to express their personal views about whether distinct, individual intelligences existed prior to spirit creation. Madsen wrote eloquently in the doctrinal tradition exemplified by his intellectual hero B. H. Roberts. Others favored the idea of undifferentiated, eternal intelligence as a building block for God's creation of human souls. All, however, agree that the human being, in its irreducible essence, is coeternal with the Father. Although Latter-day Saints use traditional theological language to talk about God creating humans in his own image and "endow[ing] them with godlike reason and intelligence," they believe that some part of that "intelligence," in some fashion, preexisted both spirit creation and physical creation and is indeed uncreated.[45] In that sense, then, all Latter-day Saints, albeit in their own way, join with Truman Madsen in affirming belief in "eternal man."

Most crucial to an LDS anthropology, though, as explained in a recent church publication, is the affirmation that humans are children of God "in a full and complete sense." Why this is said to matter is here offered as a concluding reflection: "All human beings are children of loving heavenly parents and possess seeds of divinity within them. In His infinite love, God invites His children to cultivate their eternal potential by the grace of God, through the Atonement of the Lord Jesus Christ. The doctrine of humans' eternal potential to become like their Heavenly Father is central to the gospel of Jesus Christ and inspires love, hope, and gratitude in the hearts of faithful Latter-day Saints."[46]

"How Great a Debtor"

Mormon Reflections on Grace

Camille Fronk Olson

One of the most popular and beloved hymns for Latter-day Saints (LDS), sung in conjunction with the weekly service of the Sacrament of the Lord's Supper, is "I Stand All Amazed."[1] The hymn was first included in an LDS hymnal in 1909, only ten years after the words and music were first published in a nondenominational collection of gospel songs.[2] Mormons know the words of the hymn by heart as they sing, "I stand all amazed at the love Jesus offers me, confused at the grace that so fully he proffers me." The words alert the penitent—the grace of Jesus Christ is confusing. The grace of Jesus Christ is confusing because it is not fair. He gives us his gifts of re-birth, repentance, forgiveness, enabling ability and perfect love when we did not earn or merit them. We come to him as unprofitable servants, with souls as "rebellious and proud as mine," and he molds us into new creatures—pure, loving and caring—as we bend to his will.

During the twelve years that I have participated in the LDS-evangelical dialogues, I have found that we are remarkably close in our understanding and appreciation for what Paul means by "saved through faith; . . . not of works, lest any man should boast" (Ephesians 2:8-9 KJV) and what James means by "faith, if it hath not works, is dead, being alone" (James 2:17 KJV). In fact, we probably agree more on this theological principle than any other that we have explored.

The challenge, as I have discovered, is to convince other evangelical Christians that we Mormons embrace the foundational doctrine of grace and that we believe we are justified by our faith in Christ and not by our own merits. Almost as challenging is the task to convince Latter-day Saints that evangelical Christians more often believe that their faith in Christ inherently leads to doing good for others and that by saying they are "saved" they do not mean that the actions of their daily lives are of no consequence. Both sides have suffered from misinformation and reluctance to allow the other side to accept the same truths.

C. S. Lewis observed that the devil "always sends errors into the world in pairs—pairs of opposites. And he always encourages us to spend a lot of time thinking which is the worse. . . . He relies on your extra dislike of the one error to draw you gradually into the opposite one. But do not let us be fooled. We have to keep our eyes on the goal and go straight through between both errors."[3]

EMPHASIS ON SHOWING FAITH BY OUR WORKS

In our interfaith discussions, no one has been able to definitively explain why so many of us Latter-day Saints have tended to speak less of grace and more of works. Professor Robert Millet has postulated that we avoided the doctrine of grace "because it brings us face to face with our own limitations. Perhaps we shy away from it because we sense that it may entail an alternation in our present way of viewing things."[4] Perhaps Mormons have resisted the doctrine of grace in reaction to Protestant claims to salvation by simply proclaiming Jesus their "Lord and Master." When they cite Paul to back their position, we Mormons go to our beloved epistle of James to underscore that faith must be accompanied by good works to be efficacious. We usually add a verse from the Book of Mormon (never mind that it was taken out of context!) to bolster our case: "It is by grace we are saved, after all we can do" (2 Nephi 25:23), as though it were an either/or proposition. In other words, we have feared that if we emphasize grace, we might ignore the importance of obedience and discipleship, of *living* the word of God. With our pioneer heritage of crossing the plains with handcarts and carving out a society in the desert, we know and reverence the value of hard work and sacrifice.

Early in the 1980s the ramifications of stressing "all we can do" became apparent. An article by Kenneth Woodward titled "What Mormons Believe" appeared in a 1980 edition of *Newsweek* highlighting how Mormons interpret their religious traditions. The focus was on the rank-and-file members rather than what church leaders and Scripture purported to be LDS doctrine. The report summarized our traditional understanding of the atonement in these words: "Unlike orthodox Christians, Mormons believe that men are born free of sin and earn their way to godhood by the proper exercise of free will, rather than through the grace of Jesus Christ. Thus Jesus' suffering and death in the Mormon view were brotherly acts of compassion, but they do not atone for the sins of others."[5]

RETURN TO GRACE

Reading such a conclusion in a national magazine brought numerous responses from Latter-day Saints protesting that this perspective in no way matched our doctrine. It also revealed that teachings about our profound need for the grace and mercy and merits of Jesus Christ had often been missing from formative religious instruction. The succeeding years witnessed major presentations and written works from high-profile LDS leaders and scholars who directly addressed the void.

In the mid-eighties, Bruce C. Hafen, then dean of the J. Reuben Clark Law School at BYU, addressed LDS religious educators in a speech he called "The Atonement Is Not Just for Sinners." After citing the *Newsweek* article, Hafen observed, "Despite [the] remarkable truth about the Book of Mormon, we Latter-day Saints are, for the most part, only superficially acquainted with our own doctrines of grace, mercy, justice, and the Atonement." He went on in his address to highlight the essential role of the grace of Jesus Christ in our progression.

In 1992, Professor Stephen E. Robinson followed up with his treatise on salvation through the grace of Jesus Christ in a landmark book titled *Believing Christ*. After determining that his BYU religion students were often "more comfortable defining themselves in terms of what they *didn't* believe (predestination, original sin, and so forth) than in terms of what they *did* believe," he made a concerted effort to design several lectures with the central doctrines of grace, mercy, justification and atonement to help his students make the connections.[6] The book reflects those lectures.

In 1994, shortly after the death of Ezra Taft Benson, president of the Church

of Jesus Christ of Latter-day Saints, Elder Dallin H. Oaks of the Quorum of
the Twelve Apostles reviewed President Benson's numerous discourses to the
church about the Book of Mormon, especially his frequent recitation that the
church "shall remain under . . . condemnation until they repent and remember
the new covenant, even the Book of Mormon" (Doctrines and Covenants,
84:57). After carefully considering President Benson's reasons for a more in-
depth study of the Book of Mormon, Elder Oaks concluded,

> In my opinion, one of the principal reasons our Heavenly Father had his
> prophet direct us into a more intensive study of the Book of Mormon is to
> help us counteract (the) modern tendency to try to diminish the divinity and
> mission of our Savior. . . . In too many of our classes, in too many of our
> worship services, we are not teaching of Christ and testifying of Christ in the
> way we should. This is one way we are failing to remember the new covenant.[7]

In the past two decades general leaders of the church have often focused
their official semiannual messages to the church on the essential nature of
grace in our salvation. For example, Elder Bruce C. Hafen of the Seventy, by
that time a general church officer, clarified Nephi's words by teaching that
we are saved by grace "both *during* and 'after all we can do.'"[8] Elder M. Russell
Ballard of the Quorum of the Twelve Apostles explained it this way:

> It is only through the infinite Atonement of Jesus Christ that people can
> overcome the consequences of bad choices. Thus Nephi teaches us that it is
> ultimately by the grace of Christ that we are saved even after all that we can
> do. No matter how hard we work, no matter how much we obey, no matter
> how many good things we do in this life, it would not be enough were it not
> for Jesus Christ and His loving grace.

He continued, "Unfortunately, there are some within the Church who have
become so preoccupied with performing good works that they forget that
those works—as good as they may be—are hollow unless they are accompanied by a complete dependence on Christ."[9]

From the perspective that these clarifying teachings gave to us, we as
Mormons are sometimes astounded to recognize that the principle of
grace was part of the roots of Mormonism as much as the need to manifest
our faith through our actions. The Book of Mormon is saturated with reminders that

salvation is free. . . . And by the law no flesh is justified; or, by the law men are cut off. . . . Wherefore, redemption cometh in and through the Holy Messiah; for he is full of grace and truth. Behold he offereth himself a sacrifice for sin, to answer the ends of the law, unto all those who have a broken heart and a contrite spirit; and unto none else can the ends of the law be answered. Wherefore, how great the importance to make these things known unto the inhabitants of the earth, that they may know that there is no flesh that can dwell in the presence of God, save it be through the merits, and mercy, and grace of the Holy Messiah. (2 Nephi 2:4-8)

As many of the early LDS apostles prepared for their missions to the British Isles, Joseph Smith gave them many instructions, including this advice on remembering the source of their success, from July 2, 1839:

When the Twelve or any other witnesses stand before the congregations of the earth, and they preach in the power and demonstration of the Spirit of God, and the people are astonished and confounded at the doctrine, and say, "That man has preached a powerful discourse, a great sermon," then let that man or those men take care that they do not ascribe the glory unto themselves, but be careful that they are humble, and ascribe the praise and glory to God and the Lamb; for it is by the power of the Holy Priesthood and the Holy Ghost that they have power thus to speak. What art thou, O man, but dust? And from whom receivest thou thy power and blessings, but from God.[10]

The second leader of the Church of Jesus Christ of Latter-day Saints was Brigham Young, known for his hard work and pioneer wisdom, qualities certainly needed to tame the desert of the Great Basin. He also testified that salvation is possible only through the atonement of Jesus Christ: "I will take the liberty of saying to every man and woman who wishes to obtain salvation through [Jesus Christ] that looking to him only, is not enough: they must have faith in his name, character and atonement; and they must have faith in his Father and in the plan of salvation devised and wrought out by the Father and the Son."[11]

THE GREATER CHALLENGE: CONVINCING EVANGELICALS OF OUR BELIEFS

The first LDS-evangelical student dialogue was held in 2006 in Salt Lake City, organized by Pastor Greg Johnson. Craig Blomberg of Denver Seminary and

I were paired to share our respective doctrinal understanding of the role of faith and works in our hope for salvation. Knowing that our conclusions would not be that far apart, we decided beforehand that he would use the Bible, both Old and New Testaments, as his doctrinal source and I would exclusively use the Book of Mormon to support the LDS beliefs. He went first and outlined the consistent message that humankind is lost and without hope if not for a Redeemer. But in truth, none of the students, evangelical or Mormon, were surprised to hear such a treatise on grace from an evangelical.

When I began, many expected me to argue the importance of works and ordinances in our ability to receive salvation. Among the many Book of Mormon passages that I cited, I focused on a dream had by Lehi, the first prophet-leader in the story. In the dream Lehi sees the Tree of Life, which he and his family are told represents Jesus Christ, the "love of God," and that its fruit represents the atonement of Christ. According to the dream, everyone is lost until they come to the tree. There is a path prepared, and "the word of God" is represented by a rod of iron that runs along the path to assist those who will hold to it until people finally arrive at the tree. Only by partaking of the fruit of the tree does one feel "great joy" and desire to help others to achieve the same fullness of joy by coming to the tree (1 Nephi 8).

Nephi, an early Book of Mormon prophet, gave commentary on the dream to underscore our need for the Redeemer. He explained that the gate by which we enter the path leading to the tree is "repentance and baptism by water; and then cometh a remission of your sins by fire and by the Holy Ghost" (2 Nephi 31:17). To underscore that repentance and baptism are not to be counted as our merits, Nephi wrote, "And now, my beloved brethren, after ye have gotten into this strait and narrow path, I would ask if all is done? Behold, I say unto you, Nay; for *ye have not come thus far save it were by the word of Christ with unshaken faith in him, relying wholly upon the merits of him who is mighty to save*" (2 Nephi 31:19 [emphasis added]). Nephi concluded his explanation with an unequivocal statement: "This is the way; and there is none other way nor name given under heaven whereby man can be saved in the kingdom of God" (2 Nephi 31:21).

In reviewing all the places in the Book of Mormon where the word "merit" appears (2 Nephi 2:8; 31:19; Alma 22:14; 24:10; Helaman 14:13; Moroni 6:4), the consistent message is this—we merit nothing of ourselves, but we are saved only through the merits, mercy and grace of Jesus Christ. To have faith in Christ therefore means that we are *faithful* to Christ and sincerely desire to obey his commands out of love and gratitude to him. We will want to show our faith in Christ by trying to be like him. That includes being baptized "to fulfill all righteousness" and following the Savior's example. Indeed, "can we follow Jesus save we shall be willing to keep the commandments of the Father?" (2 Nephi 31:5-12).

The best interpretation of Nephi's teaching that "it is by grace we are saved, after all we can do" comes from considering the context of the rest of the chapter, which all focuses on our need for a Redeemer. Salvation by grace "after all we can do" is understood in its context by such phrases as *above and beyond* all we can do, *notwithstanding* all we can do or *in spite of* all we can do. Additionally, an analysis from a later passage in the book about another group of people who were converted to belief in Jesus Christ after a tradition of bloodshed and war is instructive. The leader of the group observed, "Since it has been *all that we could do* (as we were the most lost of all mankind) to repent of all our sins and the many murders which we have committed, and to get God to take them away from our hearts, for it was *all we could do* to repent sufficiently before God that he would take away our stain" (Alma 24:11 [emphasis added]). According to the Book of Mormon, "all *we* can do" is repent of our sins in faith that Jesus Christ will remit them.

So why do Mormons also speak of the need for good works? According to the Book of Mormon, we will be judged by our manifestations that we have allowed Christ to change our nature to become more like him, not by the merits of our work (Alma 42:27). Robert Millet explains,

> The works and deeds of man, though insufficient of themselves for salvation, are necessary. They are necessary because they evidence our desire to keep our covenant, to be true to our promise to follow the Lord and keep his commandments. True faith always results in faithfulness. Discipleship is inextricably linked with full acceptance of Christ and his gospel.[12]

As we respond with love and gratitude to Christ, we become more humble, long-suffering, diligent and thereby increase in "faith, hope, and charity, and then" are enabled to do "good works" to further God's purposes (Alma 7:24).

Our efforts to do good for others are the natural expression of our love and gratitude for Christ, not our work to merit salvation.

The evangelical students' reaction to my presentation was very positive. They acknowledged that my witness carried power and truth. One of them asked during the question-and-answer portion of the session, "Is it possible that your Church had it wrong at first but is now correcting its doctrine?" My response was instantaneous: "The Book of Mormon hasn't changed; I changed. And in so doing I discovered a core tenet of my religious tradition—I am saved by the grace, mercy and merits of Jesus Christ."

In other settings when I have been invited to explain to evangelical Christians my understanding of the role of grace in good works, I have also been met with anger. People tell me point-blank, "You do not really believe that!" They claim that none of the other Mormons they know believe that only through the grace of Jesus Christ can we be saved, and so consequently I cannot really believe what I claim. Others have accused me of purposefully misrepresenting our doctrine to make Mormonism more acceptable to mainline Christians. I feel like the wind has been knocked out of me when so attacked. I do not expect others to agree with me, but why am I not allowed to witness what the Holy Spirit has communicated to me about grace from my studies of the Book of Mormon and the Bible and my subsequent desire to obey the Lord?

I teach hundreds of LDS students at Brigham Young University every year, and every year I hear their affirmations of the need for the atonement of Christ. They agree with what I and the Book of Mormon teach. But they typically use different words and expressions than evangelicals use. My experience with a fairly constant group of participants in our interfaith dialogues has taught me how to speak of grace and faith in terms more akin to their words. Consequently, I now tell my students that if someone asks them if they believe they are "saved by faith," it is imperative that, before they answer, they know the questioner's definition of faith as well as works. Once you know that, you can answer about their beliefs in words that are less likely to be misunderstood.

ACCEPTING EVANGELICAL CLAIMS THAT THEIR EFFORTS MATTER

At the same time that these dialogues have prompted me to find better ways to verbalize my faith to evangelicals, I try to help my students and LDS neighbors listen to what evangelicals really mean by their emphasis on grace. I correct those who want to simply write off any Protestant who talks about being "born again" and "saved by grace" as though their only definition of grace required no response from them in the way they live, much like the antinomians in Paul's day.

To assist me in my quest, I love to cite Dietrich Bonhoeffer (1906–1945), a theologian and German Lutheran pastor in the Confessing Church in Germany. He was the first one to coin the phrase "cheap grace" and to point out the serious problems associated with it.

> Cheap grace means grace as bargain-basement goods, cut-rate forgiveness, cut-rate comfort. . . . It is grace without a price, without costs. . . . Because grace alone does everything, everything can stay in its old ways. Our action is in vain. . . . Thus, the Christian should live the same way the world does. . . . Cheap grace is preaching forgiveness without repentance; it is baptism without the discipline of community; it is the Lord's Supper without confession of sin. . . . Cheap grace is grace without discipleship, grace without the cross.[13]

Bonhoeffer's description of "costly grace" is as beautiful and powerful as I have read.

> Costly grace is the gospel which must be sought again and again, the gift which has to be asked for, the door at which one has to knock. . . . It is costly, because it calls to discipleship; it is grace, because it calls us to follow Jesus Christ. It is costly, because it costs people their lives; it is grace, because it thereby makes them live. It is costly, because it condemns sin; it is grace because it justifies the sinner. Above all, grace is costly, because it was costly to God, because it costs God the life of God's Son—"you were bought with a price" (1 Cor. 6:20)—and because nothing can be cheap to us which is costly to God.[14]

With so many doctrines on which we might disagree, it is comforting to know that I can feel such a strong connection with my evangelical friends about Christ's amazing grace; this is something worth celebrating. I hope to always give them the benefit of the doubt when they express their heartfelt beliefs and hope for salvation. In the same token of charity, I pray that they will do the same for me and my LDS brothers and sisters when we proclaim, "I stand all amazed at the love Jesus offers me. . . . O it is wonderful, wonderful to me."[15]

Authority Is Everything

Robert L. Millet

Several years ago I hosted an academic conference at Brigham Young University titled "By What Authority?" I invited representatives from many faiths, including Roman Catholic, Eastern Orthodox, evangelical, Episcopalian, Seventh-day Adventist and Christian Science. It was a fascinating couple of days. Maybe the most interesting point of the conference came during a panel discussion in which the participants took questions from the audience. I was interested that so many Latter-day Saint (LDS) students were perplexed by the presentations made by the three evangelical presenters. More than one of the students said some variation of the following: "I still don't know where you get your authority. I can understand the Roman Catholic, Orthodox and Latter-day Saint positions, but I just don't see where your authority comes from." Perhaps I can indicate in this chapter why the Mormon kids were so confused.

Joseph Smith once remarked that "a man can do nothing for himself unless God direct him in the right way; and the priesthood is for that purpose."[1] From an LDS perspective, the New Testament clearly teaches the need for divine authority. Jesus ordained the twelve apostles (John 15:16), gave to them the keys of the kingdom of God (Matthew 16:18-19; 18:18) and empowered his servants to perform miracles and take the gospel to all nations (Matthew 10:1, 5-8; 28:19-20). Later, after the Lord's death, the apostles were divinely directed to fill the vacancy in the Twelve created by the death of Judas Iscariot, commissioned others to serve in the ministry (Acts 1:15-26; 6:1-6; 13:1-3; 14:23; 1 Timothy 4:14; 2 Timothy 1:6; Titus 1:5) and ensured that the saving ordinances (sacraments) were performed only by those properly ordained (Acts 19:1-6, 13-16).

This was a power that no man could assume, take upon himself or even purchase; it came through the laying on of hands by those holding proper authority (Acts 8:18-20; Hebrews 5:4). Mormons believe that with the death of the apostles, within one hundred years of the crucifixion of Jesus, this apostolic authority, the power to act in the name of God, was lost from the earth. Hegesippus, the second-century Jewish-Christian writer, noted that "when the sacred band of the apostles had in various ways reached the end of their life, and the generation of those privileged to listen with their own ears to the divine wisdom had passed on, then godless error began to take shape."[2]

Similarly, J. B. Philips observed that the differences between present-day Christianity and the young church of the first century are readily apparent. The early Christians

> did not make "acts of faith," they believed; they did not "say their prayers," they really prayed. They did not hold conferences on psychosomatic medicine, they simply healed the sick. . . . We in the modern Church have unquestionably lost something. Whether it is due to the atrophy of the quality which the New Testament calls "faith," whether it is due to a stifling churchiness, whether it is due to our sinful complacency over the scandal of a divided Church, or whatever the cause may be, very little of the modern Church could bear comparison with the spiritual drive, the genuine fellowship, and the gay unconquerable courage of the Young Church.[3]

The story is told that on one occasion the pope "pointed to his gorgeous Papal Palace and said [to St. Dominic], 'Peter can no longer say "Silver and gold have I none"'; and the Spanish friar answered, 'No, and neither can he now say, "Rise and walk."'"[4]

While Catholic and Orthodox Christians claim apostolic succession (that the bishops of the ancient church have conveyed their priesthood powers down to the pope and patriarch in our time), Latter-day Saints teach that God's divine authority was not to be found in the Old World by the middle of the second century A.D. Other than the formal break between Western (Roman) and Eastern (Orthodox) Christianity in A.D. 1054, the Roman Church had control of the Christian faith in the West until the sixteenth century, when bold and courageous Reformers objected to, opposed and broke away from Catholicism.

LDS apostle Jeffrey R. Holland stated:

> In the tumultuous years of the first settlements in this nation, Roger Williams, my volatile and determined 10th great-grandfather, fled—not entirely of his own volition—from the Massachusetts Bay Colony and settled in what is now the state of Rhode Island. He called his headquarters Providence, the very name itself revealing his lifelong quest for divine interventions and heavenly manifestations. But he never found what he felt was the true New Testament church of earlier times. Of this disappointed seeker the legendary Cotton Mather said, "Mr. Williams [finally] told [his followers] that being himself misled, he had [misled them, and] he was now satisfied that there was none upon earth that could administer baptism . . . so he advised them therefore to forego all . . . and wait for the coming of new apostles."[5]

In short, Williams held that there was "no regularly constituted church of Christ, on earth, nor any person authorized to administer any church ordinance, nor can there be until new apostles are sent by the great head of the Church, for whose coming I am seeking."[6]

John Wesley is considered by many to be the father of Methodism. His brother Charles is responsible for hundreds if not thousands of the magnificent hymns sung in Christendom today. Though they were very close as brothers, on one occasion Charles criticized his brother John when the latter ordained a man to an office without authority to do so. Charles wrote:

> How easily are bishops made
> By man or woman's whim:
> Wesley his hands on Coke hath laid,
> But who laid hands on him?[7]

Let's be clear, however, when we speak of the LDS notion of a falling away, a loss of priesthood power. "In our assertion that the church had apostatized," Mormon church leader Alexander Morrison has written,

> We must *not* conclude that all virtue had left the world. We must *not* for even a moment think that with the apostasy a blanket of spiritual darkness, keeping out all light and truth, descended upon humankind, suffocating and choking off every good and worthy thought and deed, erasing Christ from every heart.

That just didn't happen, and we do a grave injustice to all Christians, including ourselves, if we think otherwise.[8]

John Taylor, third president of the Church of Jesus Christ of Latter-day Saints, declared that there were persons during medieval times who "could commune with God, and who, by the power of faith, could draw aside the curtain of eternity and gaze upon the invisible world . . . , have the ministering of angels, and unfold the future destinies of the world. If those were dark ages I pray God to give me a little darkness, and deliver me from the light and intelligence that prevail in our day."[9] A modern Mormon apostle added:

> The line of priesthood authority was broken. But mankind was not left in total darkness or completely without revelation or inspiration. The idea that with the Crucifixion of Christ the heavens were closed and they opened in [Joseph Smith's] First Vision is not true. The Light of Christ would be everywhere present to attend the children of God; the Holy Ghost would visit seeking souls. The prayers of the righteous would not go unanswered.[10]

But let's go back to the question of authority. I have pondered frequently on the Protestant assertion that Mormons aren't Christian because we are not a part of the historic Christian tradition, because we cannot trace our lineage back through the Reformation, through Catholic Christianity, to the first-century church. For me, the irony of this indictment is this: neither can Protestants! How can one claim to be a part of the Christian line of authority when that line was broken in the days of the Reformers? How can one, like Martin Luther, an Augustinian monk, assert and assume a "priesthood of all believers," thereby denouncing the need for a priestly hierarchy and thus apostolic succession back to Peter? Joseph Smith taught: "I will illustrate it [the situation in the Christian world in regard to divine authority] by an old apple tree. Here jumps off a branch and says, I am the true tree, and you are corrupt. If the whole tree is corrupt, are not its branches corrupt? If the Catholic religion is a false religion, how can any true religion come out of it?"[11]

"In becoming a Catholic," Richard John Neuhaus observed,

> one is braced for certain criticisms. Among the most common, usually coming from Protestant sources, is that the person who becomes a Catholic has a "felt need for authority." This is usually said in a somewhat conde-

scending manner by people who say they are able to live with the ambiguities and tensions that some of us cannot handle. But *to say that I have a felt need for authority is no criticism at all. Of course I have, as should we all.* The allegedly autonomous self who acknowledges no authority but himself is abjectly captive to the authority of a tradition of Enlightenment rationality that finally collapses into incoherence. Whether in matters of science, history, religion, or anything else of consequence, we live amid a storm of different and conflicting ideas claiming to be the truth. Confronted by such truth claims, we necessarily ask, "Sez who?" By what authority, by whose authority, should I credit such claims to truth? Answering the question requires a capacity to distinguish between the authoritative and the authoritarian.[12]

"It is in the order of heavenly things," Joseph Smith observed, "that God should always send a new dispensation into the world when men have apostatized from the truth and lost the priesthood; but when men come out and build upon other men's foundations, they do it on their own responsibility, without authority from God."[13] Orson F. Whitney, an LDS apostle, told the following story:

> Many years ago a learned man, a member of the Roman Catholic Church, came to Utah and spoke from the stand of the Salt Lake Tabernacle. I became well-acquainted with him, and we conversed freely and frankly. A great scholar, with perhaps a dozen languages at his tongue's end, he seemed to know all about theology, law, literature, science and philosophy. One day he said to me: "You Mormons are all ignoramuses. You don't even know the strength of your own position. It is so strong that there is only one other tenable in the whole Christian world, and that is the position of the Catholic Church. The issue is between Catholicism and Mormonism. If we are right, you are wrong; if you are right, we are wrong; and that's all there is to it. The Protestants haven't a leg to stand on. For, if we are wrong, they are wrong with us, since they were a part of us and went out from us; while if we are right they are apostates whom we cut off long ago. If we have the apostolic succession from St. Peter, as we claim, there is no need of Joseph Smith and Mormonism; but if we have not that succession, then such a man as Joseph Smith was necessary, and Mormonism's attitude is the only consistent one. It is either the perpetuation of the gospel from ancient times, or the restoration of the gospel in latter days."[14]

Joseph Smith explains that while translating the Book of Mormon in May of 1829, he and his scribe encountered repeatedly the concept of divine authority and the need for the same to operate and oversee the church. Joseph and Oliver Cowdery went into a grove of trees and knelt in prayer on the banks of the Susquehanna River in Harmony, Pennsylvania. According to both of their accounts, a heavenly messenger who introduced himself as John the Baptist, the same who prepared for and baptized Jesus in the New Testament, appeared, laid his hands on their heads and conferred on them what is known as the Aaronic or Lesser Priesthood. A few weeks later they were visited by Peter, James and John, apostles of Jesus Christ in the first century, who conferred on them the Melchizedek or Higher Priesthood, including the power of the Holy Apostleship, the power they had received under the hands of the Savior himself some eighteen hundred years earlier. On April 6, 1830, the church was organized in Fayette, New York.

Latter-day Saints feel strongly that the church of Jesus Christ should and must be built on the foundation of *living* apostles and prophets, with Jesus Christ himself as the chief cornerstone (Ephesians 2:19-20). As marvelous as it is to have the writings and witness of the first-century apostles in the New Testament, one does not derive apostolic authority from a book, even a sacred book. For that reason, the Church of Jesus Christ of Latter-day Saints is presided over by fifteen men—the First Presidency and the Quorum of the Twelve Apostles—who profess to hold the apostolic office. These apostles are charged to be "special witnesses of the name of Christ in all the world." Further, they are tasked to "build up the church, and regulate all the affairs of the same in all nations" (Doctrine and Covenants, 107:23, 33).

"Some years ago," Harold B. Lee (an apostle and the eleventh president of the Church) stated,

> Two missionaries came to me with what seemed to them to be a very difficult question. A young . . . minister had laughed at them when they had said that Apostles were necessary today in order for the true Church to be upon the earth. They said that the minister said, "Do you realize that when the Apostles met to choose one to fill the vacancy caused by the death of Judas they said it had to be one who companied with them and had been a witness of all things pertaining to the witness and resurrection of the Lord? How can you say you have Apostles, if that be the measure of an Apostle?" And so these young men said, "What shall we answer?"

I said to them, "Go back and ask your minister friend two questions. First, how did the Apostle Paul gain what was necessary to be called an Apostle? He didn't know the Lord, and had no personal acquaintance. He hadn't accompanied the Apostles. He hadn't been a witness of the ministry nor of the resurrection of the Lord. How did he gain his testimony sufficient to be an Apostle? And the second question you ask him is, how does he know that all who are today Apostles have not likewise received that witness? I bear witness to you that those who hold the apostolic calling may, and do, know of the reality of the mission of the Lord."[15]

At the very end of our second gathering, which was being held in Pasadena—following a lengthy discussion of Joseph Smith's First Vision and the LDS belief that heavenly messengers had delivered priesthood power to Joseph Smith—one of our evangelical friends said: "You know, it seems to me that perhaps the biggest issue between us, above and beyond everything we have discussed or will discuss in the future, is the matter of authority: who has divine authority, and how it is conveyed." The LDS participants looked at each other and smiled. I responded: "Yes, you have just hit the nail on the head. For us, authority is everything!"

Revealed Truth

Talking About Our Differences

Richard J. Mouw

According to Terryl L. Givens and Matthew Grow in their excellent biography of Parley Pratt—they designate him as "the Apostle Paul of Mormonism"—Pratt was unusual among early Mormons for what drew him to the new religious movement. His conversion was occasioned by his reading of the Book of Mormon. "Up to this point," Givens and Grow report, "the vast majority of converts to Mormonism had been drawn from the Smiths' immediate circles." They "first encountered Joseph Smith and his revelatory claims and then read the Book of Mormon," with the book functioning in their minds primarily "as a sign of a divinely sanctioned restoration." Pratt, however, first "became convinced of Mormonism's truth claims by reading the Book of Mormon and not through association with Smith."[1]

Evangelicals have typically assumed that the key step in becoming a Mormon is an acceptance of the content of the Book of Mormon, which means that the convert now has another book in addition to the Bible as an authoritative revelation from God. Once one makes that move, we have argued, one has abandoned the precious evangelical insistence on *sola scriptura*, "the Bible alone" as our supreme and unique authority.

It certainly is true that *sola scriptura* constitutes a defining difference between evangelicalism and Mormonism. But the issue is misconstrued when the argument is simply about how many "books" we take to be authoritative. And that is why those early Mormons who began by trusting the authority of Joseph Smith provide us with an insightful picture of the real point of departure. They were clear about the fact that the founder of Mormonism was not simply giving them more writings to draw on in their efforts to understand the ways of God and humankind. They saw something new that was happening in his *person*. The ancient office of prophet was now restored.

That does not mean that Parley Pratt's path to Mormonism was the wrong one. Joseph Smith's claim to being a vehicle for divine revelation and the authenticity of the Book of Mormon are both so important that someone could start with one or the other, as long as both end up being embraced. But in terms of logical sequence, affirming the content of the book is secondary. Mormonism's differences with classical Protestant theology do not rest primarily on Mormonism's claim to have one more authoritative body of revealed writings than the rest of us acknowledge—"Another Testament of Jesus Christ," as the official subtitle to the Book of Mormon reads. Rather, the central authority issue is the present-day reality of the prophetic office.

Joseph Smith's most significant claim, then, was not that he found some golden plates which, when translated, gave us the Book of Mormon. Rather, it was that the age of revelation was being restored, with the ancient office of prophet being reestablished in his person. The Mormon poet W. W. Phelps captured the enthusiasm for new revelations in the first verse of the hymn he composed in 1836 for the dedication of the first Mormon temple, in Kirtland, Ohio:

The Spirit of God like a fire is burning;
The latter-day glory begins to come forth;
The visions and blessings of old are returning;
And angels are coming to visit the earth.

The primary significance of the Book of Mormon for the Mormon system of thought, then, is that it was one of many signals from the realm of the divine that a new era of "visions and blessings" was being initiated in the early decades of the nineteenth century. To be sure, it is to be accepted by the faithful as an authoritative text, but its authoritative status derives from that of the prophetic office, which has—to use a common Mormon term— "brought forth" the book. Indeed, the appearance of the Book of Mormon would soon be supplemented by more authoritative writings, all of them revelations that came from the utterances of Joseph Smith and his successors as prophets of the Church of Jesus Christ of Latter-day Saints (LDS).

In an important sense, of course, the idea of the authority of a human prophet is a familiar one—and an admirable one—for evangelical Christians. Much of biblical revelation itself has its origins in the declarations of human prophets. There were times in Old Testament history when godly people had no authoritative book to rely on in understanding the will of God. Noah, Abraham, Moses and Amos—none of these had anything like a Bible. God spoke directly to them. Similarly, in the New Testament and the early church, there was much reliance on oral tradition—the memories of what Jesus had taught and done, and later the memories of the teachings of the apostles.

There came a point, though, when these testimonies were written down, and eventually those writings that the church came to see as supremely authoritative became—in the forming of "the canon"—our Bible. Christians became a "people of the book."

The problem for evangelicals is that Mormons insist on going "behind" the process that produced "the book." What matters about the Bible for Mormonism is not only that it contains the teachings that had come directly from God to apostles and prophets, but also that now, Mormons argue, the prophetic office has been restored. This means that "the canon" is not "closed." Revelations continue. What binds together the Bible, then, with the Book of Mormon, the Doctrines and Covenants, the Pearl of Great Price and any new authoritative deliverances from the continuing line of the true prophets is that they receive their authority from the fact that they come to us from those who have occupied—and continue to occupy—the office of the prophet.

SOLA SCRIPTURA AND CONTINUING REVELATION

How serious is our evangelical disagreement with Mormons about this issue of prophetic authority? Let me say right off that it is a very serious topic. I am a *sola scriptura* Christian. I don't believe that we get new revelations today. On that matter I have serious disagreements with my Mormon friends.

The question, though, is: *How* serious are those disagreements? Is the theological gap between us on this particular subject so wide as to be a deal-breaker?

It would be difficult for me as an evangelical simply to draw the line between my theology and Mormonism's on the issue of *sola scriptura* as such.
The fact is that I have theological disagreements with some folks *within* the
mainstream Christian community on that subject, and I don't simply write
them off the Christian island because we disagree on the issue of extrabiblical authority. It is important, then, to see how Mormonism's insistence on
postbiblical revelation differs from those in Christian tradition who go
beyond *sola scriptura* in their understandings of the scope of revealed truth.

Catholicism is an obvious case in point. Catholics believe they must
accept as authoritative truths—truths, they believe, that come from God—
whose explicit content goes beyond anything we can find in the Bible. Take
the idea of the immaculate conception of Mary—the Catholic teaching that
God, knowing that Mary would someday give birth to the incarnate Son of
God, prepared her by seeing to it that she was born without being affected
by original sin, so that she could carry the sinless babe in her womb.

How did Catholicism come up with that notion? They arrived at it by
reflecting on what the Bible does explicitly teach, namely, that Jesus was
born of a virgin. From that biblical truth, the church reasoned that the birth
by a virgin of the Son of God could only happen if the woman giving birth
was herself free from original sin.

I don't accept that Catholic teaching because I don't accept Catholicism's
underlying idea of authority. Catholics believe in authoritative extrabiblical
deliverances, but not because they see these deliverances as coming from
direct revelation as such. They don't believe that God simply told a pope
about the need to believe in an immaculate conception of Mary. Rather, the
Catholic pope is seen as occupying an infallibly authoritative *teaching*
office—the church's *magisterium*. Popes and bishops *think* about what the
Bible explicitly says, and they draw further teachings out of that kind of
reflection. They see the relationship between these new conclusions and the
biblical ideas that generate them in their minds as—to use a common
Catholic image—an "organic growth." As an oak grows out of an acorn, so
the doctrine of the immaculate conception "grows out of" the fact of the
virgin birth.

The prophetic office in Mormonism differs significantly from this teaching
office in Catholicism. When Mormon leaders declared that it had been re-

vealed to them that plural marriage was no longer permissible (1890), and that the priesthood would now be open to African American males (1978), these teachings did not "grow out of" earlier prophetic deliverances—it reversed them. These teachings were brand new. God had directly conveyed something different, not contained in previous revelations—through the church's prophet.

I should make it clear that in my many hours of discussing theological topics with Mormons, I have never heard any of them say that what they see as their extrabiblical revelations in any way contradict or correct in their minds anything taught in the Bible. Rather, their additional Scriptures are always treated as further elaborations on—extensions of, supplements to—the contents of the Bible. That does not mean that I think their interpretations of biblical teaching are perfectly fine. But it is to point out that when they discuss these matters with care, they do give the impression of a basic compatibility between the Bible and extrabiblical Mormon teachings.

Another group within the broad Christian mainstream who look to new revelations for guidance in their lives is Pentecostalism. Pentecostals—along with those in the newer charismatic communities—also make much of the need for new messages from God. And on occasion these new "revelations" have been viewed as bizarre from the standpoint of historic Christian thought and practice, as when some leader has allegedly been told by God that the world will come to an end on such and such a date, or when someone has it on divine authority that a disaster has hit a particular city because of certain sexual sins.

But the mainstream of Pentecostal/charismatic Christianity has typically not given credence to such claims. At the very least, new messages from God are not seen as adding new *content* to the corpus of biblical truth. Pentecostal prophecies are usually set forth as a restating of biblical teachings for specific contemporary situations, often taking this form: "O my people, says the Lord, do not be discouraged or fearful of what is happening. I am still your God and I will be with you in this time of trouble." Or they may be presented in the form of a specific "word from the Lord" based on prayerful reflection on a specific challenge: "I hear the Lord saying that you should break off this relationship. It is not pleasing to him."

In all of this, the new "revelations" of the Pentecostal/charismatic variety are treated as organically continuous with biblical revelation. They do not contradict the Bible. And they must in an important sense be "organically" continuous with biblical teachings. These new words from the Lord are treated as *confirming* biblical teachings and not as *adding to* them.

THE QUESTION OF AUTHORITY

While there are some surface similarities, then, between the Mormon reliance on authoritative teachings from "extrabiblical" sources, the Mormon insistence on a continuing revelation based on the restoration of the office of prophet goes well beyond anything in the mainstream Christian tradition. Does that mean that we are simply at a stalemate in discussion on this important matter between evangelicals and Mormons? I think not. We might be able to pursue the dialogue further by paying attention, for example, to "best practices" in interfaith and ecumenical dialogue.[2]

One requirement for attempting to be clear about another person's belief about an important matter is to make an effort to understand the belief "from within that person's perspective." This means, I am convinced, that we must be clear about the spiritual dynamic that gave rise to Mormonism in the first place. And this means paying special attention to Joseph Smith's testimony about his spiritual quest as a young boy in western New York State.

During his mid-teens, Smith tells us in his account of his First Vision,[3] he experienced considerable spiritual distress. He was much disturbed by "the confusion and strife among the different denominations" that it seemed "impossible for a person young as I was, and so unacquainted with men and things, to come to any certain conclusion who was right and who was wrong." The prominent Christian groups in his environs—Baptists, Presbyterians, Methodists—were all arguing with each other, and with considerable rancor. Each group was intent on proving their own views to be the right ones and the others' as riddled with error.

And so, the Mormon prophet reports, "In the midst of this war of words and tumult of opinions, I often said to myself, what is to be done? Who of all these parties are right; or, are they all wrong together? If any one of them be right, which is it, and how shall I know it?"

It was at this point, in searching the New Testament, that he came upon the passage in the epistle of James that says, "If any of you lack wisdom, let him ask of God, that giveth to all men liberally, and upbraideth not; and it shall be given him" (James 1:5 KJV).

Evangelicals are not likely to affirm the veracity of Joseph's subsequent account of his encounter with the divine Father and Son—the idea that the members of the Godhead assured Smith that they considered the Christian "creeds" to be "an abomination" is a bit much for us to swallow! But our quite understandably negative reaction to that kind of thing should not keep us from lingering a bit over Smith's report of his youthful distress regarding the theological debates so prominent in those days.

Joseph's struggle over the "war of words and tumult of opinions" that filled the spiritual atmosphere of his youth should resonate with many of us. Many of us have asked his questions about religious disputes: "Who of all these parties are right; or, are they all wrong together? If any one of them be right, which is it, and how shall I know it?"

Those are certainly not uniquely Mormon questions. It is not uncommon, for example, to hear similar expressions of frustration over diverse claims to religious certainty in the testimonies of folks who have embraced Catholicism's doctrine of papal infallibility. When it is impossible to decide among, say, conflicting *interpretations* of the Bible, finding an infallible *interpreter* is an attractive option.

We may not accept Mormonism's solution to the quest for religious certainty. But we can at least identify with the questions that, in Joseph Smith's case, gave rise to that quest.

LOOKING CRITICALLY AT *SOLA SCRIPTURA*

Another requirement for effective dialogue between people holding to differing views about religious matters is that both parties engage in the exchanges in a spirit of humility—which means a willingness to look critically at one's own beliefs and practices. On this score, I am convinced that evangelicals need to take an honest look at our own actual practices with regard to our adherence to *sola scriptura*.

In the early years of the twentieth century, Protestant fundamentalists established a number of "Bible institutes" that offered "practical training" in evangelism, missionary work and church ministries. Reacting against what they viewed as an overintellectualized approach to education in existing graduate theological schools, many of these institutes characterized their pedagogical programs with the slogan, "the Bible is our only textbook."

There is something a little odd, of course, about having an educational institution make such a claim. One could certainly imagine a person who in his or her spiritual life never reads anything but the Bible and pays no attention to what anyone else says about the Bible. But the whole point of sitting in a *classroom* with the intention of learning about the Bible certainly means going beyond shutting out all interpretations of what the Bible says. Classrooms have teachers, and in a Bible institute the teacher presumably does not simply read the biblical text out loud, but talks *about* what the text says. When students are listening to those classroom lectures, how does that differ from their sitting and reading a commentary on a biblical passage?

And then there is the irony of what actually happened in those early twentieth-century Bible institutes. The theology of those schools was dispensational, which offered a rather elaborate scheme for—quoting a favorite dispensationalist passage from 2 Timothy 2:15—"rightly dividing the word of truth." This system of biblical interpretation was set forth in the *Scofield Reference Bible*, where headings and subheadings, along with elaborate interpretative notes, were injected into the biblical text. For those who used that Bible as their "only textbook," their divinely revealed book actually had much extra commentary contained in its pages.

And then there are sermons. The sermon—an essential feature of church worship for evangelicals—is never simply an oral presentation of words from the Bible. It is an elaboration—often an extensive commentary—on the text. Frequently these oral commentaries tell us "what this passage is saying to us today." I have no problems with that. It is crucial for nurturing the believing community in the faith. But there is no question that on many occasions we evangelicals leave a church service having been inspired by a commentary that has taken us well beyond what we would have learned simply by reading the Bible on our own. Again, I rejoice in that—but it is, in an important sense, an experience in "extrabiblical" learning.

As a Calvinist, I also look for guidance in understanding the Bible to the historic Reformed confessional documents: I personally rely heavily in this regard on the Heidelberg Catechism, the Belgic Confession and the canons of the Synod of Dordrecht. A couple of times in my life I have actually signed a "form of subscription" to those documents, affirming that I adhere to the system of theology they set forth. For me they clearly lay out the boundaries and contours of Reformed orthodoxy. Many of my disagreements with other evangelical Christians have to do with the fact that they follow other historical confessional documents—Lutheran, Anglican, Baptist, Wesleyan—in their ways of interpreting key biblical themes.

When I come across someone—as I often do—who teaches something that conflicts with the system of thought set forth in my favorite Reformation-era documents, I regard that teaching as less than fully biblical. Does that mean that I treat these documents as on a par with the Bible? Are they further revelations? No, on both counts. But I do see them as containing a reliable *explication of* the biblical message. They have an authority for me that goes beyond the kind of authority that I would attribute to, say, a very fine biblical commentary.

Having said all of that, I must also observe that there are dangers in the view that I have just been setting forth. The difference between standing under the supreme authority of the Bible as God's Word and subscribing to creedal/confessional documents that we take to be reliable "systematizings" of the teachings contained in God's Word is not always easy to maintain in practice. People who subscribe to extrabiblical creeds and confessions often blur the distinction. And in doing so, we come very close—functionally, if not in theory—to the way Mormons view the relationship between their later Scriptures and the Bible.

That is not to say—I repeat, *that is not to say*—that there is nothing wrong with the way Mormons add on to the content of biblical revelation. But in challenging those things that they have added to the biblical message, it is not enough simply to criticize them for treating with great seriousness things that they have added on to the biblical message. We all do that kind of thing. I once had a conversation with a theologian from a "no creed but Christ" church. He explained to me in great detail why his movement opposed creeds. After I had heard him out, I asked him whether anyone could have an official position in his denomination while also insisting that it is a good thing to have a few creeds. He responded with firmness that such a person would not be allowed to hold an office. The explanation he had given me about why creeds were wrong, he said, was the "officially required" teaching of his church. To my ears, that sounded a lot like something that came close to being a creedal requirement!

My basic point here is this. Those of us who claim "the Bible alone" as our authority often supplement that authority with something else that defines the boundaries of how to understand and interpret biblical authority. In our arguments with Mormons about looking to authoritative extrabiblical sources for our understanding of what God wants us to believe, we need to be very clear about how we treat the "extras" that we ourselves bring into the picture.

TAKING THE CONVERSATION FORWARD

To be sure, none of this closes the gap between Mormon and evangelical views about what we look to in setting forth the nonnegotiable elements of our respective theological systems. But perhaps it can help evangelicals to recognize that the arguments need to be characterized by more nuances than we have typically assumed in the past. And if we are willing to take some steps to find more common ground with Mormonism—even if the ground covered extends over a fairly small theological territory—we may at least be able to create the kind of humility and mutual trust that can take the argument further.

We can also hope that the LDS dialogue partners will join us in being willing to introduce some nuances into the ongoing conversation. What might those nuances look like? In the end, of course, only our Mormon friends can tell us where they find some "wiggle room" in their theological framework of moving a little closer to us. So anything I say here is not to be taken as my own nonnegotiable demands. They are merely some thoughts that are meant to stimulate the conversation.

When I began my own serious explorations of Mormon thought and practice, I was very much helped by Jan Shipps's book *Mormonism: The Story of a New Religious Tradition*. Shipps, a Methodist historian of American religion, presents Mormonism's relationship to historic Christianity as much like Christianity's relationship to Judaism.[4] This is, I am convinced, insightful, and it gives us some important agenda items to pursue.

In each case—Christianity's relationship to Judaism and Mormonism's relationship to the Christian tradition—there is the obvious factor of "adding to" that is at stake. Christianity adds the New Testament to the Old, and

Mormons add more recent prophetic deliverances and writings to the Christian canon. But there are also claims in each case to continuities. Christians insist that the New Testament message supplements and illuminates the materials of the Old Testament, and Mormonism makes a similar claim about their expanded canon.

In my own conversations with Jewish friends, I try to make the point that we Christians—certainly we evangelicals—are honoring elements of Old Testament thought and practice that we believe present-day Judaism has wrongly set aside. In replacing, for example, the sacrificial system of the Old Testament with a thoroughgoing rabbinic Judaism, evangelicals insist that something important is ignored: namely, the powerful address of the Hebrew Scriptures to our shared human guilt and shame. The animal sacrifices of ancient Israel, we believe, point forward to the once-for-all sacrifice of Jesus, the Lamb of God, who by his atoning work on Calvary has taken away sins, bringing about our reconciliation with the God of justice and mercy.

I sense that Mormons see themselves as posing a parallel challenge to those of us in the Christian tradition. They see their teachings and practices as fulfilling the hopes and fears set forth in the Christian canon. Mormonism's "more than" is not meant by the LDS as a "contrary to." They view it as providing a corrective to the ways traditional Christians have read the biblical narrative—further revelations as yet a further unfolding of the plot that gets developed in the Old and New Testaments.

We evangelicals should be willing to engage Mormonism in addressing that agenda of significant—indeed, as I have put it on many occasions, eternally important—topics. And the questions we pose to our LDS friends will not be surprising ones. What is the relationship of what Mormonism sees as later revelations to what we all agree are the revelations set forth in the Bible? Why does it seem to us that Mormonism actually treats the latter, not so much as "fulfilling" the earlier, but *correcting* it? Is there, in Mormon thought, a clear sense of the organic continuity between later and earlier? And if so, how does Mormonism see itself as holding on to what we evangelicals see as the precious themes of the gospel as set forth in the New Testament—especially the proclamation of salvation by grace alone, made possible solely by the completed work of redemption on the cross of Calvary?

Why does the strong Mormon emphasis on the eternality of the marriage relationship seem to overshadow, if not completely ignore, the blessed hope that the church as Christ's Bride, redeemed by his atoning work, will someday meet her Bridegroom face to face?

Several of my Mormon friends report an increased attention to the teachings of the Old and New Testaments in their environs during the past several decades. This is, for many of us in the evangelical world, an encouraging development, because it means that we can explore together the meaning of the good news in the presence of a Word that—however we interpret the larger questions of inspiration and authority—we both profess to accept as a revelation from the Father who sent the Son into the world. Indeed, some of us have already been exploring those matters together, in ways that we have often found to be mutually profitable.

For our part as evangelicals, there is no more exciting conversation to have than one that focuses on the fact that God has sent a Savior into the world to do for us what we could never accomplish for ourselves. Mormons and evangelicals both like to sing that we "love to tell the story of Jesus and his love." A wonderful place to start in exploring our differences about authority and revelation is to share together why it is that we find something in that story that "satisfies my longings as nothing else can do"!

Two Questions and Four Laws

Missiological Reflections on LDS and Evangelical Missions in Port Moresby

C. Douglas McConnell

THE 1980S SAW FRESH APPROACHES to mission practice in the South Pacific. A century of Christian missionary work, represented by Catholic orders, every stripe of Protestants, Pentecostals, Seventh-day Adventists and a smattering of other groups including the Latter-day Saints (LDS), had long established the Pacific Islands as a destination for missions to the ends of the earth. But by 1980 younger people were taking on missions as a short-term experience ranging anywhere from a few weeks to a couple of years. As with any new endeavor, it was long on enthusiasm and short on knowledge, illustrated by a young Youth With A Mission (YWAM) worker who announced one evening after an outreach to a local market, "Those people heard the gospel for the first time today!" Her realization was driven in part by the peculiar dramatic presentation of the YWAMers of that time, but to a larger extent their completely uninformed youthful zeal. This was particularly hard to hear around a dinner table paid for by the very limited budget of a family in their fifth year of mission service a mere two hundred yards from the "unevangelized" market, a site well known to London Missionary Society (LMS) missionary James Chalmers one hundred years earlier.

Each group of young missionaries in Papua New Guinea had some distinctive look or approach to their mission. Evangelicals seemed to be particularly fond of carrying guitars, using projectors to show *The Jesus Film*, reading from the New Testament in the local trade language *Tok Pisin* and wearing T-shirts, shorts and sandals, while riding around in a minivan. In contrast, the LDS missionaries were seen walking or riding their bikes in pairs through the hot, congested streets of Port Moresby, dressed in white shirts, ties, black pants and wearing the telltale black and white name tag with the curious title "Elder," despite their youthful appearance. To be sure both groups were easily distinguished by their physical appearances, but there were more important differences in the approaches of these young evangelicals and Mormons.

The topic of short-term missions was a source of surprising annoyance for those of us who viewed ourselves as true missionaries in the 1980s. Our missionary predecessors trekked through the jungles and highlands to bring the message of the gospel to tribes who had been isolated from the outside world for centuries. The proliferation of missionary activity in the 1950s was fueled by stories from soldiers introduced to the unreached tribes during military service in the South Pacific theater of World War II. Despite our cynicism toward short-term missions, the trend grew in strength through the decade and beyond.

There are significant missiological implications in scope and impact between short-term and longer-term, more holistic approaches, especially with regard to the long, costly history of the older established missions. However, for the purposes of this analysis the comparisons between evangelical and Mormon missions will focus on issues of context, content and contrast that are particularly relevant to missionary encounters. Our reflections will be based on similarities and differences of approach in short-term missionary service in Port Moresby during the 1980s.

The thesis of this chapter is that Mormon missionaries were the beneficiaries of over a century of evangelical missionary presence that created an environment of benign approval by the government and relatively minor challenges to their presence during a decade of proliferation of new mission efforts. The unique message of the Mormon missionaries based on their modern revelation addressed concerns of the Melanesian worldview, previously unexplained by generations of evangelicals. This chapter explores the underlying theology and assumptions that continue to undergird the missionary approaches of Mormons and evangelicals as it relates to short-term missions in the 1980s and today.

CONTEXT: FAVORABLE CONDITIONS FOR MISSIONS

In the years after World War II the city of Port Moresby experienced rapid growth as the capital of the territory of Papua and New Guinea (1945–1975) and then nation of Papua New Guinea (1975). By 1980 the population of Port Moresby was 122,761 with 93 percent being indigenous tribal peoples, doubling the population in a decade.[1] The growing urban center was a magnet for migration from the villages and rural areas. Government and private-sector efforts to keep up with the growth lagged behind, forcing many migrants into squatter settlements. The sociocultural impact created a sense of ambivalence with regard to life in the big city.[2]

Like many other capitals of commonwealth nations, Port Moresby was deeply imprinted by the mission efforts, from schools and hospitals to the growing numbers of churches that dotted the landscape. Missionary efforts were a major part of the strategy for developing a civil society within the British Commonwealth, which in turn was adopted by Australia when first Papua (1905) and then New Guinea (1918) became territories. Nowhere was this more evident than in the social services sector. In the memoirs of his years in Papua New Guinea (PNG), Sir Percy Chatterton wrote, "For the first thirty years of British-Australian rule in Papua the government's attitude to mission schools had been one of benign approval. . . . Health services, like education . . . were [also] in the hands of the mission."[3]

As the years passed and the population grew, there was a proliferation of Christian mission through voluntary associations, building on the benign approval of missionary work. Evangelistic groups such as Campus Crusade for Christ, Navigators, Boys and Girls Brigade, Prison Fellowship, Inter-Varsity and many others were in constant motion preparing or running events, which fostered a kind of continuous evangelistic outreach. Similarly, biblical literacy was of the highest priority among missions and churches alike. Groups like the United Bible Society, Wycliffe Bible Translators/ Summer Institute of Linguistics, Scripture Union, Christian Literature Crusade and other similar groups raised the awareness and accessibility of the Bible for all sectors of society.

It is unimaginable that these factors alone can adequately describe the growing complexities faced by the tribal peoples who made up the first two generations of urban dwellers. Everywhere one looked in the 1980s something new was coming into the city. However, for the purpose of this essay, limiting the focus to the presence and acceptance of missionary work provides an important context for comparing the outreach of Mormons and evangelicals.

Mormon missionary work in Port Moresby began in earnest in 1980.[4] Using the small congregation established in October 1979 as a base, missionaries primarily from Australia shared the unique message of the Church of Jesus Christ of Latter-day Saints, finding both opposition and reception in the city. The opposition came from many quarters, but among the most vocal was the Port Moresby Minister's Fraternal. Fraternal members provided vocal opposition within their congregations and considered attempts to discourage the acquisition of land for an LDS church building.[5] Despite the opposition, the Mormon missionaries persevered in their efforts, so that by 1987 there were 1,450 members in nine branches, and by 1992 the Papua New Guinea Port Moresby Mission was created.[6] Mormon missions were the beneficiaries of the long-standing "benign approval" of missionary work in Port Moresby and beyond.

To understand the missionary work of the Mormons and evangelicals, one must examine some of the central beliefs forming the content of the message as well as the cultural questions that influenced the receptivity.[7]

CONTENT: APPROACHES TO WITNESS

In a cartoon by well-known PNG artist Bob Browne, a young man is portrayed sharing his faith with the repeated assertion that "Jesus is the answer!" In the last frame, an inquisitive bystander asks, "So what is the question?" While at first it appears a simple exchange, on further reflection it is a profound missiological insight: What are the questions in the minds of those who hear the gospel? This strikes at the heart of one of the key issues in missiology, namely, how does the gospel affect the deepest issues of someone's worldview? If there is no relationship between the message of the missionary and the world of the hearer, then there is little room for a real and lasting response.

Foundational to understanding mission is God's revelation in Christ through the incarnation. In reference to the coming of Christ, the prophet Isaiah proclaimed "Look, the young woman is with child and shall bear a son, and you shall name him Immanuel" (Isaiah 7:14), which is quoted in Matthew 1:23: "'And they shall name him Emmanuel,' which means 'God is with us.'"[8] Both evangelicals and Mormons accept the statement in the Gospel of John, "And the Word became flesh and lived among us" (John 1:14).

Beyond the broad affirmation of the incarnation, evangelical theology ties its understanding to the formulations in the creeds of the early church, as seen in the Nicene Creed of A.D. 325. The creed asserts that the Lord Jesus Christ is "begotten of the Father before all worlds . . . begotten not made. . . . Who, for us men for our salvation, came down from heaven, and was incarnate by the Holy Spirit of the virgin Mary, and was made man."[9] The distinction between the LDS and creedal understandings of the incarnation is that according to the creed Jesus became flesh at the virgin birth, whereas the Mormon theology of the incarnation states that the Great Jehovah, the God of ancient Israel, would come to earth, assume a physical body, and be born as Jesus of Nazareth. From God the Father, a glorified and exalted Being—whom the LDS believe to be an embodied God—Jesus would inherit the powers of immortality, and from Mary he would inherit mortality.[10]

Seeing these statements side by side helps us to understand important aspects of the contrast between the two. First, although evangelical theology is expressed among a diverse group of people and traditions making up the evangelical movement, it is at the same time grounded in the historical orthodox Christian faith. LDS beliefs in contrast start with the Bible, both Old and New Testaments (ancient Scripture), then add the testimony of the Book of Mormon, the Pearl of Great Price and the Doctrines and Covenants (modern revelation), which together make up the Scriptures for the Church of Jesus Christ of Latter-day Saints. Second, as noted in the contrasting views of the incarnation, the level of sophistication required to understand the significant differences between evangelical and LDS theology make it very difficult for the average listener to differentiate between them. Hence the methods employed in sharing the message become critical to the mission.

Regarding missionary efforts, despite the significant theological differences between the two views, both groups conclude that witness requires presence. Both evangelicals and Mormons uphold a strong sense of the command to witness to the ends of the earth based on God's self-revelation in the incarnation. Jesus came and dwelt among us, which we follow by going and dwelling among those to whom we are called to witness. Further, both evangelicals and Mormons draw on Christ's commands to his disciples in Matthew 28:19 and Acts 1:8 to justify the global witness. As Dallin H. Oaks and Lance B. Wickman put it, "This Great Commission is obligatory on all Christians."[11]

Building on the obligatory nature of the Great Commission, Mormon teaching adds a sense of uniqueness to their mission as a result of their belief in the restored knowledge and power that is part of the Mormon faith. As Oaks and Wickman write, "For Latter-day Saints . . . the command to witness is fundamental to all their belief and practice. . . . This duty to witness and this conviction of its God-given importance are still vital to the self-image, faith, and practice of Latter-day Saints."[12] Putting this strong belief into practice, missionary service is the "prime focus of the Aaronic (lesser) Priesthood, which is held by young men aged twelve and older."[13] From birth, boys are prepared for service with the full support of their family and local congregation. The young unmarried men serve in mission for two years. Young women who are also unmarried are eligible to serve in mission normally limited to eighteen months, but are not required to serve. In a second opportunity to serve, couples nearing retirement are also encouraged to serve for a period of six to eighteen months.

At the time of this writing, the LDS Church estimates that it has 85,000 full-time missionaries in more than 125 nations and territories.[14] David B. Barrett and Todd M. Johnson estimated that all Christian foreign missionaries totaled 420,000 globally in mid-2000.[15] When one considers the estimated relative size of the LDS Church to be 15 million compared to 648 million evangelicals in 2000, the question of commitment becomes a salient factor.[16]

In contrast to this universal practice of Mormons, evangelicals have a range of traditions. In some evangelical churches missionary service is both encouraged and expected for those who are sincere in their faith commitment. One of the trends identified in the 1980s in Port Moresby was the growth of teams coming to PNG from local evangelical churches in other countries to serve specific projects (building, teaching vacation Bible schools or similar time-bound projects), usually for up to a month. The more common types of short-term service were those associated with a missionary society or other Christian organizations. Of all the groups active in Port Moresby in the 1980s, Youth With a Mission (YWAM) and Operation Mobilization (OM) were two of the most dynamic. As the decade progressed, increasing numbers of Papua New Guinean young people participated in YWAM teams overseas as well as joining the OM ministry ships for up to two years. Among evangelicals, missionary service, full-time or short term, does not carry the same expectations for the average young person.

Returning to the missiological question, "What is the question?" a critical difference between Mormon and evangelical missions is found in the approach used. The underlying assumption in LDS mission is the Golden Questions approach. That is, every person spoken to by a Mormon missionary or layperson is asked two basic questions, "What do you know about the Mormons?" and "Would you like to know more?" Mormon practice uses the gentle invitation of Christ seen in Jesus' response to the question from John's disciples in John 1:39: "Come and see." This ties directly into Brigham Young's concept of something more, leaving the LDS missionary firmly committed to persistent witness, according to Oaks and Wickman, but they "do not seek to pull others away from the truth they have but to add to their knowledge, their happiness, and their peace."[17] As Bob Millet puts it, "The burden of proof, the effort to find out, rests with honest truth seekers."[18] Perhaps one of the most telling statements about Mormon witness was made by the church's fifteenth president, Gordon B. Hinckley: "[We are] not argumentative. We do not debate. We, in effect, simply say to others, 'Bring all the good that you have and let us see if we can add to it.'"[19] This persistent gracious manner is a hallmark of LDS mission.

In a very different underlying assumption, the evangelical missionary tends to believe that persuasion is a necessary part of the equation. Bob Browne's cartoon was a spoof on the common evangelical approach of telling people what they should believe, no questions asked. In contrast to the Golden Questions, evangelicals in 1980s Port Moresby were more likely to use the Four Spiritual Laws developed by Campus Crusade for Christ (CCC) founder, Bill Bright. Outreach teams obtained copies of the CCC booklets published locally under the direction of then CCC director Kenson Kuba. Kuba attracted many of the brightest young men and women to this straightforward approach. As the decade progressed, the CCC project known as *The Jesus Film* was widely used in all types of evangelistic work. YWAM teams were more likely to use a dramatic presentation characterized by the call to repent and believe. Whatever the approach, in the background is the strong concept of calling people to follow Christ, nothing more, nothing less.

This bears further exploration, as both experience and the relevant literature make a convincing case that LDS missionaries share the same passionate desire, but the culture of the mission tends to regulate the methods more than in the movement we know as evangelical missions.

CONTRAST: DIFFERENT METHODS, DIFFERENT APPEAL

One of the most startling contrasts of the two approaches to mission in Port Moresby is the starting points. For evangelicals the message was essentially the same as the one preached by William Lawes and James Chalmers and the early London Missionary Society missionaries over a century earlier.[20] Based on the biblical record, the message holds the fourfold conviction that (1) God loves all the peoples of the world and has revealed the plan of salvation; (2) every person has sinned and is separated from God; (3) in his life, death and resurrection Jesus atoned for the sins of humankind, reconciling all those who believe to God; and (4) every individual must receive Jesus Christ as Savior and Lord, thus experiencing the fullness of God's love and plan. These basic tenets of the faith were codified in the Four Spiritual Laws developed by Campus Crusade for Christ.[21]

The diversity of churches and voluntary missionary societies making up the evangelical presence in Port Moresby adapted the characteristic fourfold message with different emphases and a multitude of methods. The range of denominational and nondenominational churches was a source of confusion to the newly converted. So common was the multiplication of Christian groups and the inherent confusion among tribal peoples that one popular missiologist at the time referred to this diversity as Western tribalism. The challenge for the evangelical missionaries was to present the timeless message of the gospel while at the same time representing the difference between the churches in the movement in such a way that it recognized the illusive reality of unity in diversity. The freshness of the presentations by the short-term mission teams provided many nominal Christians with a new sense of the timeless message.

For Mormon missionaries the primary evangelistic task was winning the opportunity to ask the Golden Questions. Dressed neatly in clothes that were uncommon in the tropics, the distinctively foreign missionaries sought to bring additional knowledge to the hearers. In contrast to the individual or teams of the evangelicals, Mormons served in pairs, making use of tracts describing the restored knowledge of the church. While the benign approval and the presence of a variety of other missions allowed the Mormons to enter the city unhindered, the fact that they were not well known was a challenge to overcome. Even in the name the Church of Jesus Christ of Latter-day Saints, the hearer was faced with the fact that this group was not part of the mix of evangelicals represented by the many churches.

If the evangelical missions were bound by the "old, old story," Mormons were equipped with modern revelation inviting "investigators" to learn things lost to other Christian groups. Having new truth to share about the questions of life appealed to traditional Melanesian beliefs. Among the many traditional beliefs were relational concerns for family both living and deceased, the ability to access power through rituals and knowledge beyond the grasp of the uninitiated, and the nature of material possessions with special reference to acquiring the material wealth so commonly held by the expatriate community. In a particularly relevant way, Mormon teaching addresses the nature of family, specifically the focus on genealogies, the temple rituals where sacred ordinances are administered and the church welfare societies, ensuring the well-being of church members. To illustrate, a particularly attractive aspect of temple worship relates to the eternal linking of families: "Linked together forever; the living are linked to their kindred dead; heaven and earth are linked as one, worshippers are linked to the Savior."[22] Whatever the specific appeal to the Melanesian mind, the widespread success of Mormon missions leaves little doubt that the witness of the Latter-day Saints is answering questions on the minds of Pacific Islanders.

PERSONAL REFLECTION

After two years of public teaching in rural Australia, our family served
with the Asia Pacific Christian Mission from 1976–1991, primarily in Australia and Papua New Guinea. During the 1980s I served as a missionary
pastor in Port Moresby, where I had the opportunity to participate actively
in the interchurch fellowships among evangelicals and beyond. My interaction with Mormons was limited, and I was one of the outspoken critics
of their attempts to acquire property for building their church building
and mission home. In the years since leaving the South Pacific, involvement
in interfaith conversations has become a more prominent part of my work
as an evangelical professor and missiologist, providing more opportunity
to reflect on my time in Papua New Guinea and how I might approach
things differently today.

For the past decade I have participated in a dialogue between Mormon
and evangelical scholars. The purpose of the dialogue was clearly established
by Mormon scholar Bob Millet in a presentation to the Trustees and President's Cabinet at Fuller Seminary. "We're not always sure we are using the
right language when we speak theologically about the Godhead, salvation,
and the like. You folks are giving us a safe space to explore these matters. We
need people to cut us some slack for a while."[23] As Richard Mouw, professor
and president emeritus of Fuller Seminary, summarized it, "Our goal is
simply to better understand each other in ways that our hostile relations in
the past did not allow for."[24] As a missiologist I appreciate the wisdom in this
approach to dialogue, particularly from the perspective of convicted civility,
a position that brings together my missionary convictions with a deep
concern for building a civil society.[25] We afford one another the opportunity
for sincere and prolonged witness while resisting the competitive drive that
so often characterizes dialogue on the one hand and universalist affirmations on the other.

One of the insights emerging from the dialogue is that I now see it as
exploring theology together with a group of dear and respected friends, with
full knowledge that we represent two distinct faith traditions. As was intended from the beginning, evangelicals afford Mormons the opportunity
to explore the vocabulary and methods of theological reflection. But what
was not stated so clearly was that Mormons afford evangelicals the oppor-

tunity to explore a prophetic, lived religion that defies the categorizations so neatly assigned in our bounded-set approaches. In our dialogues I am often faced with Mormon categories and beliefs that are more like those of majority-world Pentecostals than Western Reformed theologies. There is much to be gained for both sides.

A second insight came as a result of visiting the Mormon historical sites at Palmyra, New York; Nauvoo, Illinois; and Salt Lake City, Utah. In listening to the missionary monologues at the historical sites and walking the path in the sacred grove near Palmyra, I had to adjust to the fact that among the missionaries we were being invited to answer the Golden Questions. In a conversation at Nauvoo, a question from a Brigham Young University religion professor drove home the Mormon mission approach when he asked, "Is Joseph a possibility for you?" Clearly there is a missionary zeal embedded in every one of the dialogue participants. As an evangelical missionary I never lose hope that all of us will know salvation in Christ Jesus. For me the dialogue can only be credible if I am a faithful witness to the gospel, seeking to understand and respond to the questions being asked. This volume represents an honest attempt to deepen that understanding.

BECOMING AS GOD

Robert L. Millet

WHAT WAS FOR ME ONE OF the most stimulating and provocative of all our dialogues was our conversation on deification, *theosis*, the Latter-day Saint (LDS) doctrinal concept of the capacity of men and women to become like God. There were several occasions in the preceding years when this issue had arisen, and brief explanations had been offered by the LDS dialogists. We had agreed, however, that the subject was important enough to merit an entire dialogue and that there were a number of other theological matters that seemed to be more central and fundamental to Mormon belief and practice—authority, revelation and Scripture, the nature of fallen humanity, the atonement, grace and works.

But eventually it came time to engage what is, unfortunately, one of the most controversial features of the Mormon faith—namely, the idea, disturbing and even blasphemous to many, that it is possible for fallen and finite mortals to one day become as our exalted and infinite God. Rich Mouw and I had chatted about this topic for some time and wondered how we might approach it. Rich called me one day and said, in essence, "Bob, I think I have an idea. We have a very impressive member of our faculty here at Fuller Seminary who has done some work in this area of deification. His name is Veli-Matti Kärkkäinen." Rich agreed to speak with Kärkkäinen and see if he would be willing to lead our discussion when we next met in Pasadena. Kärkkäinen agreed, and we committed to read Kärkkäinen's short work *One With God* as well as some LDS writings on the subject.

There were certain things about this particular dialogue that impressed me. This conversation seemed far less an evaluation of Mormonism, a test of LDS Christianity or an assessment of just how close or far away we were from our evangelical counterparts. There was much less comparison and contrast, fewer "tryouts for Christianity," as Spencer Fluhman called it. Rather, the topic was so stimulating, the subject matter so penetrating, the literature so extensive, there almost didn't seem to be an "us" and a "them." Instead, we worked and learned together as a group, not as two separate or even competing faith traditions. While most of the Mormons in the group were quite familiar with quotations about deification from early church fathers and even later Eastern Orthodox scholars and churchmen, some of the evangelical participants seemed to be much less aware of this literature. That is, it was as though we had entered a realm of study and engagement that was almost foreign to evangelicals and evangelical theology, a realm, however, with which LDS participants were much more comfortable. Without getting too specific, let me say simply that both groups found themselves making comments like, "Wow! This is fascinating stuff!" or "I really need to plumb the depths of this field more." In this chapter I will offer a very brief impression (my own, admittedly) of deification—one Latter-day Saint's explanation of why Mormons hold to this belief.

Some years ago I read the following from popular Christian writer Max Lucado: "God loves you just the way you are, but he refuses to leave you that way. He wants you to be *just like Jesus*."[1] Dallas Willard, a Christian philosopher at the University of Southern California, likewise noted that "Jesus offers himself as God's doorway into the life that is truly life. Confidence in him leads us today, as in other times, to become his apprentices in eternal living."[2] Joseph Smith taught in lecture five of the *Lectures on Faith* (a series of lectures delivered in Kirtland, Ohio, in the winter of 1835–1836) that all those who keep God's commandments "shall grow up from grace to grace, and become heirs of the heavenly kingdom, and joint heirs with Jesus Christ; possessing the same mind, being transformed into the same image or likeness."[3] New Testament scholar N. T. Wright explained that "you become like what you worship. When you gaze in awe, admiration, and wonder at something or someone, you begin to take on something of the character of the object of your worship."[4]

For members of the Church of Jesus Christ of Latter-day Saints, our God is God. There is no knowledge of which he is ignorant and no power he does not possess. Scriptural passages that speak of him being the same yesterday, today and forever clearly have reference to his divine attributes—his love, justice, constancy and willingness to bless his children. For Mormons, eternal life consists in being *with* God; in addition, it entails being *like* God.

More than once I have heard the LDS view of deity described as a belief in a "finite God." I suppose because of the one statement by Joseph Smith that God was once a man, people jump to the conclusion that the God in whom Latter-day Saints put their complete trust is not the same being as the God of the omnis. I am one, however, who is very uncomfortable with stating that we believe in a finite God; all of the Scriptures state otherwise. From the Doctrine and Covenants, for example, we learn that Latter-day Saints worship "a God in heaven, who is infinite and eternal, from ever-lasting to everlasting, the same unchangeable God, the framer of heaven and earth, and all things which are in them" (20:17). Our Father in heaven is indeed omnipotent, omniscient and, by the power of his Holy Spirit, omnipresent. From our perspective, he is a gloried, exalted, resurrected being, "the only supreme governor and independent being in whom all fullness and perfection dwell; . . . in Him every good gift and every good principle dwell; He is the Father of lights; in Him the principle of faith dwells independently, and He is the object in whom the faith of all other rational and accountable beings center for life and salvation."[5] The Almighty sits enthroned "with glory, honor, power, majesty, might, dominion, truth, justice, judgment, mercy, and an infinity of fullness" (Doctrines and Covenants 109:77). He is not a student, an apprentice or a novice.

As late as 1840, Matthew S. Davis, a man not of the LDS faith, heard Joseph Smith preach in Washington, D.C. In a letter to his wife, he explained that Smith taught the following: "I believe that there is a God, possessing all the attributes ascribed to Him by all Christians of all denominations; that He reigns over all things in heaven and on earth, and that all are subject to his power." Davis also reported that he heard the Mormon prophet say: "I believe that God is eternal. That He had no beginning, and can have no end. Eternity means that which is without beginning or end."[6] That just doesn't sound like a "finite" God to me.

Some years ago, Greg Johnson, Craig Hazen and I accompanied Elder

Jeffrey Holland, one of the current Mormon apostles, to Biola University to meet with several evangelical pastors in Southern California. Elder Holland made a few brief remarks and then opened the meeting for questions. The spirit there was amiable and respectful, and the questions were fair and information-seeking in nature. One of the questions was: "Is it true that you folks believe that you will one day be like God, create worlds, preside over those worlds, travel and govern throughout the cosmos, and so on?" Elder Holland replied, in essence: "Well, I don't know anything about that planetary stuff. What I do know for sure, and the Scriptures confirm this, is that through the atonement of Jesus Christ and the sanctifying power of the Spirit, we may develop and mature in Christlike attributes, the divine nature, until we are prepared and comfortable to dwell in the presence of God and Christ, together with our families, forever."

A few years back, the following statement was placed on the official LDS Church *Newsroom* page, which contains many of the most frequently asked questions about our beliefs and practices. Question: Do Latter-day Saints believe that they will "get their own planet"? The response:

> No. This idea is not taught in Latter-day Saint scripture, nor is it a doctrine of the Church. This misunderstanding stems from speculative comments unreflective of scriptural doctrine. Mormons believe that we are all sons and daughters of God and that all of us have the potential to grow during and after this life to become like our Heavenly Father (see Romans 8:16-17). The Church does not and has never purported to fully understand the specifics of Christ's statement that "in my Father's house are many mansions (John 14:2).[7]

While Latter-day Saints believe that becoming like God is entailed in eternal life (Doctrines and Covenants, 132:19-20), we do not believe we will ever, worlds without end, unseat or oust God the eternal Father or his only begotten Son, Jesus Christ; those holy beings are and forever will be the Gods we worship. Even though we believe in the ultimate deification of human beings, I am unaware of any authoritative statement in LDS literature that suggests that men and women will ever worship any being other than the ones within the Godhead. Parley P. Pratt wrote one of the first theological treatises within Mormonism, *Key to the Science of Theology*. In describing those who are glorified and attain eternal life, Parley states: "The difference between Jesus Christ and another immortal and celestial man is this—the man is subordinate to Jesus Christ, does nothing in and of himself, but does all things in the name of Christ, and by his authority, being of the same mind, and ascribing all the glory to him and his Father."[8]

Let me now speak briefly about the frequently made comment that Mormons believe "God and man are of the same species." As we have already noted, God possesses every godly and divine attribute in perfection. There is nothing he does not know and no power he does not possess. What Joseph Smith experienced in the grove of trees in 1820 and in subsequent encounters with Deity, however, suggests to us that our heavenly Father is not simply a force in the universe, not even the most powerful force in that universe; that he is not merely a congeries of laws or the great First Cause of the philosophers; that he is a he, a man, a glorified and exalted man, as named in one of the books of our scriptural canon, the Pearl of Great Price, Man of Holiness (Moses 6:57; 7:35); that he has form; and that he is possessed of substance. We take this a step further. Joseph Smith taught that "the Father has a body of flesh and bones as tangible as man's; the Son also; but the Holy Ghost has not a body of flesh and bones, but is a personage of spirit" (Doctrines and Covenants, 130:22).

Having said that, we do not believe that the corporeality of God inhibits or confines or restrains or restricts him in any way, any more than Jesus' resurrected body confined, restrained or restricted him. The Scripture reports that the risen Lord, just prior to his ascension, said, "All power is given unto me in heaven and in earth" (Matthew 28:18 KJV). Jesus does not sound finite or limited or lacking in anything. Now, this is what we mean when we say that God and man are of the same species. To be sure, we readily acknowledge that the chasm between a fallen, mortal being and an immortal, resurrected and glorified Being is immense (see Doctrine and Covenants, 20:17; 109:77), but for Mormons who are true to their founding scriptural texts, to become like God—which to us really means to become more Christlike, more filled with the Spirit and the fruit of that Spirit (Galatians 5:22-25)—is that toward which we press.

We do not believe we can work ourselves into glory or godhood, can gain eternal life through human effort alone. One does not become more and more Christlike through sheer grit and willpower. Central to any and all spiritual progress is the atonement of Jesus Christ, and it is only by and through his righteousness and the shedding of his precious blood that we may be declared righteous. It is only by the power of that blood that we may be cleansed and sanctified from the taint and tyranny of sin. And it is only by and through the power of his everlasting life that we receive life—energy, strength, vitality, renewal, enabling power—to accomplish what we could never accomplish on our own.

Just how strange, then, is the LDS doctrine of deification? How unscriptural is it? It's fascinating to read two statements made by Martin Luther. The first, written in his Christmas sermon of 1514, affirms, "Just as the word of God becomes flesh, so it is certainly also necessary that the flesh become word. For the word becomes flesh precisely so that the flesh may become word. In other words: God becomes man so that man may become God. Thus power becomes powerless so that weakness may become powerful."[9] The second, written in 1519, says, "For it is true that a man helped by grace is more than a man; indeed, the grace of God gives him the form of God and deifies him, so that even the Scriptures call him 'God' and 'God's son.'"[10] I identify with the following from beloved evangelical scholar John Stott: "I want to share with you where my mind has come to rest as I approach the end of my pilgrimage on earth and it is—God wants his people to become like Christ. Christlikeness is the will of God for the people of God. . . . In other words, if we claim to be a Christian . . . God's way to make us like Christ is to fill us with his Spirit."[11]

To summarize, Latter-day Saints teach that through the cleansing and transforming power of the blood of Jesus Christ, and through the sanctifying and divinizing power of the Holy Spirit, men and women may over time mature spiritually, may, as our Eastern Orthodox friends would put it (and with which we would have no argument), partake of the *energies*, not the *essence* of God our Father, a process that is referred to variously as participation, transformation, union, intermingling, partaking, elevation, kingship, interpenetration, joint-heirship, son and daughterhood, adoption, re-creation and realization.[12]

Hyrum Mack Smith (a Mormon apostle in the early twentieth century) and Janne M. Sjodahl offered the following insightful commentary on the verse in the Doctrine and Covenants, "Then shall they be gods" (132:20):

> What a wonderful Revelation this is, when compared with the narrow ideas held in the world! Children of kings are princes and princesses, associating

on terms of equality with their royal parents, and having a good chance of becoming kings and queens themselves. But when we say that the privilege of God's children is to associate with Him in the eternal mansions, and that they may become gods, then the world does not understand us, and many deem us guilty of blasphemy. They seem to think that they honor God by supposing that His children are infinitely inferior to Him. What kind of Father is He, then, that He should feel it an honor to be the progenitor of an inferior off-spring? Is there a king on earth that would feel honored by having degenerates and beggars for children? Do not fathers and mothers rejoice in the progress of their children? Is it not their ambition to educate and train their loved ones, until these shall reach the highest possible degree of intelligence and efficiency? Surely, we can do no greater honor to God, our Father, than to admit the divine possibilities which He has implanted in His offspring, and which will be developed under His tuition in this life and hereafter, until His children are perfect as He is perfect.[13]

Frankly, whether the LDS doctrines of exaltation and deification are the same as that which was delivered by the church fathers, by Eastern Orthodox thinkers of the past and present, or with modern Christians like C. S. Lewis,[14] or whether Joseph Smith meant just what they mean, is absolutely immaterial. I wish to suggest simply that the doctrine of deification, divinization, *theosis* has been around for a long, long time throughout Christian history and that it should require more than a modicum of cognitive and spiritual dissonance for traditional Christians to dismiss or ignore it outright.

"The whole design of the gospel," former LDS Church president Gordon B. Hinckley declared,

is to lead us onward and upward to greater achievement, even, eventually, to godhood. This great possibility was enunciated by the Prophet Joseph Smith in the King Follett sermon and emphasized by President Lorenzo Snow. . . . Our enemies have criticized us for believing in this. Our reply is that this lofty concept in no way diminishes God the Eternal Father. He is the Almighty. He is the Creator and Governor of the universe. He is the greatest of all and will always be so. But just as any earthly father wishes for his sons and daughters every success in life, so I believe our Father in Heaven wishes for his children that they might approach him in stature and stand beside him resplendent in godly strength and wisdom.[15]

Is Mormonism Biblical?

J. B. Haws

From the get-go, it seems important to note that this chapter is more about public perception and portrayal and practice than it is about theology (although that certainly plays into it). The "public" in mind here includes the American populace generally and the Mormon and evangelical communities specifically. This focus stems from a belief that perception can become as serious an impediment to dialogue and understanding as almost anything else.

Mormons present a real taxonomy problem. Evangelical Christians (and others) have not quite known what to do with the Latter-day Saints (LDS) when they've encountered them—and the confusion is certainly understandable. Mormons want to be seen as Christians, yet they themselves do not want to be identified as Protestant or Catholic or Orthodox. What's more, Latter-day Saints do not object when they are told that they do not fit in the family of historic Christianity. One almost insurmountable difficulty has been that many evangelical Christians feel that the label "Christian" is—or at least should be, for all intents and purposes—exclusively identical to "historic" or "orthodox" or "trinitarian" Christianity; such modifiers, to them, could feel almost absurdly redundant. At least since the years of the modernist/fundamentalist controversy of the turn of the twentieth century, a number of observers have accused conservative Christians of guarding that label—"Christian"—in almost a gatekeeper role as a way to preserve Protestant, fundamental, *sola scriptura*, *sola fide* orthodoxy. Hence for some whose interpretation of "Christian" is the strictest, even Roman Catholics and Eastern Orthodox and mainline Protestants can fall outside of that narrowest "Christian" domain.[1] However, what is at stake here is public misunderstanding—and this is a big deal for Mormons.

Because of cultural familiarity and visibility—and the backing of two millennia of history—Catholic or Eastern Orthodox or Episcopalian public standing is not threatened in the same way that Mormon public standing is threatened when the "not-fully-Christian" label is used. Latter-day Saints often see being called non-Christians as such a serious affront because it conveys the impression to a mostly still-uninformed public that Mormons do not believe in the divinity of Jesus Christ—a crucial misconception— rather than the reality that they do not believe in the *traditional* Christian doctrine of a triune God.[2]

Whether the perpetuation of such an impression is intentional is almost beside the point. Richard Mouw has eloquently called for reconsideration about "bear[ing] false witness against our neighbors."[3] So in the spirit of getting things right and giving people a better way to understand their religious neighbors, this essay offers an alternative label that could go a long way in fostering conversation. That label centers on this word: *biblical*.

When someone asks, "Are Mormons Christians?" in reality neither a "yes" nor a "no" brings appropriate clarity, because as Jan Shipps has articulated so well, it is not always easy to know what the inquirer has in mind by *Christian*.[4] "It depends" can be a better answer because it calls for more conversation, but it still could leave far too much ambiguity—especially if someone does not wait around for more than that initial sound bite. So in the spirit of seeking brevity *and* clarity, what if the standard answer on websites and in college textbooks and in Sunday School courses were something like this: "Mormons are biblical Christians, but not trinitarian or traditional Christians"? Or, even better, the formulation suggested by Philip Barlow: Mormons are "Bible-believing Christians—but with a difference."[5] Such a label, this essay suggests, is merited on a number of counts, and it does justice to both evangelical and Mormon sensitivities and concerns. Most important, the contention here is that only by labeling Mormons in this way can that "difference" be fairly represented and understood. That's the place where these conversations should lead, in any case.

"Mormons as Biblical" Fits with Evangelical Diversity

It almost goes without saying that a descriptor like *biblical* might be just as contested *within* evangelical circles as it would be in Mormon-evangelical dialogue. With recent titles (let alone historic ones) like Christian Smith's *The Bible Made Impossible: Why Biblicism Is Not a Truly Evangelical Reading of Scripture*, or Kenton Sparks's *Sacred Word, Broken Word: Biblical Authority and the Dark Side of Scripture*, or Carlos Bovell's *Rehabilitating Inerrancy in a Culture of Fear*, it quickly becomes obvious that Mormons who seek the "biblical" label are jumping into an already lively debate.[6]

But that seems precisely the point: *biblical* matches a degree of diversity that is already well tolerated within the evangelical community. And applying that label to Mormons fits the way parishioners in the pews *and* professors in their publications are currently treating that accepted diversity.

Brian Malley's interesting anthropological study, *How the Bible Works*, contains some very telling interviews with members of Creekside Baptist Church. Malley asked Sandra, a "middle-aged woman who had attended the church for some years" (and Malley called this interview "fairly representative"), "Do you consider yourself an evangelical Christian?" When Sandra replied, "Yes," Malley followed with this question: "And what do you mean by that?" Sandra's answer: "Again, the born again thing enters into it. The literal belief in the Bible. Those are the two basic components of what I deem to be evangelical."[7]

If we set aside for now the very tricky issue of what qualifies as being "born again"—which is, of course, a topic worthy of many more evangelical-Mormon conversations!—there is something important in Sandra's "literal belief in the Bible" category. Most Latter-day Saints would not hesitate or squirm in the least if they were asked to subscribe to that qualifier. If by "literal belief" one means to say that God delivered his Word to human scribes and mouthpieces, Mormons would heartily affirm that. If by "literal belief" one means to say that the Bible recounts events of history that actually took place—no matter how unlikely or miraculous those events seem—Mormons would heartily affirm that. If by "literal belief" one means to say that the Bible bears witness to the full divinity of Jesus Christ, Mormons would heartily affirm that.[8]

None of this is meant to dismiss the reality that Sandra and an equally representative Mormon might conceive of "literal belief" in different ways; of course that's possible, even likely. But what matters more here, it seems, is the reality that Sandra and a *fellow* Creekside Baptist attendee might conceive of "literal belief" in different ways—yet in that case, those differences would probably never be seen as irreconcilable, theological, "in communion" deal-breakers. What this means is that the points of contention *between* Mormons and evangelical Christians on questions related to biblical inerrancy would probably boil down to be essentially the same as the points of contention *among* evangelical Christians themselves. (Scholars who have participated in Mormon-evangelical dialogue sessions have speculated that this might be a deeper reality on a number of presumed points of divergence for Mormons and evangelicals.)

Brian Malley's conclusion that "the *closure* of the canon affords *openness* in interpretation" might make many evangelicals uncomfortable, but he does seem to have captured a sense of the shared assumptions that can go a long way in explaining why many Christians balk at calling Mormons "biblical": Mormons are anomalous because of their expanded canon. Yet when it comes to approaching the Bible, this same interpretive reality that Malley identifies might bring Mormons into that biblical fold.

> Evangelical Christians do indeed maintain a sharp boundary between the Bible and all other texts, and a stereotypical one at that: they maintain a boundary around the Bible that they expect to be recognized as such by all evangelicals. . . . This conventional boundary affords a different kind of flexibility. . . . The contents of the text can be left unspecified [so] long as evangelicals can know what counts as a biblical text.[9]

The contention here is that, with a little more consideration, it becomes harder to argue that Latter-day Saints do things with the Bible that are *functionally* different from what evangelical Christians do, extrabiblical texts aside for the moment (and more on those extrabiblical texts later).

Here's another interview excerpt from Creekside Baptist: Scott told Malley, "I have several Bibles, and I have like a bookshelf, like a little section in that room [his reading room] where I keep the Bible I'm reading. And usually I'll read a paraphrase like *The Message*. I like *The Message* because it makes me think in a new way about things. I don't always agree with his interpretations and his paraphrase, but. . . ."[10]

It is this question of interpretation—and this tolerated diversity of interpretation—that deserves more attention, particularly here on questions about the acceptability of Mormons-as-biblical. Craig Blomberg of Denver Seminary offered a thoughtful response to Christian Smith's *The Bible Made Impossible*. One of Blomberg's general tacks was to argue that Smith had used one type of "biblicism"—that of "grass-roots pure fundamentalists"—to create a "straw man" that stood in for "an entire movement" but might be "true only of a largely untutored minority within it." Christian Smith contends that "biblicism fails due to 'pervasive interpretive pluralism.'" Blomberg counters that this interpretive pluralism does not affect the fundamentals of the Christian faith—and here's what Blomberg enumerated along those lines: "I know of no pervasive interpretive pluralism in evangelicalism, for example, concerning the full deity and full humanity of Jesus, about the moral attributes of God, about the universal sinfulness of humanity (as distinct from the origins of that universality), about Christ's bodily resurrection and bodily return, or about the centrality of a love ethic." The point that cannot be missed about Blomberg's list is that evangelicals and Mormons would find real agreement on each one of those issues. On this count, then, interpretive differences should not disqualify Latter-day Saints as "biblical."[11]

At this point in this essay, readers on both sides of this question have probably already asked themselves this: "Okay, but what about Article of Faith 8?" This is the well-known affirmation that Mormons "believe the Bible to be the word of God as far as it translated correctly; [Mormons] also believe the Book of Mormon to be the word of God." At least two things seem to be happening in this statement (which Joseph Smith composed in an 1842 letter to a Chicago newspaper editor).[12] First, Latter-day Saints *seem* to be casting aspersions at the Bible's trustworthiness. And second, Latter-day Saints elevate another book to the level of Scripture, the level of the Bible.

The trustworthiness issue is the easiest to deal with. To the degree that evangelicals find Article of Faith 8 troubling, much of that trouble has been, admittedly, self-inflicted by Mormons. With a nod again to Jan Shipps's insightful analysis, for most of their history Latter-day Saints sought to distinguish themselves from historic Christianity in order to draw attention to their church's raison d'être. In this effort Mormons have been quick to point out the translation and transmission problems in the Bible's long and colorful history. For Mormons, that history only underscores the need for new revelation to transcend the fractious infighting that has long characterized Christian denominationalism.[13]

But the significance of the "as far as it is translated correctly" phrase for Latter-day Saints essentially matches several articles in the Chicago Statement on Biblical Inerrancy—a point Robert Millet persuasively made in a presentation at the 2008 Society of Biblical Literature meetings.[14] And this may be of surprise to many evangelicals. Latter-day Saints would not hesitate to affirm, with Carl F. H. Henry and J. I. Packer and a host of other signatories of the Chicago Statement, that "inspiration, strictly speaking, applies only to the *autographic text of Scripture*, which in the providence of God can be ascertained from available manuscripts with *great* accuracy. We further affirm that copies and translations of Scripture are the Word of God *to the extent* that they faithfully represent the original."[15]

Mormons would see the phrases "to the extent" (from the Chicago Statement) and "as far as" (from Article of Faith 8) as synonymous, and they would note, appreciatively, that the Chicago Statement avows "great accuracy" but not "*perfect* accuracy." Joseph Smith even said, "I believe the Bible as it read when it came from the pen of the original writers."[16]

It might be worth repeating at this point that this advocating for the appropriateness of labeling Mormons "biblical" is more concerned with questions of public perception and common ground than with technical theological classifications. That will not satisfy all readers, especially informed ones. Yet in many ways this essay is aimed at helping the uninformed, because public perception often makes common ground seem unreachable. The surprise, then, is that the similarities in article ten of the Chicago Statement and in Joseph Smith's testimony of the Bible's original authors show that common ground exists, and it's not a far country either. For that reason, the similarities need to be better publicized. Latter-day Saint beliefs in the Bible need wider play.

Still, what about the stickier issue of elevating another book (or books) to the level of Scripture? Should that disqualify Mormons as a "biblical" faith? The contention here is no—little surprise there. But while there is no question that Mormons do not meet the *sola Scriptura* standard that many evangelicals would say is a critical component of their faith, a reconsideration of what might be called Joseph Smith's theological project can suggest that even Mormonism's additional standard works do not do hazard to the "biblical" standard.

"Biblical" Fits Joseph Smith's Theological Project

Regardless of how one feels about the Book of Mormon—its origins, its claims, its translator—it is hard to deny that a major thrust of that book is its witness of the Bible. Sprinkled throughout the pages of the Book of Mormon are reminders that its various authors (again, however one views that authorship) saw their work as constituting a last-days witness to the world that what would come from the Jews—what we now know as the Bible—was true and trustworthy. This (the Book of Mormon) was written that future readers might believe that (the Bible)—not the other way around. The Book of Mormon offers a second witness, for example, that Jacob's son Joseph really did save Egypt and, by so doing, saved his formerly murderous brothers as well; that Moses really did cross the Red Sea on dry ground; that Isaiah really did prophesy of him who would be "bruised for our iniquities"— and that Jesus Christ did emerge from the tomb triumphant and gloriously embodied. Debates about the Book of Mormon's divinity can in this case be temporarily set aside in favor of what is repeatedly apparent: the Book of Mormon sees itself, and conscientiously so, as evidence that the Bible is the Word of God.[17]

And Joseph Smith's other work has this same feel. In the spring of 1838, Joseph Smith published, in a church periodical, answers to "questions which were frequently asked me." Some of the answers take on a playful tone, a reflection perhaps of Joseph Smith's exasperation with repeated misunderstandings. But underneath that playfulness, the answers are often straightforward and direct. In response to the question "Wherein do you differ from other sects?" Joseph Smith wrote: "In that we believe the Bible, and all other sects profess to believe their interpretations of the Bible, and their creeds."[18] Of course a statement like this can be off-putting, even offensive, in its presumptuousness. But it also can be seen as expressing Joseph Smith's deepest self-understanding. Philip Barlow put a statistical point to this: "Mormon periodicals in the 1830s cited the Bible nineteen times as often as the Book of Mormon, and in the 173 discourses given in Nauvoo, Illinois, for which contemporary records exist, Smith himself paraphrases the Book of Mormon only twenty-three times but quoted or paraphrased the Bible more than six hundred times."[19]

John Brooke won the prestigious Bancroft Prize with his 1994 book, *The Refiner's Fire*. Brooke argues throughout that Joseph Smith's cosmology bore the marks of medieval hermeticism, even though the ties of transmission of such ideas from sometimes obscure European thinkers to Joseph Smith's rural New York environs were admittedly thin.[20] What three prominent historians of Mormonism all agreed on was that John Brooke failed to acknowledge the key source for Joseph Smith's worldview: the Bible! In the words of Jan Shipps: "Although [Richard Bushman and Philip Barlow] apparently did not compare notes about what they would write [in their reviews of *The Refiner's Fire*], both . . . pointed to Brooke's failure to recognize how much of what he described as hermetic or occult came directly from the New Testament." Shipps then adds, "Brooke concentrates too much on the recondite and radical aspects of this new faith. At no point does he acknowledge that the religious and cultural situation into which Mormonism made its way was one in which . . . authority continued to rest in the Bible—the Bible alone, *sola scriptura*."[21]

As significant an example as any other of this reliance on the Bible is Joseph Smith's revelation that has since come to be known in Mormonism simply as "the Vision" because of its fundamental importance in shaping Latter-day Saint belief in a multitiered heaven. While many Christians find that belief surprising, to say the least (Craig Blomberg suggested that the Vision hits evangelical Christians "like a bolt out of the blue with its elaboration of *four* possible destinies of humanity"[22]), Joseph Smith nevertheless expressed it in a string of biblical phrases. Readers familiar with the Bible will recognize in that revelation (now Doctrine and Covenants 76 in the LDS canon) one biblical passage after another—that's how Joseph Smith and Sidney Rigdon chose to describe their visionary experience: John 5:29; 1 Corinthians 3:22-23; 15:40-42; 2 Corinthians 12:2-4; Hebrews 6:6; Revelation 22:15; and so on.[23] One thinks of John Nelson Darby or Cyrus Scofield linking specific biblical passages to build a systematic dispensationalism. And while Joseph Smith was obviously claiming more, in terms of revelatory authority, he nevertheless expounded his vision of the afterlife by thoroughly blending literal readings of the Bible into a revolutionary view of heaven.

Joseph Smith saw his theological work as Bible-centered, and so did his followers—so much so that it has almost become a truism among Mormon historians that serious and widespread study of the Book of Mormon is a recent development in Mormonism. For most of its history, the Book of Mormon has been seen as a sign of the restoration of the prophetic office more than a doctrinal repository.[24]

Even the rites that take place in LDS temples are thoroughly grounded in biblical characters, stories, themes and analogs. Joseph Smith presented the theological underpinnings of those rites in biblical terms: baptism for the dead, the "sealing" of families for postmortal perpetuation and proxy rites for deceased ancestors are explicitly connected in the LDS canon to Malachi 4:5-6; Matthew 16:19; 1 Corinthians 15:29; 1 Peter 3:18-20; 4:6; and especially Hebrews 11:40.[25]

This is not to say that an acknowledgment of just how Bible-centered Joseph Smith's starting points were necessarily implies even a tacit acceptance of the validity of Joseph Smith's interpretive work. But that acknowledgment could go a long way as an important corrective in terms of popular understanding. And it seems worth repeating here that Richard Mouw notes in this volume that evangelicals also rely on a variety of extrabiblical authorities in coming to apprehend their faith. His statement seems to be generous in its aim to allow for a space for the extrabiblical authorities that are also important to Mormons.

"Biblical" Fits Latter-day Saints Beliefs About Jesus Christ

Perhaps the most compelling reason to argue for the appropriateness—and necessity—of applying the "biblical" label to Mormons is that the Bible is, for Latter-day Saints and evangelical Christians, the prime locus of agreement about Jesus Christ. To be sure, Latter-day Saints and evangelical Christians hold different beliefs about Jesus Christ—but technically speaking, those differences are *not* Bible-based. Latter-day Saints and evangelical Christians can *both* say (and have said) that they believe *everything* the Bible says about Jesus Christ. Latter-day Saints would say, and not disingenuously either, that they cannot think of a single biblical description of Jesus Christ that they would disavow.[26]

That statement calls for some qualification, since readers might already be thinking, "Wait—what about this passage? Or that one?" In some ways, this assertion must be taken in the spirit of the earlier point about tolerated interpretive variation. That is, Latter-day Saints and evangelical Christians have no disagreements in accepting the same *words* that the Bible uses to describe Jesus Christ. Disagreements arise over the *meaning* of the words, or what each faith tradition reads back into those words. But again, interpretive variation of the Bible seems to be the rule among Christians. And remember how Craig Blomberg framed that variety: "I know of no pervasive interpretive pluralism in evangelicalism, for example, concerning the full deity and full humanity of Jesus, about the moral attributes of God, about the universal sinfulness of humanity (as distinct from the origins of that universality), about Christ's bodily resurrection and bodily return, or about the centrality of a love ethic." On the points of consensus he lists, Latter-day Saints heartily join in.

Latter-day Saints and evangelical Christians both witness that Jesus Christ is the only begotten Son of God, the only name by which humanity can be saved, *the* way, *the* truth and *the* life. Latter-day Saints and evangelical Christians both agree that "in the beginning was the Word, and the Word was with God, and the Word was God" (John 1:1).[27]

Earlier in this chapter, the contention was that only by labeling Mormons as "Bible-believing Christians with a difference" could that "difference" be properly understood and communicated. The reason behind that contention becomes clearest on this point of Christology. This label would encourage both Latter-day Saints and evangelicals, it seems, to be more explicit in their admissions that their respective readings of the Bible are not always as straightforward and commonsensical as we sometimes like to portray them. We need more of the forthrightness of Roger Olson and Christopher Hall, who in their excellent exposition on the Trinity begin at this important starting point: "Although there is no written word 'Trinity' in the Bible, there is evidence that the concept is biblically supported in the Old Testament," and the "practices and doctrines of the church finally led early Christian leaders to propose a Trinitarian model of God, but the formation of this model took place over many years and in many contexts."[28] And we need more from Latter-day Saints of what we hear from the highest levels of their leadership—

statements like this one from church apostle Jeffrey R. Holland: "Our view of the Godhead breaks with post-New Testament Christian history."[29]

Obviously, millions of Bible-believers—the majority of them—accept the trinitarian understanding of Scripture, but not all of them do.[30] Olson and Hall's helpful "seeds that blossomed" model about the way they see inspiration moving the early Christian fathers to settle on trinitarian formulations finds analogs in the way Mormons see biblical "seeds" blossoming through the prayerful inquiries of Joseph Smith and his successors.[31] Latter-day Saints could even comfortably borrow Olson and Hall's same words from above—"there is evidence that the concept is biblically supported"—when discussing unique LDS doctrines like pre-earth existence, or evangelizing in the postmortal spirit world, or the perpetuity of the marriage relationship beyond the grave. Where the label "biblical" could move Mormon-evangelical conversations is to this place: to have participants from both sides of this dialogue say, "I can see how you read the Bible that way—that seems reasonable, but it's not the way I read the Bible because of the extrabiblical thinking, conventions, inspiration and so on, that my tradition brings to bear on Scripture." In other words, there would be fewer contests over whether or not someone really *believes* in the Bible and more conversations about how and why one *reads* the Bible the way they do.

CONCLUSION: CLARITY OVER OBSCURITY

"We love and revere the Bible," LDS apostle Jeffrey Holland said in 2008. "The Bible is the word of God. It is always identified first in our canon, our 'standard works.'"[32] And Mormon devotional and institutional curriculum practices offer evidence that these are not just idle words. One example: hundreds of thousands of LDS high schoolers around the world participate in a daily religion class ("seminary" in Mormon parlance). Two of the four seminary years are devoted to the study of the Bible.

Although Elder Holland was speaking at an LDS General Conference when he gave the above affirmation, it also seemed apparent that he had in mind a wider audience. He prefaced his witness of the Bible with these words: "Please do not misunderstand." This concern over misunderstandings fits the thesis of this chapter, and in many ways, the larger project this book represents.

In that quest for mutual understanding, though, there seem to be no substitutes for engagement and empathy, and so this discussion of labels and public perception might seem to be overexuberance for a proposed panacea. Still, as a starting point, whether someone wants a sound bite or sound doctrine, the "biblical" label seems to satisfy. If more and more people hear, "Mormons are biblical Christians, but not trinitarian Christians like Protestants or Catholic or Orthodox Christians," they will begin to better appreciate the centrality of both Jesus Christ and the Bible in Mormonism on the one hand—something Mormons deem crucial—and the distinctiveness (sometimes radically so) of Mormon beliefs on the nature of God on the other hand—something evangelical Christians deem crucial.

This label can move conversations in the direction of similarities (shared moral values, for example) *and* differences (like doctrinal divergence). Franklin Graham gave glimpses of that potential utility when he invoked the word "biblical" in his open letter to fellow Christians who wondered if an evangelical could vote for Mormon presidential candidate Mitt Romney: "While there are major differences in the theology of evangelical Christians and that of Mormons, as well as those who practice the Catholic faith or the Jewish faith, we do share common values that are biblically based."[33]

Such is the explanatory power of descriptions along the lines of Philip Barlow's "Latter-day Saints are Bible-believing Christians—but with a difference." Making the Bible common ground rather than battleground would move conversations to a place suggested by N. T. Wright, someone many evangelical Christians and Mormons are happy to quote. "The risen Jesus, at the end of Matthew's Gospel, does not say, 'All authority in heaven and on earth is given to the books you are all going to write,' but [rather] 'All authority in heaven and on earth is given to me.'" And "Scripture itself points . . . away from itself and to the fact that final and true authority belongs to God himself."[34] That's where conversations by and about evangelicals and Mormons could point, too.

And agreeing on just a few words can do a lot of this work.

Afterword

Robert L. Millet

LOOKING BACK ON FIFTEEN-PLUS YEARS of interaction between Latter-day Saint (LDS) and evangelical scholars, I find myself deeply grateful for a number of things:

1. There is a God, he actually exists, he cares a great deal about the way his children treat one another and, for our purposes, how they deal interpersonally with the often-difficult but eternally significant matters of religion, the religious life and spirituality. While evangelicals and Mormons certainly have their theological differences, particularly in regard to the Trinity or the Godhead, we have been able to acknowledge and agree on the existence; divine perfections; and attributes, goodness and grace of Deity, as made known through the Old and New Testaments. Rich Mouw said once to our combined group, our dialogue team, as we came to the close of one of our twenty-two sessions together, "Let's now lift our voices to the only God who is worthy of our worship and our prayers!" I appreciated that insightful sentiment a decade ago, and I appreciate it even more now.

2. We rejoice in the fact that we all, every one of us, loves and adores the person Jesus Christ as described in the New Testament; that his was and is the only name by which salvation comes; that an acceptance of his divine Sonship and his gospel is absolutely necessary for any person to qualify for eternal life; that while our good works manifest our love and gratitude and desire to be his true disciples, we are saved now and forevermore through his unmerited divine favor; that his sufferings and death open the door to forgiveness, rebirth, transformation, resurrection and glorification; and that

he will come again, this time in might and majesty and power, to cleanse the earth and initiate a thousand years of goodness and glory, to reign as King of kings and Lord of lords.

3. There is something very meaningful and worthwhile, even soul-transforming, about women and men coming together to pray and sing hymns and read Scripture and speak and listen and reflect and ruminate and question and probe, all in the spirit of kindness and respect, in an attitude of convicted civility. When we truly listen to better understand and even empathize—rather than simply pausing momentarily in order to prepare our denunciations and refutations—an edifying Spirit enters the room. We begin to sense that as vital as doctrine is, there is something even deeper than our perception of the infinite, and that is our shared humanity, the position each of us holds as children of God created in his image and likeness. That subtle but certain sense, that inner awareness, is precious, akin to inspiration. Now obviously I could go on and on about what we've learned from this most unusual endeavor, but the three items mentioned above are a cause for celebration and expressions of thanks to a benevolent and beneficent God who loves all of us and no doubt wishes that his children would get along a little better than they do.

We have all learned a few things along the way:

- that a person need not compromise one iota of their faith or religious practice in order to have meaningful dialogue on tenets of faith;

- that building relationships takes time and cannot be hurried;

- that while theological differences do and will exist, it is crucial that we understand exactly what those differences are, so that when we do disagree we disagree over the right things, not over what we had supposed the differences were;

- that engaging in intense and rigorous discussions provides not only significant insights into the "other's" faith but also surprising insight into our own;

- that respectful dialogue is far more difficult to accomplish than debate and argument;

- that conversion to your way of thinking is not the only measure of a successful dialogue;

- that the process of preparing for, carrying out and contemplating what was said and done during the dialogue is rewarding and enriching, both intellectually and spiritually; and

- that because God's ways are not our ways and his thoughts are not our thoughts (Isaiah 55:8-9), we cannot always comprehend and appreciate what he might be bringing to pass.

We recently brought our LDS-evangelical conversation to its close, feeling as though this particular body of participants had probed and investigated about as much as we could. Some of us plan to begin a new dialogue, to tweak slightly the dialogists and the topics, and to dig deeper, much deeper into both vexing differences and startling similarities. I think it would be safe to say that many of us are persuaded, more so now than ever, that there is a requisite humility associated with effective dialogue, a sobering awareness that we simply don't have all the answers, that even some of our answers are mere approximations to the way things really are. Such a realization does not weaken one's faith or commitment; rather, it motivates us to be appropriately tentative, meekly nonjudgmental and cautiously open and receptive to both the common and saving grace of Almighty God. In the words of the beloved apostle,

> "For who has known the mind of the LORD,
>   or who has been his counselor?"
> "Or who has given a gift to him
>   that he might be repaid?"

> For from him and through him and to him are all things. To him be glory forever. Amen. (Romans 11:33-36 ESV)

Notes

Chapter 1: The Dialogue: Backgrounds and Context

[1] Martin Forward, *Inter-religious Dialogue: A Short Introduction* (Oxford: Oneworld, 2001), p. 28.

[2] Reid L. Neilson, *Exhibiting Mormonism: The Latter-day Saints and the 1893 Chicago World's Fair* (New York: Oxford University Press, 2011), p. 144; see also Davis Bitton, "B. H. Roberts at the Parliament of World Religion, 1893, Chicago," *Sunstone* 7, no. 1 (January–February 1982): 46-51.

[3] John P. Burris, *Exhibiting Religion: Colonialism and Spectacle at International Expositions 1851–1893* (Charlottesville: University Press of Virginia, 2002), p. 151.

[4] See George M. Marsden, *Understanding Fundamentalism and Evangelicalism* (Grand Rapids: Eerdmans, 1991), p. 11.

[5] Mark Noll, *A History of Christianity in the United States and Canada* (Grand Rapids: Eerdmans, 1992), p. 361.

[6] Roger Finke and Rodney Stark, *The Churching of America, 1776–2005: Winners and Losers in Our Religious Economy* (New Brunswick, NJ: Rutgers University Press, 2005), p. 121.

[7] The Pew Forum on Religion and Public Life, "U.S. Religious Landscape Survey: Religious Affiliation: Diverse and Dynamic, February 2008," Pew Research Center, February 25, 2008, http://religions.pewforum.org/pdf/report-religious-landscape -study-full.pdf.

[8] See Burris, *Exhibiting Religion*, p. 150.

[9] See Kathleen Flake, *The Politics of American Religious Identity: The Seating of Senator Reed Smoot, Mormon Apostle* (Chapel Hill: University of North Carolina Press, 2004), pp. 1-2.

[10] See Thomas G. Alexander, *Mormonism in Transition: A History of the Latter-day Saints, 1890–1930* (Chicago: University of Illinois Press, 1986), pp. 261-64.

[11] See Armand L. Mauss, *The Angel and the Beehive: The Mormon Struggle with Assimilation* (Chicago: University of Illinois Press, 1994), pp. 157-95.

[12] See O. Kendall White Jr., *Mormon Neo-Orthodoxy: A Crisis Theology* (Salt Lake City: Signature, 1987).

[13] Ibid., p. xvi.

[14] Richard J. Mouw, "Evangelical Mormonism?," *Christianity Today*, November 11, 1991, p. 30.

[15] See John-Charles Duffy, "Conservative Pluralists: The Cultural Politics of Mormon-Evangelical Dialogue in the United States at the Turn of the Twenty-First Century" (PhD diss., University of North Carolina at Chapel Hill, 2011).

[16] Ibid., p. 132.

[17]Greg Johnson, interviews by author, Salt Lake City, UT, January 13, 20, 27, 2011; February 10, 22, 24, 2011; March 3, 2011; December 21, 26, 2011.

[18]For a good summary of both Mormon and evangelical reactions to *How Wide the Divide*, see Matthew R. Connelly and *BYU Studies* Staff, "Sizing Up the Divide: Reviews and Replies," *BYU Studies* 38, no. 3 (1999): 163-90.

[19]Robert L. Millet, "The Mormon/Evangelical Dialogue: Retrospect and Prospect" (paper presented at the annual meeting of the American Academy of Religion, Montreal, Canada, November 7, 2009).

[20]Ibid.

[21]Ibid.

CHAPTER 3: WHAT DREW ME TO DIALOGUE . . . AND WHY I'M STILL TALKING

[1]Boyd K. Packer, *Conference Report* (Salt Lake City: Church of Jesus Christ of Latter-day Saints, October 1985), p. 107. See also Boyd K. Packer, "Be Not Afraid" (address at Ogden, Utah, LDS Institute of Religion, November 16, 2008), p. 5.

[2]Doctrine and Covenants 88:118.

CHAPTER 4: LOOKING AHEAD: MY DREAMS FOR MORMON-EVANGELICAL DIALOGUES

[1]Craig L. Blomberg and Stephen E. Robinson, *How Wide the Divide? A Mormon and an Evangelical in Conversation* (Downers Grove, IL: InterVarsity Press, 1997).

[2]The term is championed and modeled by Richard J. Mouw, *Uncommon Decency: Christian Civility in an Uncivil World*, 2nd ed. (Downers Grove, IL: InterVarsity Press, 2010), pp. 11-20.

[3]The proceedings of one such conference are published as Roger R. Keller and Robert L. Millet, eds., *Salvation in Christ: Comparative Christian Views* (Provo, UT: Religious Studies Center, BYU, 2005). A sample of the Millet-Johnson dialogue has been published as Robert L. Millet and Gregory C. V. Johnson, *Bridging the Divide: The Continuing Conversation between a Mormon and an Evangelical* (Rhinebeck, NY: Monkfish, 2007).

[4]The NAE was already meeting at an Evangelical Free Church in Park City, UT, for their regular board meetings. I was privileged to be invited to participate in this event as well. Elder Holland's address is now published as "Standing Together for the Cause of Christ," *Religious Educator* 13 (2012): 11-19.

[5]"Evangelicals and Catholics Together: The Christian Mission in the Third Millennium," *First Things*, May 1994, pp. 15-22.

[6]In addition to the works cited in nn. 1-2, see Robert L. Millet and Gerald R. McDermott, *Evangelicals and Mormons: Exploring the Boundaries* (Vancouver: Regent College Press, 2010) and several of the additional articles in *Religious Educator* 13 (2012). Some of us have also written forewords or commendatory blurbs for each other's works.

[7]Very much in the spirit of Catherine Cornille, *The Im-possibility of Interreligious Dialogue* (New York: Crossroad, 2008), which we have read and discussed together.

[8]Quoting pollster George Gallup Jr., in the article "Religion: Counting Souls," *Time*, October 4, 1976, www.time.com/time/magazine/article/0,9171,918414,00.html.

[9]See Randall L. Balmer, *Redeemer: The Life of Jimmy Carter* (New York: Basic Books, 2014). Media attention, of course, hardly equates with accurate understanding, especially in matters theological. The cynics among us might even muse that at times such attention guarantees theological misrepresentation!

[10]The closest approximation is the excellent little book by Richard J. Mouw, *Talking with Mormons: An Invitation to Evangelicals* (Grand Rapids: Eerdmans, 2012). But there is still more to share.

[11]Far preferable, therefore, is the language of the title of and the approach adopted in Ronald Enroth, ed., *A Guide to New Religious Movements* (Downers Grove, IL: InterVarsity Press, 2005).

[12]Or at least read introductions to those movements written by their own adherents, and the more recent and up-to-date the sources, the better. In the case of the LDS, see esp. Robert L. Millet, *The Vision of Mormonism: Pressing the Boundaries of Christianity* (St. Paul: Paragon House, 2007).

[13]For both of these errors see, e.g., Richard Hopkins, *Biblical Mormonism: Responding to Evangelical Criticism of LDS Theology* (Bountiful, UT: Horizon, 2005).

[14]For just one illustration, see the varied responses to Blomberg and Robinson, *How Wide the Divide?* discussed in "Sizing Up the Divide: Reviews and Replies," *BYU Studies* 38 (1999): 163-90.

CHAPTER 6: A SERIOUS CALL TO DEVOUT AND HOLY DIALOGUE: GOING DEEPER IN INTERFAITH DISCUSSIONS

[1]William Law, *A Serious Call to a Devout and Holy Life* (1728).

[2]It is likely that Law's *A Practical Treatise Upon Christian Perfection* (1726) had some impact on John Wesley's doctrine of Christian perfection.

[3]William Law, *Case of Reason* (1732).

[4]William Law, *Remarks on Mandeville's Fable of the Bees* (1723).

[5]It was published as Gerald R. McDermott, "Jesus, Paul, and Israel's Covenant: What Can Christians and Jews Learn from One Another?" in *Covenant and Hope: Christian and Jewish Reflections*, ed. Robert Jenson and Eugene Korn (Grand Rapids: Eerdmans, 2012), pp. 19-40.

[6]Jon D. Levenson, *Inheriting Abraham: The Legacy of the Patriarch in Judaism, Christianity, and Islam* (Princeton: Princeton University Press, 2012).

[7]Ibid., p. 202.

[8]Ellen T. Charry, *By the Renewing of Your Minds: The Pastoral Function of Christian Doctrine* (New York: Oxford University Press, 1999).

[9]Stanley Hauerwas, "Which Church? What Unity? Or, An Attempt to Say What I May Think About the Future of Christian Unity," *Pro Ecclesia* 22, no. 3 (Summer 2013): 273.

[10]Ibid., p. 277.

[11]The fruit of the Jewish-Christian dialogue can be seen in Korn and Jenson, eds. *Covenant and Hope*.

Chapter 7: Apologetics as if People Mattered

[1]James K. A. Smith, *Who's Afraid of Postmodernism: Taking Derrida, Lyotard, and Foucault to Church* (Grand Rapids: Baker Academic, 2006), p. 51.

[2]William Placher, *Unapologetic Theology: A Christian Voice in a Pluralistic Conversation* (Louisville, KY: Westminster John Knox Press, 1989), p. 117.

[3]Ibid., p. 148.

Chapter 8: From Calvary to Cumorah: The Significance of "Sacred Space"

[1]Personal diary of Richard E. Bennett, entries for July and August 1956.

[2]Delbert L. Stapley, "The Importance of Church History," in *Speeches of the Year*, Brigham Young University, April 15, 1969 (Provo, UT: Brigham Young University Press, 1969), pp. 2, 13-14.

[3]The term *New Mormon History* suggests a Renaissance-like return to original manuscripts with emphasis on revised interpretation, on seeing things as they really were and on professional historical study.

[4]Richard J. Mouw, *The Smell of the Sawdust—What Evangelicals Can Learn from Their Fundamentalist Heritage* (Grand Rapids: Zondervan, 2000), p. 8.

[5]Jesse Lyman Hurlbut, *Hurlbut's Story of the Bible for Young and Old* (Philadelphia: Universal Book and Bible House, 1952).

[6]J. Gresham Machen, *Christianity and Liberalism* (Grand Rapids: Eerdmans, 1923), pp. 25, 28-29, 53.

[7]Adolf Koberle, "Jesus Christ, the Center of History," in *Jesus of Nazareth: Saviour and Lord*, ed. Carl F. H. Henry (Grand Rapids: Eerdmans, 1966), pp. 64-65, 70.

[8]Koberle, "Jesus Christ, The Center of History," p. 68.

[9]Charles Colson, "Keynote Address," in *Evangelical Affirmations*, ed. Kenneth S. Kantzer and Carl F. H. Henry (Grand Rapids: Academie, 1990), pp. 48-49.

[10]J. Gresham Machen, *What Is Christianity?* (Grand Rapids: Eerdmans, 1951), p. 171.

[11]LeGrand Richards, "Faith in Action," radio address delivered April 10, 1955 (Salt Lake City: The Church of Jesus Christ of Latter-day Saints, 1955).

[12]Gordon B. Hinckley, *Teachings of Gordon B. Hinckley* (Salt Lake City: Deseret, 1997), p. 227.

[13]Ibid.

[14]Leonard I. Sweet, "The 1960s: The Crisis of Liberal Christianity," in *Evangelicalism and Modern America*, ed. George Marsden (Grand Rapids: Eerdmans, 1984).

[15]Ibid., pp. 42-43.

[16]Timothy George, "Evangelicals and Others," *First Things*, February 2006, p. 23.

Chapter 9: Mormon-Evangelical Dialogue: Embracing a Hermeneutic of Generosity

[1]Ron and Carol Harris, *In This Very Room* (Woodland Hills, CA: Ron Harris Publications, 1979). Ironically enough, this song's lyrics are about the inclusivity of Christ's love.

[2]Names have been changed.

[3]As I recall, there were just over one hundred students in that class. To my knowledge, Sam Jones was the only student in that group who was not LDS.

[4]Richard L. Bushman, *Joseph Smith: Rough Stone Rolling* (New York: Vintage, 2007), p. ix.

[5]Ibid.

[6]Stuart Parker, "The Hermeneutics of Generosity," *Journal of Mormon History* 38, no. 3 (2012): 12-25.

[7]Ibid., p. 16.

[8]Bushman, *Rough Stone Rolling*, p. xii.

[9]Richard J. Mouw, "The Possibility of Joseph Smith: Some Evangelical Probing," in *Joseph Smith Jr.: Reappraisals After Two Centuries*, ed. Reid L. Neilson and Terryl L. Givens (Oxford: Oxford University Press, 2009), p. 189.

[10]Dan Vogel, "The Prophet Puzzle Revisited," in *The Prophet Puzzle: Interpretive Essays on Joseph Smith*, ed. Bryan Waterman (Salt Lake City, UT: Signature, 1999), p. 50.

[11]Mouw, "The Possibility of Joseph Smith," p. 191.

[12]Ibid.

[13]Ibid.

[14]Ibid., p. 195.

[15]Richard L. Bushman, "The Visionary World of Joseph Smith," *BYU Studies* 37, no. 1 (1997–1998): 199.

[16]Laura Barnett, *When Death Enters the Therapeutic Space: Existential Perspectives in Psychotherapy and Counselling* (New York: Routledge, 2009), p. 211.

[17]Richard Sennett, *Together: The Rituals, Pleasures and Politics of Cooperation* (New Haven, CT: Yale University Press, 2012), p. 19.

[18]Ibid., pp. 18-19.

[19]Ibid., p. 21.

[20]This kind of approach is described by Martin Buber in *Between Man and Man*, trans. Ronald Gregor-Smith (New York: Routledge, 2002), p. 22.

[21]See Martin Buber, *The Knowledge of Man: Selected Essays*, trans. Maurice Friedman and Ronald Gregor-Smith (Amherst, NY: Prometheus, 1998), pp. 71, 74.

[22]Richard L. Bushman, *Believing History: Latter-day Saint Essays*, ed. Reid L. Neilson and Jed Woodworth (New York: Columbia University Press, 2004).

[23]Bushman, *Rough Stone Rolling*.

[24]Sennett, *Together*, p. 19.

[25]Ned Noddings, *Educating for Intelligent Belief or Unbelief: The John Dewey Lecture* (New York: Teachers College Press, 1993), p. 23.

CHAPTER 10: TEMPLE GARMENTS: A CASE STUDY IN THE LIVED RELIGION OF MORMONS

[1]A transcript of Mouw's address can be found at "We Have Sinned Against You," *Beliefnet*, http://www.beliefnet.com/Faiths/Christianity/2004/11/We-Have -Sinned-Against-You.aspx?p=1 (accessed November 1, 2013).

[2]Richard J. Mouw, *Uncommon Decency: Christian Civility in an Uncivil World* (Downers Grove, IL: InterVarsity Press, 2010), p. 60.

[3]William Dyrness, *Senses of Devotion: Interfaith Aesthetics in Buddhist and Muslim Communities* (Eugene, OR: Cascade, 2013), pp. 1-2.

[4]Lesslie Newbigin, "The Basis, Purpose, and Aims of Inter-Faith Dialogue," *Scottish Journal of Theology* 30, no. 3 (1977): 263-64; William A. Dyrness, *Invitation to Cross-Cultural Theology: Case Studies in Vernacular Theologies* (Grand Rapids: Zondervan, 1992), p. 30.

[5]James K. A. Smith, *Imagining the Kingdom: How Worship Works* (Grand Rapids: Baker Academic, 2013), pp. 12-13.

[6]John D. Witvliet, "For Our Own Purposes: The Appropriation of the Social Sciences in Liturgical Studies," in *Foundations in Ritual Studies: A Reader for Students of Christian Worship*, ed. Paul Bradshaw and John Melloh (Grand Rapids: Baker Academic, 2007), pp. 37-40.

[7]The decision to analyze the temple garment is based on the minimal theological discussion from Latter-day Saint authorities on this practice. This dynamic requires that evangelicals look beyond a traditional doctrinal analysis of written texts and engage their Mormon neighbors in dialogue to gain a more accurate understanding of the significance of this ritual. Colleen McDannell, *Material Christianity: Religion and Popular Culture in America* (New Haven, CT: Yale University Press, 1995), p. 199.

[8]Richard Lyman Bushman, *Mormonism: A Very Short Introduction* (New York: Oxford University Press, 2008), p. 56.

[9]See McDannell, *Material Christianity*, pp. 198-99. A recent Google search for "Mormon undergarments" produced an array of websites, blogs and news articles on the practices, origins and meanings surrounding Mormon garments. Mitt Romney's involvement in the 2012 GOP race factors into the frequent references to him in many of these websites and blogs. For example, see www.buzzfeed.com /mckaycoppins/a-brief-guide-to-mormon-underwear (accessed December 2, 2014).

[10]Gary C. Lawrence, *Mormons Believe . . . What?! Fact and Fiction About a Rising Religion* (Orange, CA: The Parameter Foundation, 2011), p. 84. Stephen Webb's article "Mormonism Obsessed with Christ" offers a commentary on the vitriolic commentaries against Mormonism found in the media (*First Things*, February 2012, www.firstthings.com/article/2012/02/mormonism-obsessed-with-christ. On the distinction between secrecy and sacredness among Mormons, see Boyd K. Packer, *The Holy Temple* (Salt Lake City: Bookcraft, 1980), pp. 26, 28-33, 78.

[11]During the final editing process of the chapter, the Church of Jesus Christ of Latter-day Saints website posted this short video, in which it explains to the public some of the practices and purposes for the garment. See www.mormonnewsroom .org/article/temple-garments (accessed December 2, 2014).

[12]Andrew C. Skinner, "Temple," in *LDS Beliefs: A Doctrinal Reference,* ed. Robert L. Millet, Camille Fronk Olson, Andrew C. Skinner and Brent L. Top (Salt Lake City: Deseret, 2011), p. 612; Packer, *Holy Temple*, p. 10.

[13]Bushman, *Mormonism*, p. 58. Gordon B. Hinckley, *Teachings of Gordon B. Hinckley* (Salt Lake City: Deseret, 1997), p. 636.

[14]The centrality of Jesus in the LDS tradition is well attested in the relevant scholarship. See, e.g., Tad R. Callister, *The Infinite Atonement* (Salt Lake City: Deseret, 2000); and Robert Millet, *A Different Jesus? The Christ of the Latter-day Saints* (Grand Rapids: Eerdmans, 2005), pp. 110-13.

[15]Packer, *Holy Temple*, p. 262.

[16]Words and music by Janice Kapp Perry. See www.lds.org/music/text/childrens -songbook/i-love-to-see-the-temple?lang=eng (accessed February 26, 2015).

[17]Packer, *Holy Temple*, 241.

[18]Ibid., pp. 267, 260.

[19]Millet, *A Different Jesus?*, 134-36; Terryl L. Givens, *The Latter-day Saint Experience In America* (Westport, CT: Greenwood Press, 2004), pp. 174-75; Packer, *Holy Temple*, pp. 10-16; Bushman, *Mormonism*, pp. 57, 61. The New Testament basis for this is found in John 3:5; ; 1 Corinthians 15:29; 1 Peter 3:18-19; 4:6. Joseph Smith saw baptism for the dead as a fulfillment of Malachi 4:6.

[20]Givens, *Latter-day Saint Experience*, pp. 174-75; Bushman, *Mormonism*, pp. 57-62.

[21]Packer, *Holy Temple*, pp. 153-54.

[22]*Handbook of Selected Church Policies*, 21.1.42. Inside the temple, all participants wear white clothing—symbolizing purity, worthiness and cleanliness—providing a sense of oneness and equality as they take part in the ordinances and covenants (Packer, *Holy Temple*, pp. 71, 77-78). The garment also cultivates an atmosphere of spiritual contemplation and meditation.

[23]*Handbook of Selected Church Policies*, 21.1.42 (emphasis added).

[24]Packer, *Holy Temple*, pp. 75, 79, 265; Givens, *Latter-day Saint Experience*, p. 174. According to the *Handbook* the garment's religious significance is derived from its sacred markings. Other sources indicate that these markings are copies of those found at various places inside the temple (McDannell, *Material Christianity*, pp. 209-10). Once removed, however, the garment is no longer sacred and may be discarded by shredding the remaining fabric (see paragraphs seven and eight of the *Handbook of Selected Church Policies*, 21.1.42).

[25]See the LDS *Handbook of Instruction*, http://www.lds.org/handbook/handbook -2-administering-the-church/selected-church-policies?lang=eng#21.1.42 (accessed January 31, 2012).

[26]For an account of Mormon apostle Boyd Packer's presentation to a non-Mormon audience of Navy chaplains about temple garments, see Packer, *Holy Temple*, pp. 75-79. See also LDS.org under "Temple Garment."

[27]McDannell, *Material Christianity*, p. 199.

[28]Mark Searle, "Ritual," in *Foundations in Ritual Studies: A Reader for Students of Christian Worship*, ed. Paul Bradshaw and John Melloh (Grand Rapids: Baker Academic, 2007), pp. 11-13.

[29]Witvliet, "For Our Own Purposes," p. 26.

[30]Paul G. Hiebert, R. Daniel Shaw and Tite Tiénou, *Understanding Folk Religion: A*

Christian Response to Popular Beliefs and Practices (Grand Rapids: Baker, 1999), p. 73.
[31]Ibid., pp. 73-75.
[32]For a colorful and illuminating discussion of ritual generation and authorization, see Ronald L. Grimes, "Liturgical Supinity, Liturgical Erectitude: On the Embodiment of Ritual Authority," *Studia Liturgica* 23 (1993): 51-69. See also Dyrness, *Senses of Devotion*, pp. 4-5.
[33]Lawrence A. Hoffmann, "How Ritual Means: Ritual Circumcision in Rabbinic Culture and Today," *Studia Liturgica* 23 (1993): 78-97.
[34]Consider, for example, the tenor of conversation that might emerge if these were the types of questions that were posed:

> When you put on your garment every day, what purpose would you say this plays in your life? Your identity and sense of belonging? Commitment and obedience to God? Your sexuality?
>
> Many religions have special or sacred coverings. In what ways do you think the LDS garment is similar and different?
>
> In your process of eternal progression, what significance does the garment play in your connection with God? Do you feel closer to God or more spiritually enriched when clothed in the garment?
>
> How do you explain to your children (or younger members of the faith) the significance of the garment?
>
> In addition to the instructions in the *Church Handbook*, what are some of the unspoken or implied messages communicated within the Latter-day Saint community concerning garment wearing? How have you interpreted and personalized these messages?

[35]Newbigin, "The Basis, Purpose, and Aims," pp. 263-66.
[36]Terry Muck's notion of "participant theologizing" is a helpful framework for this process. See Terry C. Muck, "Theology of Religions after Knitter and Hick: Beyond the Paradigm," *Interpretation* (January 2007): 7-22, here at 20.
[37]Saint Augustine, *Confessions,* trans. Henry Chadwick, Oxford World Classics (New York: Oxford University Press, 2008), p. 3; John Calvin, *Institutes of the Christian Religion* 1.1.3 and 1.1.4.
[38]Hiebert, Shaw and Tiénou describe critical contextualization as a third-way alternative to a wholesale rejection of culture on the one hand and an uncritical acceptance of culture on the other. The critical contextualization process involves phenomenological analysis, ontological reflections (theological criteria and reality testing), critical evaluation, missiological transformation and critical contextualization (*Understanding Folk Religion*, pp. 21-29).

Chapter 11: Mormons and Evangelicals in the Public Square

[1]See Thomas G. Alexander, *Mormonism in Transition: A History of the Latter-day Saints, 1890–1930* (Urbana: University of Illinois Press, 1996), p. 258. For an example of this kind of early twentieth-century evangelical endorsement of Mormon mo-

rality, see Janice P. Dawson, "Frederick Vining Fisher: Methodist Apologist for Mormonism," *Utah Historical Quarterly* 55, no. 4 (Fall 1987): 359-69. Dawson's article also highlights that expressed support for Mormons was still highly divisive among religionists. For Mormon-evangelical tension in the turn-of-twentieth-century Reed Smoot–hearing era, see Jonathan H. Moyer, "Dancing with the Devil: The Making of the Mormon-Republican Pact" (PhD diss., University of Utah, 2009), p. 348, where Moyer calls the Women's Christian Temperance Union "the most important single group opposing Smoot"; and, importantly, Kathleen Flake, *The Politics of American Religious Identity: The Seating of Senator Reed Smoot, Mormon Apostle* (Chapel Hill: University of North Carolina Press, 2004), pp. 85-87, where Flake discusses evidence of a perceived Mormon aloofness, because of a Mormon "ethic of self-reliance," giving way to examples of Latter-day Saints' "willingness to act for the common good," such that "it became more difficult for mainstream Protestants to argue that Mormons were un-American and ought to be excluded from the privileges of citizenship."

[2]See, e.g., Matthew Bowman, "A Dubious Friendship: Conservative Mormons and Evangelicals in the Twentieth Century" (paper presented at the annual meetings of the American Academy of Religion, Baltimore, Maryland, November 24, 2013).

[3]See Molly Worthen, *Apostles of Reason: The Crisis of Authority in American Evangelicalism* (New York: Oxford University Press, 2013), p. 10. See also pp. 15-35 for Worthen's discussion of the rise of "neo-evangelicals" and the National Association of Evangelicals in the 1940s.

[4]For the "Year of the Evangelical," see Kenneth L. Woodward, John Barnes and Laurie Lisle, "Born Again," *Newsweek*, October 25, 1976, p. 69; their article was the issue's cover story. For the voting numbers and George Bush's disclaimer, see Adam Clymer, "Bush Says No Single Group Gave Reagan His Victory," *New York Times*, November 18, 1980, B10.

[5]To some national writers, the religious conservatism of Mormons made them identical to fundamentalist Christians. That was the implication of Peter Bart's piece, "The Mormon Nation," *New York Times*, July 3, 1981, p. A19, and his suggestion that "anyone interested in peeking into the new American Dream" of the "ubiquitous 'moral activists'" should "look no further than that part of the United States that Westerners call 'the Mormon Nation.'" Bart's essay and equation of Mormonism with the "moral activists" of the Christian Right drew a corrective letter to the editor from Kenneth L. Woodward, religion reporter for *Newsweek*. Woodward wrote that "the Mormon ethos is unique and not transferable to Americans who do not share the Mormons' singular mythos about the origin and destiny of man. Mr. Falwell, for example, regards Mormonism as a heretical cult and to date has neither solicited nor received support from the L.D.S. General Authorities" (Kenneth L. Woodward, "A Distorted View of Mormonism," *New York Times*, July 23, 1981, A22). For Mormons in the Moral Majority, see, e.g., Jerry Falwell, "Maligned Moral Majority," as a "My Turn" feature in *Newsweek*, September 21, 1981, p. 17: "The Moral Majority is not a Christian or a religious orga-

nization (however, as a fundamentalist, I personally object to categorizing funda-mentalists as bellicose and anti-intellectual). We are made up of fundamentalists, evangelicals, Roman Catholics, conservative Jews, Mormons and even persons of no religious belief who share our concern about the issues we address." In reality, it appears that the small segment of Mormons who actively participated in Fal-well's coalition represented what one set of researchers called "political fringe groups on the Mormon periphery" (Merlin B. Brinkerhoff, Jeffrey C. Jacob and Marlene M. Mackie, "Mormonism and the Moral Majority Make Strange Bed-fellows? An Exploratory Critique," *Review of Religious Research* 28, no. 3 [March 1987]: 236-51). Their article came in response to Anson Shupe and John Heinerman, "Mormonism and the New Christian Right: An Emerging Coalition?" *Review of Religious Research* 27, no. 2 (December 1985): 146-57. Shupe and Heinerman focus on the Freemen Institute and the John Birch Society, both of which were right-wing political organizations that attracted a relatively small number of Mormon participants.

[6]For more on these 1980s tensions, see chap. 5 of J. B. Haws, *The Mormon Image in the American Mind: Fifty Years of Public Perception* (New York: Oxford University Press, 2013).

[7]Kenneth L. Woodward and Barbara Bugower, "Bible-Belt Confrontation," *Newsweek*, March 4, 1985, p. 65.

[8]Ibid.

[9]"An Interview with the Lone Ranger of American Fundamentalism," *Christianity Today*, September 4, 1981, pp. 23-24.

[10]Val Edwards (LDS Public Affairs Department staffer under Richard Lindsay), in-terview by author, August 21, 2008, transcript in possession of the author, pp. 3-4. This paragraph and the next two are taken from Haws, *The Mormon Image in the American Mind*, pp. 109, 161-62.

[11]Richard P. Lindsay, interview by Jonice Hubbard, August 24, 2006, transcript in-cluded in the appendix of Hubbard, "Pioneers in Twentieth Century Mormon Media: Oral Histories of Latter-day Saint Electronic and Public Relations Profes-sionals" (master's thesis, Brigham Young University, 2007), pp. 98-99; Hubbard, "LDS Official Testifies on Families," *Deseret News*, September 23, 1983, B-1; Hubbard, "Religious Leaders Join Together, Pledge to Fight Drug-Related Crime," *Church News*, June 17, 1989, p. 5; Richard P. Lindsay, interview by author, February 22, 2007, transcript in possession of the author, p. 3.

[12]Richard P. Lindsay, interview by the author, February 22, 2007, transcript in pos-session of the author, p. 3.

[13]For an overview of the organization and evolving emphasis of Ex-Mormons for Jesus, see Sara M. Patterson, "'A P.O. Box and a Desire to Witness for Jesus': Identity and Mission in the Ex-Mormons for Jesus/Saints Alive in Jesus, 1975–1990," *Journal of Mormon History* 36, no. 3 (Summer 2010): 54-81. For estimates about screenings and audience sizes, see Bob Keeper, "Ex-Mormons' Film Sparks Controversy," *Eugene (Oregon) Register-Guard*, January 14, 1984; photocopy in possession of the

author; also Janet Barker, "Anti-Mormon Film Makes Impact on South Bay," *Torrance (California) South Bay Breeze*, January 21, 1984, p. B2.

[14]Stephen E. Robinson, *Are Mormons Christians?* (Salt Lake City: Bookcraft, 1991).

[15]See Greg Johnson, interview with author, March 2, 2010, transcript, pp. 3-4.

[16]Craig L. Blomberg and Stephen E. Robinson, *How Wide the Divide? A Mormon and an Evangelical in Conversation* (Downers Grove, IL: InterVarsity Press, 1997).

[17]Standing Together ministries produced a DVD that included Richard Mouw's and Ravi Zacharias's addresses: *In Pursuit of Truth* (2004).

[18]See Sarah Pulliam, "A Latter-day Alliance," *Christianity Today*, December 2008 (web-only edition), www.christianitytoday.com/ct/2008/decemberweb-only /149-22.0.html. Pulliam's article reported that Charles Colson, James Dobson, Tony Perkins and Richard Land were among the people who "signed an online petition thanking the LDS Church for its Proposition 8 efforts." See also statements released by the Catholic Bishops of Sacramento and Salt Lake City, "Catholic Bishop Decries Religious Bigotry Against Mormons," *Newsroom, The Church of Jesus Christ of Latter-day Saints*, November 7, 2008, http://newsroom.lds.org/ldsnewsroom /eng/news-releases-stories/catholic-bishop-decries-religious-bigotry-against -mormons. For criticism of Mormon involvement in supporting the ballot measure, see Nicholas Riccardi, "Mormons Feel the Backlash over Their Support of Prop. 8," *Los Angeles Times*, November 17, 2008, http://articles.latimes.com/2008/nov/17 /nation/na-mormons17; Jennifer Dobner, "Film Blasts LDS Role in Prop 8," *Salt Lake Tribune*, January 24, 2010, B7. For the church's response to claims that it did not report its donations to the cause, see "Media Reports on Proposition 8 Filing Uninformed," *Newsroom, The Church of Jesus Christ of Latter-day Saints*, November 17, 2008, http://newsroom.lds.org/ldsnewsroom/eng/commentary/media-reports -on-proposition-8-filing-uninformed.

[19]Michael Otterson, interview by author, October 25, 2013, transcript, pp. 6-7.

[20]For Jeffress's comments, see Rachel Weiner, "Mormonism Takes Center Stage at Conservative Event," *Washington Post*, October 7, 2011, www.washingtonpost.com /politics/mormonism-takes-center-stage-at-conservative-event/2011/10/07 /gIQA9rXoTL_story.html; and the CNN clip with Anderson Cooper in Frances Martel, "Anti-Mormon Pastor to Anderson Cooper: Romney May Belong to a 'Cult,' but He Is Better Than Obama," October 8, 2011, *Mediaite.com*, www.mediaite .com/tv/anti-mormon-pastor-to-anderson-cooper-romney-may-belong -to-a-cult-but-he-is-better-than-obama. Martel said Jeffress "stole the Friday news cycle."

[21]Richard J. Mouw, "My Take: This Evangelical Says Mormonism Isn't a Cult," special to CNN, October 9, 2011, http://religion.blogs.cnn.com/2011/10/09/my-take-this -evangelical-says-mormonism-isnt-a-cult; John Mark Reynolds, "Why Evangelicals Must Stand Up to Anti-Mormon Bigotry," *Civitate.org*, October 10, 2011, www .civitate.org/2011/10/why-evangelicals-must-stand-up-to-anti-mormon-bigotry.

[22]See Kathleen Flake's comments about "antipathy" toward the "present administration" [of President Barack Obama] as accounting for "the silencing of evan-

gelical anti-Mormonism," in Liz Halloran, "What Romney's Run Means for Mormonism," *National Public Radio*, November 1, 2012, www.npr.org/blogs /itsallpolitics/2012/11/01/164101548/what-romneys-run-means-for-mormonism. See also "Panel Asks: Can Christians Vote for a Mormon?" *Baptist Press News*, September 11, 2012, www.bpnews.net/bpnews.asp?ID=38688; Robert Jeffress, "Romney and the Disappearing Evangelical Dilemma," *FoxNews.com*, September 19, 2012, www.foxnews.com/opinion/2012/09/19/mitt-romney-and-disappearing -evangelical-dilemma.

[23]Holland presented these views, and suggested that Christian voters might have simply chosen to sit out the election, at a Utah Valley University panel sponsored by the university's Interreligious Engagement Initiative, November 15, 2013. Richard Mouw was another invited panelist.

[24]Jonathan Merritt, "Election 2012 Marks the End of Evangelical Dominance in Politics," *The Atlantic*, November 13, 2012, www.theatlantic.com/politics /archive/2012/11/election-2012-marks-the-end-of-evangelical-dominance-in-pol itics/265139. See also "The Media, Religion and the 2012 Campaign for President," Pew Research Center's Project for Excellence in Journalism, December 14, 2012, which calculated 79 percent of white evangelicals voted for George W. Bush in 2004 and Mitt Romney in 2012, while 73 percent of evangelicals voted for John McCain in 2008, based on exit polling; www.journalism.org/analysis_report /media_religion_and_2012_campaign_president. In fact, evangelicals voted for Romney at a rate one percentage point higher than even Mormons did. For Pew's estimate that 79 percent of evangelicals and 78 percent of Mormons voted for Romney, see "How the Faithful Voted: 2012 Preliminary Analysis," Pew Research Religion and Public Life Project, November 7, 2012, www.pewforum.org/2012/11/07 /how-the-faithful-voted-2012-preliminary-exit-poll-analysis.

[25]Franklin Graham, "Can An Evangelical Christian Vote for a Mormon?" *Decision Magazine*, October 22, 2012, http://billygraham.org/decision-magazine /october-2012/can-an-evangelical-christian-vote-for-a-mormon; Daniel Burke, "Billy Graham Faces Backlash over Mormon 'Cult' Removal," *Washington Post*, October 24, 2012, http://articles.washingtonpost.com/2012-10-24/national /35501066_1_mormonism-evangelicals-christians.

[26]Tad Walch, "At BYU, Baptist Says Mormons and Evangelicals 'May Go to Jail Together,'" *Deseret News*, October 21, 2013, www.deseretnews.com/article /865588850/At-BYU-Baptist-says-Mormons-and-evangelicals-may-go-to -jail-together.html?pg=all.

[27]See John-Charles Duffy, "Conservative Pluralists: The Cultural Politics of Mormon-Evangelical Dialogue in the United States at the Turn of the Twenty-first Century" (PhD diss., University of North Carolina at Chapel Hill, 2011), for Duffy's argument that evangelicals found a rhetorical place for dialogue and interaction with Mormons by avoiding doctrinal compromise—and this essentially allowed support for Mitt Romney, as long as that political cooperation did not require tacit acceptance of Mormons as Christians. Also see Michael Otterson interview, transcript,

p. 8: "People may not agree with us theologically, but they don't dismiss us. We are
not the curiosity, 'Utah' . . . church that we used to be."

[28]See Michael Otterson interview, transcript, pp. 9-10: "For example, the [Af-
fordable Care Act] mandate really doesn't affect the [LDS] Church but it certainly affects the Catholic Church and their hospitals and their facilities. So we
have been willing to sign on to some of their letters to government or petitions.
We've been willing to attach a church general authority's signature to those because we recognize the broader issue of religious freedom is what's at play here
even though it doesn't affect us directly." See also the justserve.org volunteerism
website sponsored by the LDS Church with partners such as Catholic Charities
and the Salvation Army. For the participants in the 2013 International Law and
Religion Symposium, see www.iclrs.org/content/blurb/files/Symposium%20
Program%202013.pdf.

[29]On immigration reform see, e.g., the LDS Church's support of the "Utah Compact"
and legislation that "will allow those who are now here illegally to work legally,
provide for their families and become better contributing members of our community"; "Immigration Response," *Newsroom, The Church of Jesus Christ of Latter-
day Saints*, www.mormonnewsroom.org/article/immigration-response. On explicit LDS support for nondiscrimination statutes in Salt Lake City in November
2009, see Matt Canham, Derek P. Jensen and Rosemary Winters, "Salt Lake City
Adopts Pro-Gay Statutes—With LDS Church Support," *Salt Lake Tribune*, November 11, 2009, where they quote the statement by LDS spokesman Michael Otterson: "The church supports these ordinances because they are fair and reasonable
and they do not do violence to the institution of marriage." Some Utah gay rights
activists called the church's support "historic," and even afterward described the
church as a "caring, loving, concerned institution." In this it seems that Mormon
leaders sought to distance themselves from antigay hardliners and strike the difficult balance between two essential tenets of the faith—the sanctity and eternal
nature of marriage and the need for compassion and respect for the "human
dignity" of every individual, as Otterson said, "even when we disagree." See also
the Alliance for Unity statement of purpose, www.allianceforunity.org/purpose
.html: "We, the undersigned, are concerned that acceptance of diversity in Utah
today is not of the scope or at the level it ought to be. We ask Utahns of every
background to cast a broader look at diversity and to nurture a deeper respect for
our differences. It is only when we respect differences that we can be united in a
healthy community." One of the signatories of the alliance is M. Russell Ballard,
LDS apostle.

[30]See Michael Otterson interview, transcript, p. 10: "We do maintain our independence and there have been some things where we said 'that's really not our fight.
We don't think that's one we would want to get into.' . . . Working with a coalition
always runs the risk of losing your independence so it's carefully watched and it's
carefully balanced." For the most comprehensive look at American Mormons and
their sometimes surprisingly moderate political views, see David E. Campbell,

John C. Green and J. Quin Monson, *Seeking the Promised Land: Mormons and American Politics* (New York: Cambridge University Press, 2014). While the LDS Church is officially and adamantly nonpartisan, see p. 246, where Campbell, Green and Monson note that one effect of Mitt Romney's 2012 presidential run was the opening up of a new "wide party gap" in the public's perception of Mormons: "Republicans became much more favorable toward Mormons, independents became slightly more so, and Democrats became sharply less favorable"—and this, ironically, at the same time that Harry Reid, a Mormon and a Democrat, served as the Senate's Majority Leader. Campbell, Green and Monson note that in 2006 "there [were] no partisan differences" in that perception.

CHAPTER 13: HOW MANY GODS? MORMONS AND EVANGELICALS DISCUSSING THE DEBATE

[1]Larry W. Hurtado, *How on Earth Did Jesus Become a God? Historical Questions about Earliest Devotion to Jesus* (Grand Rapids: Eerdmans, 2005).

[2]In addition to the works cited in nn. 1, 3, 4 and 5, see his *At the Origins of Christian Worship: The Context and Character of Earliest Christian Devotion* (Grand Rapids: Eerdmans, 2000); Hurtado, *God in New Testament Theology* (Nashville: Abingdon, 2010); Hurtado, "Early Devotion to Jesus: A Report, Reflections and Implications," *Expository Times* 122 (2011): 167-76; Hurtado, "The Origins of Jesus Devotion: A Response to Crispin Fletcher-Louis," *Tyndale Bulletin* 61 (2010): 1-20; Hurtado, "To Live and Die for Jesus: Social and Political Consequences of Devotion to Jesus in Earliest Christianity," *Svensk Exegetisk Årsbok* 70 (2005): 309-31; Hurtado, "Homage to the Historical Jesus and Early Christian Devotion," *Journal for the Study of the Historical Jesus* 1 (2003): 131-46; Hurtado, "Pre-70 C.E. Jewish Opposition to Christ Devotion," *Journal of Theological Studies* 50 (1999): 35-58; Hurtado, "First Century Jewish Monotheism," *Journal for the Study of the New Testament* 71 (1998): 3-26; Hurtado, "Christ-Devotion in the First Two Centuries: Reflections and a Proposal," *Toronto Journal of Theology* 12 (1996): 17-33; Hurtado, "The Origins of the Worship of Christ," *Themelios* 19 (1994): 4-8.

[3]Larry Hurtado, *One God, One Lord: Early Christian Devotion and Ancient Jewish Monotheism,* 2nd ed. (London: Continuum, 1998).

[4]Larry Hurtado, *Lord Jesus Christ: Devotion to Jesus in Earliest Christianity* (Grand Rapids: Eerdmans, 2003).

[5]Larry W. Hurtado, "The Gospel of Mark: Evolutionary or Revolutionary Document?" *Journal for the Study of the New Testament* 40 (1990): 15-32.

[6]The classic study is Philip Schaff, ed., *The Creeds of Christendom: With a History and Critical Notes,* 6th ed., rev. David S. Schaff (New York: Harper & Row, 1931), 1:14-29.

[7]Stephen E. Robinson, *Are Mormons Christians?* (Salt Lake City: Bookcraft, 1991), pp. 71-89; Robert L. Millet, "Trinity," in *LDS Beliefs: A Doctrinal Reference*, ed. Robert L. Millet, Camille Fronk Olson, Andrew C. Skinner and Brent L. Top (Salt Lake City: Deseret, 2011), pp. 642-43.

[8]Brent L. Top, "Restoration," in Millet, Olson, Skinner and Top, *LDS Beliefs*, pp. 529-32.

[9]See esp. the reviews by Nick Overduin, *Calvin Theological Journal* 41 (2006): 392-94; Michael J. Kruger, *Westminster Theological Journal* 68 (2006): 369-72; Peter H. Davids, *Bulletin for Biblical Research* 16 (2006): 365-66; and Christoph Stenschke, *Evangelical Quarterly* 81 (2009): 175-77.

[10]Roger R. Keller, "Jesus is Jehovah (YHWH): A Study in the Gospels," in *Jesus Christ: Son of God, Savior*, ed. Paul H. Peterson, Gary L. Hatch and Laura D. Card (Provo, UT: BYU Religious Studies Center, 2002), p. 151.

[11]See esp. Margaret Barker, *The Great Angel: A Study of Israel's Second God* (Louisville, KY: Westminster John Knox, 1992).

[12]E.g., Barry R. Bickmore, *Restoring the Ancient Church: Joseph Smith and Early Christianity* (Salt Lake City: FAIR, 1999), pp. 106-21.

[13]Hurtado, *How on Earth Did Jesus Become a God?*, 113 n. 5; 128 n. 50; 131; 168 n. 53.

[14]All Scripture quotations, unless otherwise indicated, are from the New International Version.

[15]For the range of options throughout Jewish and Christian history for the interpretation of Daniel 7:9, see Ernest C. Lucas, *Daniel*, Apollos Old Testament Commentary (Downers Grove, IL: InterVarsity Press, 2002), pp. 181-82.

[16]On which see now esp. Larry W. Hurtado and Paul L. Owen, eds., *"Who Is This Son of Man?" The Latest Scholarship on a Puzzling Expression of the Historical Jesus* (London: T & T Clark, 2011).

[17]A rare recent defense by anyone of prominence in the scholarly guild is Richard B. Gaffin Jr., "A Cessationist View," in *Are Miraculous Gifts for Today? Four Views*, ed. Wayne A. Grudem (Grand Rapids: Zondervan, 1996), pp. 25-64, and even that was in the last millennium.

[18]See, e.g., throughout Blake T. Ostler, *Exploring Mormon Thought: Of God and Gods* (Salt Lake City: Greg Kofford, 2008).

[19]E.g., R. Philip Roberts, *Mormonism Unmasked: Confronting the Contradictions Between Mormon Beliefs and True Christianity* (Nashville: B & H, 1998), pp. 45-62.

[20]Cf. Robert L. Millet, *Getting at the Truth: Responding to Difficult Questions about LDS Beliefs* (Salt Lake City: Deseret, 2004), pp. 115-16.

[21]E.g., Kevin Giles, *The Trinity and Subordinationism: The Doctrine of God and the Contemporary Gender Debate* (Downers Grove, IL InterVarsity Press, 2002), who argues for temporal subordination only; and Mark Baddeley, "The Trinity and Subordinationism: A Response to Kevin Giles," *Reformed Theological Review* 63 (2004): 1-14, who argues for eternal (functional not ontological) subordination.

[22]Cf. Robert Letham, *The Holy Trinity: In Scripture, History, Theology, and Worship* (Phillipsburg, NJ: P & R, 2004), pp. 489-96, who supports eternal, functional subordination, and Millard J. Erickson, *God in Three Persons: A Contemporary Interpretation of the Trinity* (Grand Rapids: Baker, 1995), pp. 291-310, who supports functional subordination only in the incarnation.

[23]Stephen E. Robinson, "Christ and the Trinity," in *How Wide the Divide? A Mormon*

and an Evangelical in Conversation, ed. Craig L. Blomberg and Stephen E. Robinson (Downers Grove, IL: InterVarsity Press, 1997), pp. 134-36.

[24]Gordon R. Lewis and Bruce A. Demarest, *Integrative Theology*, 3 vols. (Grand Rapids: Zondervan, 1987–1994), 2:284-86.

[25]Millard J. Erickson, *Christian Theology*, 3rd ed. (Grand Rapids: Baker Academic, 2013), p. 711.

[26]Millet, *Getting at the Truth*, pp. 107-8.

[27]Cf. Marcel Sarot, *God, Possibility, and Corporeality* (Leuven: Peeters, 1992).

[28]Craig L. Blomberg and Stephen E. Robinson, "Joint Conclusion," in Blomberg and Robinson, *How Wide the Divide?*, p. 142.

[29]Cornelius Plantinga Jr., "Social Trinity and Tritheism," in *Trinity, Incarnation, and Atonement: Philosophical and Theological Essays*, ed. Ronald Geenstra and Cornelius Plantinga Jr. (Notre Dame, IN: University of Notre Dame Press, 1989), pp. 21-47. For Plantinga, this means that each person of the Trinity must be a distinct center of knowledge, will, love and action yet tightly enough related to be a particular social unit.

[30]David L. Paulsen, "Response to Professor Pinnock," in *Mormonism in Dialogue with Contemporary Christian Theologies*, ed. Donald W. Musser and David L. Paulsen (Macon, GA: Mercer University Press, 2007), pp. 538-41, 546-47.

[31]E.g., Michael W. Horton, *Pilgrim Theology: Core Doctrines for Christian Disciples* (Grand Rapids: Zondervan, 2011), p. 102. Intriguingly, although Horton rejects social trinitarianism as tritheism, he goes on to maintain that unless Christian *experience* is trinitarian, i.e., unless we experience Father, Son and Holy Spirit each differently according to their distinctive roles, "it is not properly Christian" (p. 104). If this is true, then most LDS are more properly Christian than most evangelicals in this respect!

[32]See, e.g., Eliza R. Snow Smith, *Biography and Family Record of Lorenzo Snow* (Salt Lake City: Deseret News, 1884), p. 46. The quotation is often wrongly cited as ending with "man may become."

[33]Stephen E. Robinson, "God and Deification," in Blomberg and Robinson, *How Wide the Divide?*, p. 82.

[34]Ibid.

[35]Richard J. Mouw, *Talking with Mormons: An Invitation to Evangelicals* (Grand Rapids: Eerdmans, 2012), p. 54.

[36]Ibid., pp. 83, 95.

[37]George B. Arbaugh, *Revelation in Mormonism* (Chicago: University of Chicago Press, 1932) traces the development of Mormonism from what he terms a sectarian form of Campbellite restorationism to full-fledged heterodoxy.

[38]Numerous editions exist. See, e.g., Joseph Smith, *Lectures on Faith* (Salt Lake City: Deseret, 1985).

[39]Cf. Robert L. Millet, *A Different Jesus? The Christ of the Latter-day Saints* (Grand Rapids: Eerdmans, 2005), pp. 141-42.

[40]On which, see esp. Robert L. Millet, *Grace Works: After All We Can Do* (Salt Lake City: Deseret, 2003).

[41]Cf. Robert L. Millet, *What Happened to the Cross? Distinctive LDS Teachings* (Salt Lake City: Deseret, 2007), p. 33.

[42]Erickson, *Christian Theology*, pp. 304-5.

[43]Lewis and Demarest, *Integrative Theology*, 1:272-75.

[44]Andreas J. Köstenberger is worth quoting in some detail: "Jesus' statement that the Father is greater than he is not meant to indicate ontological inferiority on his part. Elsewhere, Jesus affirms that he and the Father are one (10:30). Rather, Jesus stresses his subordination to the Father, which, as the NT makes clear, is not merely a part of his incarnate ministry but is rooted in his eternal sonship (cf. esp. 1 Cor. 15:28; . . . see also Barrett 1982a: 19-26)." Andreas J. Köstenberger, *John*, Baker Exegetical Commentary on the New Testament (Grand Rapids: Baker Academic, 2004), p. 445. The reference is to the classic study by C. K. Barrett, "'The Father Is Greater Than I' (John 14.28): Subordinationist Christology in the New Testament," in his *Essays on John* (Philadelphia: Westminster, 1982), pp. 19-36, all the more significant because Barrett was not an evangelical.

[45]One answer could be that the language of being in the Father and the Son refers back to the nearer antecedent of remaining in Christ in John 15:1-7, rather than all the way to chapter 14. See D. A. Carson, *The Gospel according to John*, Pillar New Testament Commentary (Grand Rapids: Eerdmans, 1991), p. 558.

Chapter 14: The Trinity

[1]Robert L. Millet and Gerald R. McDermott, *Claiming Christ: A Mormon-Evangelical Debate* (Grand Rapids: Brazos, 2007), p. 80.

[2]Steven D. Boyer and Christopher A. Hall, *The Mystery of God: Theology for Knowing the Unknowable* (Grand Rapids: Baker Academic, 2012), p. 52.

[3]Ibid., p. 117.

[4]Stephen Webb, *What Other Christians Can Learn from the Latter-Day Saints* (Oxford: Oxford University Press, 2013), p. 191.

[5]Boyer and Hall, *Mystery of God*, p. 118.

[6]Ibid.

[7]Gregory of Nyssa, *Against Eunomius* 2.9, *Nicene and Post-Nicene Fathers*, ed. Philip Schaff et al., 2nd series (1887–1894; repr., Peabody, MA: Hendrickson, 1994), 5:114, (emphasis added).

[8]Joseph Smith, *Doctrine and Covenants* 130:22; quoted in Webb, *What Other Christians Can Learn*, p. 84.

[9]Webb, *What Other Christians Can Learn*, p. 84.

Chapter 15: Divine Investiture: Mormonism and the Concept of Trinity

[1]In sum, the Nicene position was articulated in the doctrine of three persons (*hypostases*) in one divine substance (*ousia*). To put the issue in more precise language, the Greek term *ousia* is often translated as "essence" while *hypostasis* is often translated as "substance." Hence, three substances in one essence. In the Latin, however, the term *ousia* is translated into the term *substantia*, while *hypostasis* is translated

as "person." Hence, three persons in one substance. For more on these terms, see R. P. C. Hanson, *The Search for the Christian Doctrine of God: The Arian Controversy, 318–381* (1988; Grand Rapids: Baker Academic, 2005); and Lewis Ayres, *Nicaea and Its Legacy: An Approach to Fourth-Century Trinitarian Theology* (Oxford: Oxford University Press, 2004).

[2] This language was employed in the Athanasian Creed, which was used in later centuries to demonstrate the middle path between modalism and tritheism. See John H. Leith, ed., *Creeds of the Churches: A Reader in Christian Doctrine from the Bible to the Present*, 3rd ed. (Louisville, KY: Westminster John Knox, 1982), p. 704.

[3] A handful of issues informed the efforts to unify the church's position on the nature of God and the relationship between the Father and the Son. These included the idiosyncratic teachings of Brigham Young that Adam and God the Father were one and the same being. Though never dominant, this "Adam-God" doctrine maintained some currency throughout the nineteenth century and until the 1916 statement. See David Buerger, "The Adam-God Doctrine," *Dialogue: A Journal of Mormon Thought* 15, no. 1 (1985): 14-58.

[4] See James E. Talmage, *Jesus the Christ: A Study of the Messiah and His Mission According to the Holy Scriptures both Ancient and Modern* (Salt Lake City: Deseret, 1915).

[5] Doctrine and Covenants, 130:22.

[6] Ronald Huggins, "Joseph Smith's Modalism: Sabellian Sequentialism or Swedenborgian Expansionism?" (paper delivered at the Salt Lake Theological Seminary, July 26, 2003, document in author's possession).

[7] Space does not permit a robust treatment of these issues. For a sample of the debates, see Ari D. Bruening and David L. Paulsen, "The Development of the Mormon Understanding of God and Other Myths," *FARMS Review of Books* 13, no. 2 (2001): 109-69; and Robert L. Millet, "By What (Whose) Standards Shall We Judge the Text: A Closer Look at Jesus Christ in the Book of Mormon," *Review of Books on the Book of Mormon* 6, no. 1 (1994): 187-99. For stronger developmental views, see Thomas G. Alexander, "The Reconstruction of Mormon Doctrine," in *Line upon Line: Essays on Mormon Doctrine*, ed. Gary J. Bergera (Salt Lake City: Signature, 1989), pp. 53-66; and Alexander, *Mormonism in Transition: A History of the Latter-day Saints, 1890–1930* (Urbana: University of Illinois Press, 1996), chap. 14; Kurt Widmar, *Mormonism and the Nature of God: A Theological Revolution, 1830–1915* (Jefferson, NC: MacFarland, 2000); Melodie Moenoch Charles, "Book of Mormon Christology," in *New Approaches to the Book of Mormon: Explorations in Critical Methodology*, ed. Brent L. Metcalfe (Salt Lake City: Signature, 1993), pp. 81-114; and Dan Vogel, "The Earliest Mormon Concept of God," *Line upon Line: Essays on Mormon Doctrine*, ed. Gary J. Bergera (Salt Lake City: Signature, 1989), pp. 17-33.

[8] Book of Mormon, Mosiah 3:5, 8.

[9] Ether 3:14, 16. Later in the same discourse, God declares that "he that will not believe me will not believe the Father who sent me. For behold, I am the Father..." (Ether 4:12).

[10] Scott H. Faulring, Kent P. Jackson and Robert J. Matthews, eds., *Joseph Smith's New*

Translation of the Bible: Original Manuscripts (Provo, UT: Religious Studies Center, Brigham Young University, 2004), p. 393.

[11]Doctrine and Covenants, 29.

[12]A similar conceptualization is found in 3 Nephi 1:14. "Behold, I come unto my own, to fulfil all things which I have made known unto the children of men from the foundation of the world, and to do the will, both of the Father and of the Son—of the Father because of me, and of the Son because of my flesh. And behold, the time is at hand, and this night shall the sign be given."

[13]1 Nephi 11:18 (emphasis added). A similar change was made in 1 Nephi 11:32. The original 1830 edition read: "I looked and beheld the Lamb of God, that he was taken by the people; yea, the Everlasting God, was judged of the world." The 1837 edition reads: "I looked and beheld the Lamb of God, that he was taken by the people; yea, the *Son of* the everlasting God was judged of the world; and I saw and bear record" (emphasis added).

[14]David Paulsen argues that "disambiguation, as opposed to a sudden radical change in theology, provides the best explanation of these editorial revisions." See "Development of the Mormon Understanding," pp. 131-32. Though this may very well have been the intent, the theological question remained unclear. For example, the "Testimony of Three Witnesses" document to the Book of Mormon reads "And honor be to the Father, and to the Son, and to the Holy Ghost, which is one God." However, in the original 1830 "Articles and Covenants" document, the passage that originally read "which Father and the Son, and the Holy Ghost is one God" was edited in 1835 to read "Which Father, Son, and Holy Ghost are one God" (20:28).

[15]*History of the Church of Jesus Christ of Latter-day Saints* (Salt Lake City: Deseret, 1912), 6:474.

[16]To put the issue syllogistically: P1. The Son is a divine being; P2. All divine beings are eternal; C1. Therefore the Son is eternal. A second argument might go as follows: P1. The Bible is correct and authoritative in its descriptions of the Son; P2. The Bible affirms that the Son was begotten of the Father; P3: The Bible affirms that the Son is a divine being (and thus eternal); C1: The Son is both eternal and begotten.

[17]As printed in the Lutheran Book of Worship and the Anglican Book of Common Prayer. The Nicene Creed was later modified by the Council of Constantinople in 381. Technically, the above is the Niceno-Constantinopolitan Creed (emphasis added).

[18]Quoted in Rowan Williams, *Arius: History and Tradition*, 2nd ed. (Grand Rapids: Eerdmans, 2002), p. 271.

[19]Doctrine and Covenants 93:21, 23.

[20]"The Father and the Son: A Doctrinal Exposition," *The Improvement Era* (August 1916): 934-42.

[21]In general terms, adoptionism (or "dynamic monarchianism") is the view that Jesus was adopted as the Son of God at some point during his mortal life through sinless devotion to the will of the Father (though its advocates have differed over the key event in question).

[22]Many thanks are to due to my friend and collaborator Grant Underwood for his insights on these points.

[23]Talmage, *Jesus the Christ*, p. 34 (emphasis added).

[24]Robert L. Millet, *A Different Jesus? The Christ of the Latter-day Saints* (Grand Rapids: Eerdmans, 2005), p. 20. The quotation from McConkie is taken from *The Promised Messiah* (Salt Lake City: Deseret, 1978), p. 46 (emphasis added). See also Andrew C. Skinner, "The Premortal Godhood of Christ: A Restoration Perspective," in *Jesus Christ: Son of God, Savior*, ed. Paul H. Peterson, Gary L. Hatch and Laura D. Card (Provo, UT: Religious Studies Center, Brigham Young University, 2002), pp. 50-78. BYU professor Stephen Robinson offers a relatively refined treatment of trinitarian distinctions in his book-length dialogue with Denver Seminary professor Craig Blomberg. See the chapter titled "Christ and the Trinity," in *How Wide the Divide: A Mormon and an Evangelical in Conversation* (Downers Grove, IL: InterVarsity Press, 1997), pp. 77-110. For an alternative account, see Blake Ostler, *Exploring Mormon Thought: Of God and Gods* (Salt Lake City: Greg Kofford Books, 2008).

CHAPTER 17: THEOLOGICAL ANTHROPOLOGY: THE ORIGIN AND NATURE OF HUMAN BEINGS

[1]Truman G. Madsen, *Eternal Man* (Salt Lake City: Deseret, 1966), p. 22.

[2]This is the consensus view of Semitic philologists and Hebrew Bible scholars reaching back to Theodor Noldeke and Herman Gunkel at the turn of the twentieth century. See Claus Westermann, *Genesis 1–11: A Commentary*, trans. John J. Scullion (Minneapolis: Augsburg, 1984); and Stanley L. Jaki, *Genesis 1 Through the Ages* (London: Thomas More, 1992).

[3]Gerhard von Rad, *Genesis*, Old Testament Library, rev. ed. (Philadelphia: Westminster, 1972), p. 58.

[4]Augustine is representative of most Christian accommodationists. He acknowledged that in the Scriptures "God's eyes are mentioned, and his ears, and lips, and feet, and the Son is proclaimed in the gospel as being seated at the right hand of God the Father." But "all those who have a spiritual understanding of the scriptures have learned to take these names as meaning, not parts of the body, but spiritual powers. . . . They should know that in the Catholic school of doctrine the faithful who have a spiritual understanding do not believe that God is circumscribed in a bodily shape; and when man is said to have been made to the image of God, it is said with reference to the interior man, where reason is to be found and intelligence . . . not to the body." *On Genesis* 1.17.27, trans. Edmund Hill, *The Works of St. Augustine* (Hyde Park, NY: New City Press, 2002), pp. 56-57.

[5]Scott H. Faulring, Kent P. Jackson and Robert J. Matthews, eds., *Joseph Smith's New Translation of the Bible: Original Manuscripts* (Provo: BYU Religious Studies Center, 2004), pp. 97, 608. The different page numbers reflect the fact that there are *two* manuscript versions of Smith's revision. The first is unpunctuated and thus could be read either as an addition to verse 1 (as shown above) or as a new prefatory

phrase to verse 2 ("Male and female created he them"). In the second manuscript version, which was a copy of the original, punctuation was added. In this case, a period followed "in the image of his own body," thus linking it to verse 1. However, when the LDS Church eventually published this portion of Smith's Bible revision, the phrase was included as the opening line of verse 2. See Moses 6:9.

[6]Joseph Smith, *Gospel Doctrine* (Salt Lake City: Deseret, 1919), p. 76.

[7]Augustine, *Confessions* 1.1, trans. Henry Chadwick, Oxford World Classics (New York: Oxford University Press, 2009), p. 3.

[8]See Anthony Hoekema, *Created in God's Image* (Grand Rapids: Eerdmans, 1986).

[9]"The Origin of Man," *Improvement Era* 13 (Nov 1909): 81. See also "Becoming Like God" on the LDS Church's website, https://www.lds.org/topics/becoming-like -god?lang=eng.

[10]Walther Eichrodt, *Theology of the Old Testament* (Philadelphia: Westminster, 1967), 2:147.

[11]Joel B. Green, *Body, Soul, and Human Life: The Nature of Humanity in the Bible* (Grand Rapids: Baker Academic, 2008), esp. pp. 3-16.

[12]Rudolf Bultmann, *Theology of the New Testament*, trans. Kendrick Grobel (1953; repr., Waco: Baylor University Press, 2007), 1:194, 201. See also Hans Dieter Betz, "The Concept of the 'Inner Human Being' (*eso anthropos*) in the Anthropology of Paul," *New Testament Studies* 46 (July 2000): 315-41.

[13]Joel B. Green and Stuart L. Palmer, *In Search of the Soul: Four Views of the Mind-Body Problem* (Downers Grove, IL: IVP Academic, 2005); Green, *Body, Soul, and Human Life*; Nancey Murphy, *Bodies and Souls, or Spirited Bodies* (Cambridge: Cambridge University Press, 2006); and John W. Cooper, *Body, Soul, and Life Everlasting: Biblical Anthropology and the Monism-Dualism Debate*, 2nd ed. (Grand Rapids: Eerdmans, 2000).

[14]Phillip Cary, *Augustine's Invention of the Inner Self: The Legacy of a Christian Platonist* (New York: Oxford University Press, 2003).

[15]Madsen, *Eternal Man*, p. 45.

[16]Richard Hanson, "The Achievement of Orthodoxy in the Fourth Century AD," in *The Making of Orthodoxy: Essays in Honour of Henry Chadwick*, ed. Rowan Williams (Cambridge: Cambridge University Press, 1989), pp. 151-52.

[17]See Tertullian, *De Anima* 9.7-8. The quotation is from Carly Daniel-Hughes, *The Salvation of the Flesh in Tertullian of Carthage: Dressing for the Resurrection* (New York: Palgrave Macmillan, 2011), p. 67. Daniel-Hughes adds: "This logic extends to sexual difference, too, which in Tertullian's view is not some accidental property of the flesh alone, thus discarded with the corruptible flesh at death, as a Platonist might conclude, but a distinction that pertains to soul and flesh alike" (ibid., p. 67).

[18]John Anthony McGuckin, "Soul," in *The Westminster Handbook to Patristic Theology* (Louisville, KY: Westminster John Knox, 2004), p. 318. Decisive in this development was Origen's *Dialogue with Heracleides*.

[19]Lynne Rudder Baker, "Death and the Afterlife," in *The Oxford Handbook of Phi-*

losophy of Religion, ed. William J. Wainwright (Oxford: Oxford University Press, 2005), p. 370.

[20]Paula Fredriksen, "Beyond the Body/Soul Dichotomy: Augustine's Answer to Mani, Plotinus, and Julian," in *Paul and the Legacies of Paul*, ed. William S. Babcock (Dallas: Southern Methodist University Press, 1990), p. 245.

[21]On the later censuring of aspects of Origen's theology, see Elizabeth A. Clark, *The Origenist Controversy: The Cultural Construction of an Early Christian Debate* (Princeton, NJ: Princeton University Press, 1992).

[22]Madsen, *Eternal Man*, p. 22.

[23]In their 1909 pronouncement, the church's First Presidency declared: Jesus "is the firstborn among all the sons of God—the first begotten in the spirit, and the only begotten in the flesh. He is our elder brother, and we, like Him, are in the image of God" ("The Origin of Man," p. 78).

[24]"My Father in Heaven," *Times and Seasons* 6 (November 15, 1845): 1039. See also, "O My Father," *Hymns of the Church of Jesus Christ of Latter-day Saints* (Salt Lake City: The Church of Jesus Christ of Latter-day Saints, 1985), no. 292. Madsen remarked that this hymn "expresses the heart of 'Latter-day Saintliness'" (*Eternal Man*, p. 42). For a full discussion of this poem/hymn and its importance to Latter-day Saints, see Jill Mulvay Derr, "The Significance of 'O My Father' in the Personal Journey of Eliza R. Snow," *BYU Studies* 36 (1996–1997): 84-126.

[25]"The Family: A Proclamation to the World," *Ensign* 25 (November 1995): 102 (emphasis added). These words echo language used at the beginning of the twentieth century in the First Presidency's "Origin of Man" statement: "All men and women are in the similitude of the universal Father *and Mother* and are literally the sons and daughters of Deity," and "man, as a spirit, was begotten and born of heavenly *parents* and reared to maturity in the eternal mansions of the Father, prior to coming upon the earth in a temporal body" ("Origin of Man," pp. 78, 80 [emphasis added]). The 1995 Proclamation adds: "Gender is an essential characteristic of individual premortal, mortal, and eternal identity and purpose."

[26]A comprehensive discussion of LDS ideas about "Mother in Heaven" can be found in David L. Paulsen and Martin Pulido, "'A Mother There': A Survey of Historical Teachings," *BYU Studies* 50 (2011): 71-97. Some Mormons have assumed that a reverential veil should be drawn over any discussion of a Heavenly Mother, but church leaders have not so insisted. What church authorities have done, though, with regard to a related issue is to specifically direct church members not to pray to Heavenly Mother, emphasizing the pattern in the "Lord's Prayer" of addressing prayers to "Our Father which art in heaven" (Matthew 6:9). See, for instance, Gordon B. Hinckley, "Daughters of God," *Ensign* 31 (November 1991): 100.

[27]As cited in R. P. C. Hanson, *The Search for the Christian Doctrine of God: The Arian Controversy, 318–381* (1988; Grand Rapids: Baker Academic, 2005), p. 506. As with human reproduction, official Latter-day Saint doctrine understands the divine procreation of spirit children to require both male and female, although it says nothing about *how* and *why* this is so. An official "Doctrinal Exposition" by the

First Presidency in 1916 includes these comments: "Jesus Christ is not the Father of the spirits who have taken or yet shall take bodies upon this earth, for He is one of them. He is The Son, as they are sons or daughters of Elohim [God the Father]. So far as the stages of eternal progression and attainment have been made known through divine revelation, we are to understand that only resurrected and glorified beings can become parents of spirit offspring. . . . And the spirits born to them in the eternal worlds will pass in due sequence through the several stages or estates by which the glorified parents have attained exaltation" ("A Doctrinal Exposition by the First Presidency and the Quorum of the Twelve Apostles," *Improvement Era* 19 [August 1916]: 942).

[28]Smith, *Doctrines of Salvation*, 1:76.

[29]Madsen, *Eternal Man*, p. 35.

[30]Origen, *On First Principles* 2.9.6-7 (*Ante-Nicene Fathers*, ed. A. Roberts and J. Donaldson, trans. A. Cleveland Coxe [1889; repr., Peabody, MA: Hendrickson, 1994], 4:292-93).

[31]The varieties of preexistentialism that have flourished along the periphery of orthodox Christianity since its inception, as well as a substantive overview of Mormon thought about the preexistence, can be found in Terryl L. Givens, *When Souls Had Wings: Pre-Mortal Existence in Western Thought* (New York: Oxford University Press, 2009). Shorter treatments of Mormon preexistentialism focusing on its historical development are Charles R. Harrell, "The Development of the Doctrine of Preexistence, 1830–1844," *BYU Studies* 28 (Spring 1988): 75-96; and Blake T. Ostler, "The Idea of Preexistence in the Development of Mormon Thought," *Dialogue: A Journal of Mormon Thought* 15 (Spring 1982): 59-78.

[32]Madsen, *Eternal Man*, pp. 73, 75-76.

[33]Ibid., p. 58.

[34]*Doctrine and Covenants Student Manual: Religion 324 and 325* (Salt Lake: The Church of Jesus Christ of Latter-day Saints, 2001), p. 219.

[35]Joseph Smith, *Church History and Modern Revelation* (Salt Lake City: Council of the Twelve Apostles of the Church of Jesus Christ of Latter-day Saints, 1953), 2:162.

[36]Bruce R. McConkie, *Mormon Doctrine* (Salt Lake City: Bookcraft, 1958), pp. 73-74.

[37]Madsen, *Eternal Man*, p. 17.

[38]Stan Larson, "The King Follett Discourse: A Newly Amalgamated Text" (Provo: BYU Studies, 1978), pp. 11-12. In an 1839 discourse, Smith is reported as saying, "The Spirit of Man is not a created being; it existed from Eternity & will exist to eternity" (Andrew F. Ehat and Lyndon W. Cook, eds., *Words of Joseph Smith: The Contemporary Accounts of the Nauvoo Discourses of the Prophet Joseph* [Provo, UT: Religious Studies Center, Brigham Young University, 1980], p. 9).

[39]Mormons are currently cautioned on the church's official website that "while the King Follett discourse represents Joseph Smith's most detailed known discussion of divine nature and exaltation, it is important to note that because of the wind on the day the sermon was delivered and the limitations of transcription techniques,

we are left without certainty about Joseph Smith's exact or complete wording during the sermon. The partial accounts of four witnesses and an early published account give us a record, if only an imperfect one, of what Joseph Smith taught on the occasion, and what he taught gives us insight into the meaning of numerous passages of scripture. *But the surviving sermon text is not canonized and should not be treated as a doctrinal standard in and of itself* ("Becoming Like God," n. 35 [emphasis added]).

[40]Madsen, *Eternal Man*, pp. 24-25.

[41]Anthon H. Lund journal, August 29, 1911, as cited in Ostler, "Idea of Preexistence," p. 69.

[42]Lund journal, December 11, 1914, as cited in Ostler, "Idea of Preexistence," p. 69.

[43]Cited in Kenneth W. Godfrey, "The History of Intelligence in Latter-day Saint Thought," in *The Pearl of Great Price: Revelations from God*, ed. H. Don L. Peterson and Charles D. Tate (Provo: BYU Religious Studies Center, 1989), p. 230.

[44]John A. Widtsoe, *Evidences and Reconciliations*, 3 vols. (Salt Lake City: Bookcraft, 1943–1951) 3:76-77.

[45]The quoted phrase is from the First Presidency statement "The Origin of Man," p. 81.

[46]"Becoming Like God."

CHAPTER 18: "HOW GREAT A DEBTOR": MORMON REFLECTIONS ON GRACE

[1]*Hymns of the Church of Jesus Christ of Latter-day Saints* (Salt Lake City: The Church of Jesus Christ of Latter-day Saints, 1985), no. 193.

[2]Karen Lyn Davidson, *Our Latter-day Hymns: The Stories and the Messages* (Salt Lake City: Deseret, 1988), pp. 206-7.

[3]C. S. Lewis, *Mere Christianity* (New York: Macmillan, 1960), p. 160.

[4]Robert Millet, *After All We Can Do . . . Grace Works* (Salt Lake City: Deseret, 2003), p. 115.

[5]Kenneth Woodward, "What Mormons Believe," *Newsweek*, September 1, 1980, p. 68.

[6]Stephen E. Robinson, *Believing Christ* (Salt Lake City: Deseret, 1992), p. x.

[7]Dallin H. Oaks, "Another Testament of Jesus Christ," *Ensign*, March 1994, p. 65.

[8]Bruce C. Hafen, "The Atonement: All for All," *Ensign*, May 2004, p. 97.

[9]M. Russell Ballard, "Building Bridges of Understanding," *Ensign*, June 1998, p. 65.

[10]James B. Allen, Ronald K. Esplin and David J. Whittaker, *Men With a Mission, 1837–1841: The Quorum of the Twelve Apostles in the British Isles* (Salt Lake City: Deseret, 1992), p. 352.

[11]Brigham Young, *Journal of Discourses* (Liverpool: F. D. Richards & Sons, 1851–1886), 13:56.

[12]Millet, *After All We Can Do*, p. 118.

[13]Dietrich Bonhoeffer, *Discipleship*, ed. John D. Godsey and Geffrey B. Kelly, trans. Barbara Green and Reinhard Krauss, Dietrich Bonhoeffer Works 4 (Minneapolis: Fortress Press, 2001), pp. 43-44.

[14]Ibid., pp. 44-45.

[15]*Hymns*, no. 193.

Chapter 19: Authority Is Everything

[1]B. H. Roberts, ed., *History of the Church of Jesus Christ of Latter-day Saints* (Salt Lake City: Deseret Book, 1957), 6:363.

[2]Eusebius, *The History of the Church*, trans. G. A. Williamson, rev. Andrew Louth (New York: Penguin, 1965), p. 96.

[3]J. B. Philips, *The Young Church in Action* (London: Collins, 1955), pp. 11, 20-21; cited in Alexander Morrison, *Turning from the Truth: A New Look at the Great Apostasy* (Salt Lake City: Deseret, 2005), pp. 51-52.

[4]Cited in G. K. Chesterton, *St. Thomas Aquinas* (New York: Sheed & Ward, 1954), pp. 34-35.

[5]Jeffrey R. Holland, *Conference Report*, October 2004, p. 6; citing *Magnaliua Christi Americana* (1853), 2:498.

[6]Cited in LeGrand Richards, *A Marvelous Work and a Wonder* (Salt Lake City: Deseret, 1950), p. 29; see also Milton V. Backman, *American Religions and the Rise of Mormonism* (Salt Lake City: Deseret, 1965), pp. 180-81.

[7]Charles Wesley, cited in Jeffrey R. Holland, *Conference Report*, April 2005, p. 48.

[8]Morrison, *Turning from the Truth*, p. 52.

[9]John Taylor, *Journal of Discourses,* 26 vols. (Liverpool: F. D. Richards & Sons, 1851–1886), 16:197.

[10]Boyd Packer, "The Light of Christ," *Ensign* (April 2005): 11.

[11]Roberts, *History of the Church*, 6:478.

[12]Richard John Neuhaus, *Catholic Matters: Confusion, Controversy, and the Splendor of Truth* (New York: Basic Books, 2006), p. 70 (emphasis added).

[13]Roberts, *History of the Church*, 6:478-79.

[14]Orson F. Whitney, cited in Richards, *A Marvelous Work and a Wonder*, pp. 3-4.

[15]*Teachings of Harold B. Lee*, ed. Clyde J. Williams (Salt Lake City: Bookcraft, 1996), pp. 546-47.

Chapter 20: Revealed Truth: Talking About Our Differences

[1]Terryl L. Givens and Matthew J. Grow, *Parley P. Pratt: The Apostle Paul of Mormonism* (New York: Oxford University Press, 2011), pp. 33, 90.

[2]The best-known account of these "best practices" is Leonard Swidler's highly influential "The Dialogue Decalogue: Ground Rules for Interreligious, Interideological Dialogue," The Dialogue Institute, http://institute.jesdialogue.org/file admin/DI/DIALOGUE%20DECALOGUE%20MAY%202011.pdf. My comments here draw on Swidler's "ten commandments."

[3]"Joseph Smith Tells His Own Story," Mormon Literature website, http://mldb.byu .edu/jsmith.htm.

[4]Jan Shipps, *Mormonism: The Story of a New Religious Tradition* (Urbana: University of Illinois Press, 1987).

CHAPTER 21: TWO QUESTIONS AND FOUR LAWS: MISSIOLOGICAL
REFLECTIONS ON LDS AND EVANGELICAL MISSIONS IN PORT MORESBY

[1]National Statistical Office, March 1983.

[2]Hal B. Levine and Marlene W. Levine, *Urbanization in Papua New Guinea: A Study of Ambivalent Townsmen* (New York: Cambridge University Press).

[3]Percy Chatterton, *Day That I Loved* (Sydney: Pacific Publications, 1980), pp. 17, 24.

[4]A brief history of the work in Papua New Guinea can be found at "Facts and Statistics," *Newsroom, The Church of Jesus Christ of Latter-day Saints*, www.mormon newsroom.org/facts-and-statistics/country/papua-new-guinea (accessed January 3, 2014).

[5]The conversations surrounding the presence of the Mormon missionaries are part of my memory of the events; however, the work of the Port Moresby Minister's Fraternal can be found in C. Douglas McConnell, *Networks and Associations in Urban Mission: A Port Moresby Case Study* (Fuller Theological Seminary, School of World Mission, 1990).

[6]"Facts and Statistics."

[7]The chapter by Dallin H. Oaks and Lance B. Wickman, "The Missionary Work of The Church of Jesus Christ of Latter-day Saints," in *Sharing the Book: Religious Perspectives on the Rights and Wrongs of Proselytism*, ed. John Witte Jr. and Richard C. Martin (Maryknoll, NY: Orbis, 1999) provides an excellent overview of the missionary work of Mormons, from which I have drawn extensively in this chapter.

[8]All Scripture references are taken from the New Revised Standard Version.

[9]*Christian Classics Ethereal Library*, "Nicene Creed," www.ccel.org/creeds/nicene .creed.html (accessed January 3, 2014).

[10]See Andrew C. Skinner, "Incarnation/Incarnate God," in *LDS Beliefs: A Doctrinal Reference*, ed. Robert L. Millet, Camille Fronk Olson, Andrew C. Skinner and Brent L. Top (Salt Lake City: Deseret, 2011), p. 319.

[11]Oaks and Wickman, "Missionary Work," p. 248.

[12]Ibid., p. 250.

[13]Ibid, p. 261.

[14]Ibid., p. 247.

[15]David B. Barrett and Todd M. Johnson, *World Christian Trends, AD 30–AD 2200* (Pasadena, CA: William Carey Library, 2001), p. 384. Mormons are not included in their statistical analysis.

[16]Krista Cook, "Mormons: World Population Numbers by Year," *About.com*, http:// lds.about.com/od/mormons/a/church_membership.htm; and "Growth of the Church," *Newsroom, The Church of Jesus Christ of Latter-day Saints*, www .mormonnewsroom.org/topic/church-growth (both accessed January 3, 2014). Barrett and Johnson, *World Christian Trends*, p. 384.

[17]Oaks and Wickman, "Missionary Work," pp. 248, 255.

[18]Robert L. Millet, *The Vision of Mormonism: Pressing the Boundaries of Christianity* (St. Paul: Paragon, 2007), p. 202.

[19]President Gordon B. Hinckley, "The BYU Experience," *Brigham Young University*

Speeches (1997–1998): 64. Quoted in Oaks and Wickman, "Missionary Work," p. 264.

[20]For more on the approach of the Chalmers and the LMS, see Patricia A. Prend-ergast, "Chalmers, James (1841–1901)," *Australian Dictionary of Biography*, National Centre of Biography, Australian National University, http://adb.anu.edu.au /biography/chalmers-james-3187 (accessed January 5, 2014).

[21]The Four Spiritual Laws can be found at "Four Spiritual Laws: English," Cru website, www.campuscrusade.com/fourlawseng.htm.

[22]Skinner, "Temple," in Millet, Olson, Skinner and Top, *LDS Beliefs*, p. 616.

[23]The purpose of the dialogue was recounted by Richard Mouw in a personal correspondence to several participants on November 9, 2013.

[24]Ibid.

[25]Convicted civility is discussed in depth in Richard J. Mouw, *Uncommon Decency: Christian Civility in an Uncivil World* (Downers Grove, IL: InterVarsity Press, 2010).

Chapter 22: Becoming as God

[1]Max Lucado, *Just Like Jesus* (Dallas: W Publishing Group, 2003), p. 3 (emphasis added).

[2]Dallas Willard, *The Divine Conspiracy: Rediscovering Our Hidden Life in God* (San Francisco: HarperSanFrancisco, 1998), p. 12.

[3]Joseph Smith, *Lectures on Faith* (Salt Lake City: Deseret, 1985), 5:2.

[4]N. T. Wright, *Simply Christian: Why Christianity Makes Sense* (San Francisco: HarperSanFrancisco, 2006), p. 148.

[5]Smith, *Lectures on Faith*, 2:2.

[6]B. H. Roberts, ed., *History of the Church of Jesus Christ of Latter-day Saints* (Salt Lake City: Deseret, 1957), 4:78-79.

[7]"Mormonism 101: What Is Mormonism," *Newsroom, The Church of Jesus Christ of Latter-day Saints*, www.mormonnewsroom.org/article/mormonism-101.

[8]Parley P. Pratt, *Key to the Science of Theology* (Salt Lake City: Deseret, 1978), pp. 21-22.

[9]Luther, cited in Veli-Matti Kärkkäinen, *One with God: Salvation as Deification and Justification* (Collegeville, MN: Liturgical Press, 2004), p. 47.

[10]Ibid.

[11]John Stott, "The Model: Becoming More Like Christ," sermon delivered at the Keswick Convention, July 17, 2007.

[12]See, e.g., Daniel B. Clendenin, *Eastern Orthodox Christianity: A Western Perspective* (Grand Rapids: Baker Academic, 2003), p. 131.

[13]Hyrum Mack Smith and Janne M. Sjodahl, *Doctrine and Covenants Commentary* (Salt Lake City: Deseret, 1965), pp. 826-27.

[14]See C. S. Lewis, *Mere Christianity* (New York: Touchstone, 1996), pp. 137-40, 153-54, 176, 186; Lewis, *Miracles* (New York: Touchstone, 1996), p. 178; Lewis, *A Grief Observed* (New York: Seabury, 1961), p. 57; Lewis, *The Weight of Glory* (New York: Touchstone, 1996), pp. 39-40.

[15]Gordon B. Hinckley, *Conference Report*, October 1994, p. 64.

Chapter 23: Is Mormonism Biblical?

[1]See, e.g., a historical perspective in John Fea, *Was America Founded as a Christian Nation? A Historical Introduction* (Louisville, KY: Westminster John Knox Press, 2011), pp. 26-27; and a personal perspective in Jan Shipps, *Sojourner in the Promised Land: Forty Years Among the Mormons* (Urbana: University of Illinois Press, 2000), pp. 348-49, 355.

[2]See, e.g., the results of Gary Lawrence's nationwide survey, published in *Mormons Believe . . . What?! Fact and Fiction About a Rising Religion* (Orange, CA: Parameter Foundation, 2011), especially chaps. 1 and 2, which suggest that there is a 75 percent "uncertainty level" about whether Mormons are Christians or believe in the Bible.

[3]Richard J. Mouw, *Talking with Mormons: An Invitation to Evangelicals* (Grand Rapids: Eerdmans, 2012), p. 3.

[4]See Shipps, *Sojourner in the Promised Land*, pp. 335-36.

[5]Philip L. Barlow, *Mormons and the Bible: The Place of the Latter-day Saints in American Religion*, rev. ed. (New York and Oxford: Oxford University Press, 2013), p. xxiii. Barlow's book, first published in 1991, is the seminal study on the topic of the place of the Bible in Mormonism, and I am indebted to his keen insights throughout.

[6]See Christian Smith, *The Bible Made Impossible: Why Biblicism Is Not a Truly Evangelical Reading of Scripture* (Grand Rapids: Brazos, 2012); Kenton L. Sparks, *Sacred Word, Broken Word: Biblical Authority and the Dark Side of Scripture* (Grand Rapids: Eerdmans, 2012); Carlos Bovell, *Rehabilitating Inerrancy in a Culture of Fear* (Eugene, OR: Wipf & Stock, 2012). Peter Enns hosts an important blog, "Rethinking Biblical Christianity," under the "Evangelical Channel" on Patheos.com, where he has engaged a number of these authors; accessible at www.patheos.com/blogs/peterenns. Enns was also one of five contributors to a recent volume in the Counterpoints: Bible and Theology series from Zondervan: J. Merrick and Stephen M. Garrett, eds., *Five Views on Biblical Inerrancy* (Grand Rapids: Zondervan, 2013).

[7]Brian Malley, *How the Bible Works* (Walnut Creek, CA: AltaMira, 2004), p. 22.

[8]There is, of course, a danger in speaking in generalities like these, and that danger is portraying Mormonism as monolithic—which it is not. With that noted, however, these broad strokes can serve the purpose here of highlighting beliefs among practicing Mormons that find remarkably wide acceptance. For example, Pew found in 2007 that 91 percent of Mormons surveyed believed the Bible to be the Word of God, and 98 percent believed in the resurrection of Jesus. See Pew Research Center, "Mormons in America: Certain in Their Beliefs, Uncertain of Their Place in Society," The Pew Forum on Religion & Public Life (January 12, 2012), p. 41, for a report of Mormon beliefs from the Pew Forum's 2007 "U. S. Religious Landscape Survey," as well as additional information about majority Mormon beliefs from Pew's Fall 2011 survey.

[9]Ibid., pp. 150-51.

[10]Ibid., p. 55.

[11]Craig L. Blomberg, "Review of Christian Smith, *The Bible Made Impossible: Why Biblicism Is Not a Truly Evangelical Reading of Scripture*," *Review of Biblical Literature* (August 2012): 3-4, www.bookreviews.org/pdf/8205_8969.pdf.

[12]The "Articles of Faith" comprise thirteen statements of faith that have been canonized as part of the LDS scriptural book Pearl of Great Price; accessible at www .lds.org/scriptures/pgp/a-of-f/1?lang=eng. For the critical edition of the so-called Wentworth Letter, in which these statements originally appeared, see Karen Lynn Davidson, David J. Whittaker, Mark Ashurst-McGee and Richard L. Jensen, eds., *Histories, vol. 1, Joseph Smith Histories, 1832–1844*, vol. 1 of the Histories series of *The Joseph Smith Papers*, ed. Dean C. Jessee, Ronald K. Esplin and Richard Lyman Bushman (Salt Lake City: Church Historian's Press, 2012), p. 500; see also the Joseph Smith Papers website, "'Church History,' 1 March 1842," http://joseph smithpapers.org/paperSummary/church-history-1-march-1842?dm=image -and-text&zm=zoom-inner&tm=expanded&p=4&s=undefined&sm=none.

[13]See, e.g., Jan Shipps as quoted in Kenneth L. Woodward, "A Mormon Moment," *Newsweek*, September 10, 2001, p. 48. *Newsweek* asked historian Jan Shipps if the fact that "Mormon rhetoric [was] becoming more overtly evangelical" signaled that "the Mormons [were] going mainstream." "Not at all" was her response. "After a century of cultivating their separate identity as a religious people, Mormons now want to stress their affinities with traditional Christianity yet highlight their uniqueness." BYU professor Robert Millet has made an important argument that the LDS Church's perceptible shift to more Christian or "evangelical" themes since the 1980s corresponded with church president Ezra Taft Benson's call that Mormons study and teach from the Book of Mormon, a Scripture replete with discourses on grace and the need for an atoning Savior. See, e.g., Millet, "Joseph Smith and Modern Mormonism: Orthodoxy, Neoorthodoxy, Tension, and Tradition," *BYU Studies* 29, no. 3 (1989): 49-68. Renowned LDS historian Richard Bushman raised essentially the same point in a discussion with journalists and academics at the Pew Forum's biannual Faith Angle Conference, May 14, 2007. Bushman was the forum's guest speaker, and *Newsweek's* Kenneth Woodward asked about the place of grace in Mormon theology. Bushman responded: "In dialogues with evangelical Christians, Mormons are recovering their own grace theology, which is plentifully presented in the Book of Mormon. And they are recovering it not just at the high level of discussion between BYU faculty and Baylor faculty, but right down in the congregation" ("Mormonism and Democratic Politics: Are They Compatible?," Pew Research Religion and Public Life Project, p. 16; transcript accessible at http://pewforum.org/2007/05/14/mormonism-and -politics-are-they-compatible).

[14]See Robert L. Millet, "A Latter-day Saint Perspective on Biblical Inerrancy," *Religious Educator* 11, no. 1 (2010): 82-83.

[15]Bible Research website, "Chicago Statement on Biblical Inerrancy," art. 10, www .bible-researcher.com/chicago1.html.

[16]The statement was reported by Willard Richards as part of a synopsis of a sermon

Joseph Smith gave on October 15, 1843, in *History of the Church of Jesus Christ of Latter-day Saints*, ed. B. H. Roberts (Salt Lake City: Deseret, 1978), 6:57.

[17]See, among other passages in the Book of Mormon, Mormon 7:9 and 1 Nephi 13:40. On this point, see also Jeffrey R. Holland, "My Words . . . Never Cease" (address at the LDS annual General Conference, April 2008), www.lds.org/general -conference/2008/04/my-words-never-cease?lang=eng.

[18]Joseph Smith in the *Elders' Journal*, July 1838, p. 42, http://josephsmithpapers.org /paperSummary/elders-journal-july-1838#!/paperSummary/elders-journal-july -1838&p=15.

[19]Barlow, *Mormons and the Bible*, 47.

[20]See John L. Brooke, *The Refiner's Fire: The Making of Mormon Cosmology, 1644–1844* (Cambridge: Cambridge University Press, 1994). Brooke himself concedes in his preface that his argument "poses a series of methodological problems. First and foremost, it is not entirely clear how hermeticism might have been conveyed from late-sixteenth-century Europe to the New York countryside in the early nineteenth century" (p. xiv).

[21]Shipps, *Sojourner in the Promised Land*, pp. 205, 210-11. Compare also the reviews she cites: Richard Bushman, "The Mysteries of Mormonism," *Journal of the Early Republic* 15, no. 3 (1995): 501-5; and Philip Barlow, "Decoding Mormonism," *Christian Century*, January 17, 1996, pp. 52-53.

[22]Craig L. Blomberg and Stephen E. Robinson, *How Wide the Divide? A Mormon and an Evangelical in Conversation* (Downers Grove, IL: InterVarsity Press, 1997), p. 177.

[23]For an analysis of the context and import of "the Vision," see Richard Lyman Bushman, *Joseph Smith: Rough Stone Rolling* (New York: Alfred A. Knopf, 2005), pp. 196-202; Bushman contends that "'the Vision' used language common to Protestants" (p. 201). For "the Vision's" biblical ties, see also J. B. Haws, "Joseph Smith, Emanuel Swedenborg, and Section 76: Importance of the Bible in Latter-day Revelation," in *Doctrine and Covenants: Revelations in Context* (Salt Lake City: Deseret; Provo, UT: Religious Studies Center, 2008), pp. 142-67.

[24]See Terryl L. Givens, *By the Hand of Mormon: The American Scripture that Launched a New World Religion* (New York: Oxford University Press, 2002), pp. 63-64; also Noel B. Reynolds, "The Coming Forth of the Book of Mormon in the Twentieth Century," *BYU Studies* 38, no. 2 (1999): 7-47; and Barlow, *Mormons and the Bible*, p. xxxviii, 47.

[25]Cf., e.g., Doctrine and Covenants 127:7, 128:16-18, and 138:6-10.

[26]See this point by Stephen Robinson in Blomberg and Robinson, *How Wide the Divide?*, p. 128. For an "outsider" perspective on the way the Book of Mormon supports biblical Christology, see Stephen H. Webb, "Mormonism Obsessed with Christ," *First Things*, February 2012, www.firstthings.com/article/2012/02 /mormonism-obsessed-with-christ.

[27]Some readers might wonder about the "Joseph Smith Translation" of this passage. Joseph Smith worked his way through the Bible and made changes to hundreds

of verses. While Latter-day Saints esteem Joseph Smith's contributions as inspired and helpful, the changes have never been canonized, although many of them are included in LDS editions of the Bible as study footnotes rather than in the biblical text itself. It is also worth noting that it seems apparent that Joseph Smith saw this "translation" work along several lines, from restoring original meaning to clarifying awkward passages. See the excellent discussion of what Joseph Smith seemed to be doing in his translation work in Barlow, *Mormons and the Bible*, pp. 49-67. Regardless, and to settle any questions about Latter-day Saint beliefs about the full divinity of Jesus Christ, remember that several passages in the Book of Mormon refer to Jesus Christ as "God Himself." See, e.g., Mosiah 15:1 and Alma 42:15.

[28]Roger E. Olson and Christopher A. Hall, *The Trinity*, Guides to Theology (Grand Rapids: Eerdmans, 2002), pp. 5, 15.

[29]Jeffrey R. Holland, "The Only True God and Jesus Christ Whom He Hath Sent" (address at the LDS semiannual General Conference, October 2007), www.lds.org /general-conference/2007/10/the-only-true-god-and-jesus-christ-whom-he -hath-sent.

[30]The Christian Church (Disciples of Christ), for example, takes a "no creed but Christ" position, so that belief in the Trinity is not a formalized part of their confession. See Christian Church (Disciples of Christ), "Our Mission, Vision and Confession," www.disciples.org/our-identity/our-mission-vision-and-confession.

[31]Olson and Hall, *The Trinity*, p. 6. Some examples in the Latter-day Saint canon include Doctrine and Covenants 74, 77, 113, 130, 132 and 138.

[32]Holland, "My Words . . . Never Cease" (address at the LDS annual General Conference, April 2008).

[33]Franklin Graham, "Can an Evangelical Christian Vote for a Mormon?," *Decision Magazine*, October 2012, http://billygraham.org/decision-magazine/october-2012 /can-an-evangelical-christian-vote-for-a-mormon.

[34]N. T. Wright, *The Last Word: Beyond the Bible Wars to a New Understanding of the Authority of Scripture* (San Francisco: HarperSanFrancisco, 2005), pp. xi, 24, as quoted in Holland, "My Words . . . Never Cease."

Contributors

Richard E. Bennett worked as head of the Department of Archives and Special Collections at the University of Manitoba in Winnipeg, Canada, before joining the faculty of the Department of Church History and Doctrine at Brigham Young University, where he now serves as chair. He has authored several books and articles on the Mormon exodus from Nauvoo, Illinois, to the Great Basin in Utah.

Brian D. Birch is professor of philosophy at Utah Valley University, where he jointly directs the Religious Studies Program and the Center for the Study of Ethics. He is a cofounder of the Society for Mormon Philosophy and Theology and served as editor of the society's journal *Element* from 2005 to 2010. His current book project is titled *Mormonism Among Christian Theologies* for Oxford University Press (coauthored with Grant Underwood).

Craig L. Blomberg is distinguished professor of New Testament at Denver Seminary. His PhD is from the University of Aberdeen, Scotland. Blomberg has authored fourteen books and coauthored or coedited eight more, including, with Stephen E. Robinson, *How Wide the Divide? A Mormon and an Evangelical in Conversation*. His books also include *Jesus and the Gospels*, *The Historical Reliability of the Gospels*, *The Historical Reliability of John's Gospel* and *A Handbook of New Testament Exegesis*.

Derek Bowen is the director of the Fullerton West LDS Institute of Religion in Southern California. He also teaches online religion courses for Brigham Young University—Idaho. He has an MA in religious education from Brigham Young University in Provo, Utah. His article is based on his master's thesis, titled "'Love Your Enemy': Evangelical Opposition to Mormonism and Its Effect upon Mormon Identity."

James E. Bradley is the Geoffrey W. Bromiley Professor of Church History at Fuller Theological Seminary. His books include *Religion, Revolution, and English Radicalism* and *Religion and Politics in Enlightenment Europe*, co-edited with Dale K. Van Kley. He contributed the chapter "Toleration and Movements of Christian Reunion" for the *Cambridge History of Christianity*.

Rachel Cope is assistant professor of church history and doctrine at Brigham Young University. Her research and publication interests include female spirituality and conversion in the late eighteenth and early nineteenth centuries. She is lead series editor of the Farleigh Dickinson University Press Mormon Studies series.

J. Spencer Fluhman is associate professor of history at Brigham Young University. He is the author of *"A Peculiar People": Anti-Mormonism and the Making of Religion in Nineteenth-Century America* and is currently editor of the *Mormon Studies Review*.

Christopher A. Hall is distinguished professor of theology and director of academic spiritual formation at Eastern University, where he also has served as chancellor of the University and dean of Palmer Theological Seminary. An acknowledged authority on the patristic period, some of his books include *Worshiping with the Church Fathers*, *The Trinity* (coauthored with Roger Olson) and *The Mystery of God* (coauthored with Stephen D. Boyer).

J. B. Haws is assistant professor of church history and doctrine at Brigham Young University. Before joining the BYU faculty he worked with the LDS Church educational system as a religion instructor. He has a PhD in American history from the University of Utah, and he is the author of *The Mormon Image in the American Mind: Fifty Years of Public Perception*.

Bill Heersink completed his doctoral work at Fuller Theological Seminary and was a member of the faculty of the Salt Lake Theological Seminary for several years. He has been involved in pastoral ministry and lived among the Latter-day Saints in Ogden, Utah, for almost four decades.

C. Douglas McConnell is provost and senior vice president of Fuller Theological Seminary. The McConnells spent fifteen years as missionaries in Australia and Papua New Guinea. Prior to his work at Fuller, McConnell was associate professor and chair of the Department of Missions/Intercultural Studies and Evangelism at Wheaton College and international director of PIONEERS.

Gerald R. McDermott is Jordan-Trexler Professor of Religion at Roanoke College. A recognized authority on the life of Jonathan Edwards, some of his books include *Seeing God: Jonathan Edwards and Spiritual Discernment*, *Jonathan Edwards Confronts the Gods* and *The Theology of Jonathan Edwards*, coauthored with Michael J. McClymond. He and Robert Millet coauthored *Claiming Christ: A Mormon-Evangelical Debate*.

Robert L. Millet is coordinator of the office of religious outreach and professor emeritus of religious education at Brigham Young University. At BYU he has served as chair of the Department of Ancient Scripture and dean of the College of Religious Education. He is the author of *A Different Jesus? The Christ of the Latter-day Saints*, *Claiming Christ: A Mormon-Evangelical Debate* (coauthored with Gerald R. McDermott) and *Bridging the Divide: The Continuing Conversation Between a Mormon and an Evangelical* (coauthored with Gregory C. V. Johnson).

Richard J. Mouw holds the chair for the Center of Faith and Public Life at Fuller Theological Seminary. Mouw taught for many years as a professor of philosophy at Calvin College and then joined the faculty at Fuller Theological Seminary, where he was appointed provost and then president of the seminary for twenty years. Some of his books include *Uncommon Decency*, *Praying at Burger King*, *He Shines in All That's Fair*, *Calvinism in the Las Vegas Airport* and *Talking With Mormons: An Invitation to Evangelicals*. Mouw has for many years been involved in dialogues with Mormons, Roman Catholics, Jews and Muslims.

Dennis Okholm is professor of theology at Azusa Pacific University and adjunct professor at Fuller Theological Seminary. He is a priest and canon theologian in the Anglican Church in North America. His most recent book is *Dangerous Passions, Deadly Sins: Learning from the Psychology of Ancient Monks*.

Camille Fronk Olson is professor and department chair of ancient Scripture at Brigham Young University. Before joining the BYU faculty, she worked with the LDS Church educational system as an instructor of religion. Her publications include *In the Hands of the Potter, Mary, Martha, and Me, Too Much to Carry Alone, Women of the Old Testament* and *Women of the New Testament*. She is also a coauthor of *LDS Beliefs*, an encyclopedic reference work.

Sarah Taylor is a contributing writer for Fuller Theological Seminary's *Evangelical Interfaith Dialogue* journal. She has degrees from Brigham Young University and Fuller Theological Seminary and currently resides in Provo, Utah.

Grant Underwood is professor of history at Brigham Young University. He is the author of *The Millennarial World of Early Mormonism* and *Voyages of Faith: Explorations in Mormon Pacific History*. He is also a contributing editor of the Joseph Smith Papers series. He was founding cochair of the American Academy of Religion's Mormon Studies group and twice has served on the board of directors of the Mormon History Association.

Cory B. Willson is a PhD candidate at Fuller Theological Seminary and the Vrije Universiteit Amsterdam. He is assistant professor of missiology and missional ministry at Calvin College. He is a cofounding editor of the journal *Evangelical Interfaith Dialogue*, and he has worked in ministry to college students and young adults and been involved in Christian-Jewish dialogue.